E. Lofts.
Xmas. '92.

HORÆ SUBSECIVÆ.

By JOHN BROWN, M.D.

LL.D., ETC.

*'Ce fagotage de tant si diverses pièces, se faict en cette condition :
que je n'y mets la main, que lors qu'une trop lasche oysifveté me
presse.'*—MICHEL DE MONTAIGNE.

NEW EDITION IN THREE VOLUMES.

THIRD SERIES.

EDINBURGH:

DAVID DOUGLAS.

MDCCCLXXXIX.

JOHN LEECH

AND OTHER PAPERS

Héliog.ᵉ et Imp A. Durand Paris

JOHN LEECH

AND OTHER PAPERS

By JOHN BROWN, M.D.

LL.D., ETC.

SIXTH EDITION

EDINBURGH

DAVID DOUGLAS

MDCCCLXXXIX.

Edinburgh: Printed by Thomas and Archibald Constable,

FOR

DAVID DOUGLAS.

LONDON	. . . .	HAMILTON, ADAMS, AND CO.
CAMBRIDGE	. . . . . .	MACMILLAN AND BOWES.
GLASGOW	. . . .	JAMES MACLEHOSE AND SONS.

CONTENTS.

The portrait of the author prefixed to the present edition has been engraved by M. AMAND DURAND, *from a sketch made by* MR. GEORGE REID, R.S.A., *in February* 1882.

PREFACE TO FIRST EDITION.

EVERY man is two men—at the least.
Sydney Smith says St. Paul was a thousand men. But every man is good and bad,
wise and foolish, conceited and not. It is the
preponderance that makes the difference and
the outward man. As one of the bravest
men in the British army once said to me,
'When we go into battle we are all afraid,
but we don't all show it.'

Well, when my friend and publisher spoke
to me of putting these odds and ends into a
volume, I said at first 'No;' now I am saying
'Yes,' though I still feel both. No one can so
well know of how little worth much of these
occasional papers—what old Creech would have
called Fugitive Pieces—are, how much better

they might and ought to have been—as their author : this was the *No*—the *Yes* was a sneaking hope that others might not altogether agree with me. This was the conceit and vanity bit having its say. The struggle, somewhat protracted, as to which would prevail, is now over. The 'bit' and David Douglas have prevailed, and I must content myself, after the manner of the deliverance of Socrates and Voltaire on a more important matter, with the reflection that whether I said yes or no I would regret it.

With regard to the paper which gives its name to this volume, I hardly know how to excuse myself, it is so unworthy of its delightful subject, so much more so now than when it appeared in the *North British Review*, by reason of its not having the woodcuts. It may truly be said that it is dished for want of the plates—to give a twist to Rogers's well-known joke. My only hope is that the reader, in his anger at being asked to look at what he cannot see, may be driven to *Punch* and elsewhere, and then I am sure his anger will be appeased. He will be grateful, indeed, to Canon Hole for what he has said of his friend, and the friend of us all.

I cannot end without most affectionate and sorrowing mention of two dear dead friends— Thomas Constable, who had a true literary faculty as well as palate, and of whom it may be said—as of too few—that to him to live was to love ; and Miss Fleming, the sister of Pet Marjorie, who survived her seventy years, and who, I believe, seldom passed a day without thinking, and I dare say without speaking, of her darling, who had lain at her heart all these years.

RUTLAND STREET,
Jan. 3, 1882.

PREFACE TO SECOND EDITION.

I SHOULD before now have thanked Dr. W. F. Skene, Historiographer for Scotland, and *facile princeps* of Celtic scholars, for the material of 'A Jacobite Family,' written by his father, Sir Walter's friend, and the grandson of our fine old lady of Stoneywood. My readers, I am sure, will thank him too.

I also thank the 'North British Review' and 'The Scotsman' for such of the ingredients of the following dish—which Meg Dods would have called Potted Head—as had already appeared in them.

For putting 'Biggar' in, my excuse is that I am a Biggar *callant*.

J. B.

March 15, 1882.

THE RESTORATION:

UNPUBLISHED VERSES

By THOMAS DAVIDSON,

' THE SCOTTISH PROBATIONER.'[1]

My love, she walked yon forest glade,
  At the waning of the year,
She lifted a leaf from off the ground—
  A leaf full dry and sere.

My love, she bore it in her hand—
  It lived through every vein.
My love, she placed it on her breast,
  And it straight grew green again.

My love, she wears it at her heart;
  Will wear it till she die.
My love, thou hast been life to me,
  —For I trow that leaf am I.

PEASE GLEN, NEAR COCKBURNSPATH,
  Sept. 1865.

---

[1] 'The Scottish Probationer,' by James Brown, D.D.   A worthy
   record of a man of rare genius—' dead ere his prime.'

'*Morning breaks as I write, along those Coniston Fells, and the level mists, motionless and grey beneath the rose of the moorlands, veil the lower woods, and the sleeping village, and the long lawns by the lake shore.*

'*Oh that some one had told me, in my youth, when all my heart seemed to be set on these colours and clouds, that appear for a little while and then vanish away, how little my love of them would serve me, when the silence of lawn and wood in the dews of morning should be completed, and all my thoughts should be of those whom, by neither, I was to meet more!*

'J. RUSKIN.

'BRANTWOOD, 12th Feb. 1878.'

JOHN LEECH.

'*John Leech was an absolute master of the elements of character; of all rapid and condensed realisation ever accomplished by the pencil, his is the most dainty and the least fallible in the subjects of which he was cognisant, not merely right in the traits which he seizes, but refined in the sacrifice of what he refuses.*'— MR. RUSKIN, in a letter to Miss Leech on her brother's drawings.

I

SIR JOHN LEACH,
1827-34.

JOHN LEECH.

IF man is made to mourn, he also, poor fellow! and without doubt therefore, is made to laugh. He needs it all, and he gets it. For human nature may say of herself in the words of the ballad, 'Werena my heart licht, I wad dee.'

Man is the only animal that laughs; it is as peculiar to him as his chin and his *hippocampus minor*.[1] The perception of a joke, the smile, the sense of the ludicrous, the quiet laugh, the roar of laughter, are all our own; and we may be laughed as well as tickled to death, as in the story of the French nun of mature years, who, during a vehement fit of laughter, was observed by her sisters to sit suddenly still and look very 'gash' (like the Laird of Garscadden[2]), this being considered a further part of the joke, when they found she was elsewhere.

In books, old and new, there is no end of philosophising upon the ludicrous and its cause; from

[1] Professor Turner informs me that this comfort is taken from us,—the superior apes have the lesser sea-horse.
[2] *Vide* Dean Ramsay's *Reminiscences*.

Aristotle, who says it is some error in truth or propriety, but at the same time neither painful nor pernicious ; and Cicero, who defines it as that which, without impropriety, notes and exposes an impropriety ; to Jean Paul, who says it is the opposite of the sublime, the infinitely great, and is therefore the infinitely little ; and Kant, who gives it as the sudden conversion into nothing of a long raised and highly-wrought expectation ; many have been the attempts to unsphere the spirit of a joke and make it tell its secret ; but we agree with our excellent and judicious friend Quinctilian, that its *ratio* is at best *anceps*. There is a certain robust felicity about old Hobbes's saying, that 'it is a *sudden glory*, or sense of eminency above others or our former selves.' There is no doubt at least about the suddenness and the glory ; all true laughter must be involuntary, must come and go as it lists, must take us and shake us heartily and by surprise. No man can laugh any more than he can sneeze at will, and he has nearly as little to do with its ending—it dies out, disdaining to be killed. He may grin and guffaw, because these are worked by muscles under the dominion of volition, but your diaphragm, the midriff, into which your joker pokes his elbow, he is the great organ of genuine laughter and the sudden glory, and he, as you all know, when made absurd by hiccup, is masterless as the wind. 'untameable as flies ;' there·

fore is he called by the grave Haller, *nobilissimus post cor musculus;* for, ladies and gentlemen, your heart is only a hollow muscle. If you wish to know what is done in your interior when you laugh, here it is from Dr. Carpenter. He classes it along with sobbing and hiccup, and says : ' In it—the act of laughing—the muscles of expiration are in convulsive movement, more or less violent, and send out the breath in a series of jerks, the *glottis* being open,' the *glottis* being the little chink at the top of the windpipe.

As to the mental impression on the sensorium that sets these jerks agoing, and arches that noble muscle, we, as already said, think it may be left to a specific sense of its own, and that laughter is the effect and very often the cause of the laughable, and therefore of itself—a definition which has the merit of being self-contained. But is it not well that we are made to laugh, that, from the first sleepy gleam moving like sunshine over an infant's cheek, to the cheery and feeble chirrup of his great-grandfather by the fireside, we laugh at the laughable, when the depths of our strange nature are dappled and rippled, or tossed into wildest laughter by anything, so that it be droll, just as we shudder when soused with cold water—because we can't help it ?

But we are drifting into disquisition and must beware. What is it to us or the public that the pneumogastric and phrenic nerves are the telegraphs from their headquarters in the brain to this same midriff—that if cut, there would be an end of our funny messages, and of a good deal more; that the *musculus nobilissimus*, if wounded in its feelings from without or from within, takes to outrageous laughter of the dreariest sort; that if anything goes wrong at the central *thalami*, as they are called, of these nerves, the vehicles of will and feeling, they too make sad fools of themselves by sending down absurd, incoherent telegrams 'at lairge'?

One might be diffuse upon the various ways in which laughter seizes upon and deals with mankind; how it excruciates some, making them look and yell as if caught in a trap. How a man takes to crowing like a cock, or as if under permanent hooping-cough, ending his series of explosions victoriously with his well-known 'clarion wild and shrill.' How provocative of laughter such a musical performance always is to his friends, leading them to lay snares for him! We knew an excellent man—a country doctor—who, if wanted in the village, might be traced out by his convivial crow. It was droll to observe him resisting internally and on the sly the beginnings of his *bravura;* how it always prevailed. How another friend, huge, learned, and wise, whom laughter seizes and rends, is made desperate, and at times ends in crashing his chair, and concluding his burst on its ruins, and on the floor. In houses where he is familiar, a special chair is set for him, braced with iron for the stress.

Then one might discourse on the uses of laughter as a muscular exercise; on its drawing into action lazy muscles, supernumeraries, which get off easily under ordinary circumstances; how much good the convulsive succussion of the whole man does to his chylo-poietic and other viscera; how it laughs to scorn care and *malaise* of all kinds; how it makes you cry without sorrow, and ache every inch of you without wrong done to any one; how it clears the liver and enlivens the spleen, and makes the very cockles of the heart to tingle. By the by, what are these cockles of tradition, but the *columnæ carneæ*, that pull away at the valves, and keep all things tight?

But why should we trouble ourselves and you with either the physiology or the philosophy of laughter, when all that anybody needs to say or to hear, is said, so as to make all after saying hopeless and needless, by Sydney Smith, in his two chapters on Wit and Humour, in his *Notes of Lectures on Moral Philosophy*? Why it is that when any one—except possibly Mr. Tupper—hears for the first time, that wisest of wits' jokes to his doctor, when told by him to 'take a walk on an empty stomach;'—'on whose?' —he laughs right out, loud and strong, may be a question as hard to answer as the why he curls up his nose when tickled with a feather, or sneezes when he looks at the sun ; but it is not hard to be thankful for the joke, and for the tickle, and for the sneeze. Our business rather is now gratefully to acknowledge the singular genius, the great personal and artistic worth of one of our best masters of 'heart-easing mirth,' than to discourse upon the why and how he makes us laugh so pleasantly, so wholesomely and well,—and to deplore along with all his friends (who has not in him lost a friend ?), his sudden and irreparable loss (October 29, 1864). It was as if something personal to every one was gone ; as if a fruit we all ate and rejoiced in had vanished for ever ; a something good and cheery, and to be thankful for, which came every week as sure as Thursday—never to come again. Our only return to him for all his unfailing goodness and cheer, is the memory of the heart, and he has it if any man in the British empire has. The noble, honest, kindly, diligent, sound-hearted, modest, and manly John Leech—the very incarnation in look, character, and work of the best in an Englishman.

As there is and has always been, since we had letters or art of our own, a rich abounding power and sense of humour and of fun in the English nature ; so ever since that same nature was pleased to divert and express itself and its jokes in art as well as in books, we have had no lack of depicters of the droll, the odd, the terrible, and the queer. Hogarth is the first and greatest of them all, the greatest master in his own *terribile via* the world has ever seen. If you want to know his worth and the exquisite beauty of his colouring, study his pictures, and possess his prints, and read Charles Lamb on his genius. Then came the savage Gillray, strong and coarse as Church- ill, the very Tipton Slasher of political caricature ; then we had Bunbury, Rowlandson, and Woodward, more violent than strong, more odd than droll, and often more disgusting than either. Smirke, with his delicate, pure, pleasant humour, as seen in his plates to *Don Quixote*, which are not unworthy of that marvellous book, the most deeply and exquisitely humorous piece of genius in all literature ; then the *Monkeyana*, designed and engraved by Thomas Landseer, forgotten by, and we fear unknown to many, so wickedly funny, so awfully human, as almost to convert us to Mr. Huxley's pedigree—*The Duel*, for instance. Then we had Henry Alken in the Hunting Field, and poor Heath, the ex-Captain of Dragoons, facile and profuse, unscrupulous and clever. Then the greatest since Hogarth, though limited in range and tending to excess, George Cruikshank, who happily still lives and plies his matchless needle ;[1]—it would take an entire paper to expound his keen, penetrating power, his moral intensity, his gift of wild grimace, the dexterity and super-subtlety of his etching, its firm and delicate lines. Then came poor short-lived tragical

[1] Died 1878.

Seymour, whom Thackeray wished to succeed as artist
to *Pickwick;* he embodied *Pickwick* as did ' Phiz,'—
Hablot Browne,—*Messrs. Quilp,* and *Pecksniff,* and
Micky Free, and whose steeplechasing Irish cocktails
we all know and relish ; but his manner is too much
for him and for us, and his ideas are neither deep nor
copious, hence everlasting and weak repetitions of
himself. Kenny Meadows, with more genius, especially for fiends and all eldritch fancies, and still more
mannerism. Sibson,—and Hood, whose drawings
were quaint and queer enough, but his words better
and queerer. Thackeray, very great, answering wonderfully his own idea. We wonder that his *Snobs* and
Modern Novelists and miscellaneous papers were ever
published without his own cuts. What would *Mrs.
Perkins's Ball* be without *The Mulligan,* as the spread-
eagle, frantic and glorious, doing the mazurka, without *Miss Bunion,* and them all ; and the good little
Nightingale, in *Dr. Birch,* singing ' Home, Sweet
Home' to that premature young brute Hewlett.
But we have already recorded our estimate of Mr.
Thackeray's worth as an artist ;[1] and all his droll-
eries and quaint bits of himself,—his comic melancholy, his wistful children, his terrific soldans in the
early *Punches.* They should all be collected,—where-
ever he escapes from his pen to his pencil, they
should never be divorced. Then Doyle, with his

[1] *North British Review.* No. lxxix., February 1864.

wealth of dainty phantasies, his glamourie, his won
derful power of expressing the weird and uncanny,
his fairies and goblins, his enchanted castles and
maidens, his plump caracolling pony chargers, his
charm of colour and of unearthly beauty in his water-
colours. No one is more thoroughly himself and alone
than Doyle. We need only name his father, ' H. B.,'
the master of gentlemanly, political satire,—as Gillray
was of brutal. Tenniel we still have, excellent, careful, and often strong and effective ; but more an artist
and a draughtsman than a genius or a humorist.

John Leech is different from all these, and, taken
as a whole, surpasses them all, even Cruikshank,
and seats himself next, though below, William
Hogarth. Well might Thackeray, in his delightful
notice of his friend and fellow-Carthusian in *The
Quarterly*, say, ' There is no blinking the fact that
in Mr. Punch's cabinet John Leech is the right-
hand man. Fancy a number of *Punch* without
Leech's pictures ! What would you give for it ?'
This was said ten years ago. How much more true
it is now ! We don't need to *fancy* it any longer !
And yet, doubtless, nature is already preparing some
one else—she is for ever filling her horn—whom we
shall never think better, or in his own way, half so
good, but who like him will be, let us trust, new and
true, modest, and good ; let us, meanwhile, rest and
be thankful, and look back on the past. We'll move

on by and by—'to fresh fields and pastures new'—
we suppose and hope.

We are not going to give a biography, or a studied
appraisement of this great artist; that has been already
well done in the *Cornhill*,—and we trust the mighty
'J. O.' who knew him and loved him as a brother,
and whose strong and fine hand—its truth, nicety, and
power—we think we recognise in an admirable short
notice of Leech as one of the 'Men of Mark,' in the
London Journal of May 31, 1862—may employ his
leisure in giving us a memorial of his friend. No
one could do it better, not even the judicious Tom
Taylor, and it is worth his while, to go down the
great stream side by side with such a man. All that
we shall now do is to give some particulars, not, so far
as we know, given to the public, and end with some
remarks on a few selected woodcuts from *Punch*—
illustrative of his various moods and gifts.[1]

---

[1] When the history of the rise and progress of *Punch* comes
to be written, it will be found that the Weekly Dinner has
been one of the chief things which contributed to its success.
Almost from the foundation of that journal it has been the
habit of the contributors every Wednesday to dine together.
In the winter months, the dinner is usually held in the front
room of the first floor of No. 11 Bouverie Street, Whitefriars,—
the business offices of the proprietors, Messrs. Bradbury and
Evans. Sometimes these dinners are held at the Bedford
Hotel, Covent Garden. During the summer months, it is
customary to have ten or twelve dinners at places in the neighbourhood of London, Greenwich, Richmond, Blackwall, etc.
And once a year they attend the annual dinner of the firm, at

John Leech, we believe remotely of Irish extraction, was a thoroughly London boy, though never one whit of a Cockney in nature or look. He was born in 1817, being thus six years younger than Thackeray, both of them Charterhouse boys. We rejoice to learn that Lord Russell has, in the kindest way, given to Mr. Leech's eldest boy a presentation to this famous school, where so many of the best men of London birth have had their training, as Brougham and Jeffrey, Scott and Cockburn, had at the Edinburgh High School. This gift of our Foreign Minister is twice blessed, and is an act the country may well thank him for.

which compositors, readers, printers, machinemen, clerks, etc., dine. This dinner is called the 'Way Goose,' and is often referred to in *Punch*.

At the weekly dinner, the contents of the forthcoming number of *Punch* are discussed. When the cloth is removed, and dessert is laid on the table, the first question put by the editor is, 'What shall the Cartoon be?'

During the lifetimes of Jerrold and Thackeray, the discussions after dinner ran very high, owing to the constitutional antipathy existing between these two. Jerrold being the oldest, as well as the noisiest, generally came off victorious. In these rows it required all the suavity of Mark Lemon (and he has a great deal of that quality) to calm the storm; his award always being final.

The third edition of Wednesday's *Sun* is generally brought in to give the latest intelligence, so as to bring the Cartoon down to the latest date. On the Thursday morning following, the editor calls at the houses of the artists to see what is being done. On Friday night all copy is delivered and put into type.

When between six and seven years of age, some of
Leech's drawings were seen by the great Flaxman,
and, after carefully looking at them and the boy, he
said, ' That boy must be an artist ; he will be nothing
else or less.'   This was said in full consciousness of
what is involved in advising such a step.   His father
wisely, doubtless, thought otherwise, and put him to
the medical profession at St. Bartholomew's, under
Mr. Stanley.   He was very near being sent to Edinburgh, and apprenticed to Sir George Ballingall.   If
he had come to us then, he would have found one
student, since famous, with whom he would have
cordialised : Edward, afterwards Professor Forbes,

and at two o'clock on Saturday proofs are revised, the forms
made up, and with the last movement of the engine, the whole
of the type is placed under the press, which cannot be moved
until the Monday morning, when the steam is again up.   This
precaution is taken to prevent waggish tricks on the part of
practical-joking compositors.

At these dinners none but those connected with the staff
proper are permitted to attend ; the only occasional exceptions,
we believe, have been Sir Joseph Paxton, Mr. Layard, Charles
Dickens, Rev. Reynolds Hole, and Charles Dickens, junior.
As an illustration of the benefit arising from these meetings,
we may mention that Jerrold always used to say, ' It is no use
any of us quarrelling, because next Wednesday must come
round with its dinner, when we will all have to shake hands
again.'   By means of these meetings, the discussions arising
on all questions helped both caricaturist and wit to take a
broad view of things, as well as enabled the editor to get
his team to draw well together, and give a uniformity of tone
to all the contributions. [1865.]

who to his other great gifts added that of drawing, especially of all sorts of wild, fanciful, elfish pleasantries and freaks, most original and ethereal—and the specimens of which, in their many strange resting-places, it would be worth the while to reproduce in a volume. Leech soon became known among his fellow-students for his lifelike, keen, but always good-natured caricatures; he was for ever drawing. He never had any regular art-lessons, but his medical studies furnished him with a knowledge of the structure and proportions of the human form, which gives such reality to his drawing; and he never parades his knowledge, or is its slave; he values expression ever above mere form, never falsifying, but often neglecting, or rather subordinating, the latter to the former.

This intense realism and insight, this pure intense power of observation it is that makes the Greek sculptors so infinitely above the Roman.

We believe the Greeks knew nothing of what was under the skin—it was considered profane to open the human body and dissect it; but they studied form and action with that keen, sure, unforgetting, loving eye, that purely realistic faculty, which probably they, as a race, had in more exquisite perfection than any other people before or since. Objective truth they read, and could repeat as from a book. The Romans, with their hardy, penetrating, audacious nature—*rerum Domini*—wanted to know not only what appears, but what is, and what makes appear. They had no misgivings or shyness at cutting into and laying bare their dead fellows, as little as they had in killing them or being themselves killed: and as so often happens, their strength was their weakness, their pride their fall. They must needs show off their knowledge and their muscles, and therefore they made their statues as if without skin, and put on as violent and often impossible action as ever did Buonarotti. Compare the Laocoon and his boys (small men, rather) with the Elgin marbles; the riders on the frieze so comely in their going, so lissome; their skin slipping sweetly over their muscles: their modestly representing not of what they know, but of what they see.

In John Leech and Tenniel you see something of the same contrast; the one knows more than he needs, and shows it accordingly; the other knowing by instinct, or from good sense, that drawing has only to do with appearances, with things that may be seen, not with things that may be known, drew merely what he saw, but then with what an inevitable, concentrated eye and hand he did draw that! This made him so pre-eminent in reproducing the expression of action—especially intense and rapid action. No knowledge of what muscles were acting, and what are their attachments, etc., could teach a man how a horse trots, or how he gathers himself up to leap, or now a broken-backed cab-horse would lie and look, or even how *Mr. Briggs*—excellent soul—when returning home, gently, and copiously ebriose from Epsom on his *donkey*, would sway about on his podgy legs, when instructing his amazed and ancient groom and friend as to putting up and rubbing down —*the mare.* But observation such as the Greeks had, that ἀκριβεία or accuracy—carefulness, as they called it—it enabled Leech to do all this to the life.

All through his course, more and more, he fed upon nature, and he had his reward in having perpetually at hand her freshness, her variety, her endlessness. There is a pleasant illustration of this given in a letter in *Notes and Queries* for November 5, 1864 :—' On one occasion he and I were riding to town in an omnibus, when an elderly gentleman, in a very peculiar dress, and with very marked features, stepped into the vehicle, and sat down immediately in front of us. He stared so hard and made such wry faces at us, that *I* could hardly refrain from laughter. My discomfiture was almost completed when Leech suddenly exclaimed, " By the way, did Prendergast ever show you that extraordinary account which has been lately forwarded to him ?" and, producing his note-book, added, " Just run your eye up that column, and tell me what you *can* make of it ?" The page was *blank ;* but two minutes afterwards the features of that strange old gentleman gaping at us

2

were reflected with life-like fidelity upon it.' There is humour in the choice of the word 'Prendergast.' This is the true way to nurse invention, to preen and let grow imagination's wings, on which she soars forth into the ideal, 'sailing with supreme dominion through the azure depths of air.' It is the man who takes in, who can give out. The man who does not do the one, soon takes to spinning his own fancies out of his interior, like a spider, and he snares himself at last as well as his victims. It is the bee that makes honey, and it is out of the eater that there comes forth meat, out of the strong that there comes forth sweetness. In the letter we refer to, which is well worth reading, there is a good remark, that Leech had no mere *minutiæ*, as Turner had none; everything was subordinated to the main purpose he had, but he had exquisite *finesse* and delicacy when it was that he wanted. Look at his drawing of our 'Jocund Morn,' from the boots to the swallows. His pencil-work on wood was marvellous for freedom and loveliness.

The bent of his genius and external causes made him, when about seventeen, give up the study of medicine and go in stoutly and for life for art. His diligence was amazing, as witnessed by the list of his works; in *Bentley* they are in multitudes; and in *Punch* alone, up to 1862, there are more than three thousand separate drawings! with hardly the vestige of a repetition; it may be the same tune, but it is a new variation. In nothing is his realistic power more seen than in those delightful records of his own holidays in *Punch.* A geologist will tell you the exact structure of that rock in the Tay at Campsie Linn, where *Mr. Briggs* is carrying out that huge salmon in his arms, tenderly and safely, as if it were his first-born. All his sea-scapes—Scarborough, Folkestone, Biarritz, etc. etc.— any one who has been there does not need to be told their names, and, as we have already said, his men are as native as his rocks, his bathers at Boulogne and Biarritz, his gamekeepers and gillies in Blair-Athole and Lochaber—you have seen them there, the very men; Duncan Roy is one of them; and those men and women at Galway, in the Claddich, they are liker than themselves, more Irish than the Irish. In this respect his foreigners are wonderful, one of the rarest artistic achievements. Thackeray also could draw a foreigner,—as witness that dreary woman outworker in the Kickleburys. Then as to dress; this was one of the things Leech very early mastered and knew the meaning and power of, and it is worth mastering, for in it, the dress, is much of the man both given and received. To see this, look at his first large drawing in the fourth number of *Punch,* called 'Foreign Affairs.' Look, too, at what is still one of his richest works, with all the fervour and abundance, the very dew of his youth,—the *Comic Latin Grammar.* Look at the dress of Menelaus, who threatens to give poor Helen, his wife, 'a good hiding.' Look at his droll etchings and woodcuts for the otherwise tiresomely brilliant *Comic Histories*, by Gilbert A'Beckett, with their too much puns.

Leech was singularly modest, both as a man and as an artist. This came by nature, and was indicative of the harmony and sweetness of his essence; but doubtless the perpetual going to nature, and drawing out of her fulness, kept him humble, as well as made him rich, made him, what every man of sense and power must be, conscious of his own strength; but before the great mother he was simple and loving, attentive to her lessons, as a child, for ever learning and doing.

This honesty and modesty were curiously brought out when he was, after much persuasion, induced to make the coloured drawings for that exhibition which was such a splendid success, bringing in nearly £5000. Nothing could induce him to do what was wanted, call them *paintings.* 'They are mere sketches,' he said, 'and very crude sketches too, and I have no wish to be made a laughing-stock by calling them what they are not.' Here was at once modesty and honest pride, or rather that truthfulness which lay at the root of his character, and was also its 'bright, consummate flower,' and he went further than this, in having printed in the Catalogue the following words :—' These sketches have no claim to be regarded or tested as finished pictures. It is impossible for any one to know the fact better than I do. They have no pretensions to a higher name than that I have given them—SKETCHES IN OIL.'

We have had, by the kindness of Mr. John Heugh, their possessor, the privilege of having beside us for some time two of the best of those coloured sketches, and we feel at once the candour and accuracy or their author's title. It is quite touching the unaccustomedness, the boyish, anxious, laborious workmanship of the hand that had done so much, so rapidly and perfectly in another style. They do not make us regret much, that he did not earlier devote himself to painting proper, because then what would have become of these 3000 cuts in *Punch?* But he shows, especially, true powers of landscape painting, a pure and deep sense of distance, translucency, and colour, and the power of gleams and shadows on water. His girls are lovelier without colour—have, indeed, 'to the eye and prospect of the soul,' a more exquisite bloom, the bloom within the skin, the brightness in the dark eye, all more expressed than in those actually coloured. So it often is ; give enough to set the looker-on a-painting imagining, realising, submitting 'the shows of things to the desires of the mind,' and no one but the highest painter can paint like that. This is the true office of the masters of all the ideal arts, to evoke, as did the rising sun on Memnon, the sleeping beauty and music and melody of another's soul, to make every reader a poet, every onlooker an artist, every listener eloquent and tuneful, so be it that they have the seeing eye, the hearing ear, the loving and understanding heart.

As is well known, this exhibition took London captive. It was the most extraordinary record by drawing, of the manners and customs and dress of a people, ever produced. It was full 'from morn to dewy eve,' and as full of mirth; at times this made it like a theatre convulsed as one man by the *vis comica* of one man. The laughter of special, often family groups, broke out opposite each drawing, spread contagiously effervescing throughout, lulling and waxing again and again like waves of the sea. From his reserve, pride, and nicety, Leech could never be got to go when any one was in the room; he had an especial horror of being what he called 'caught and talked at by enthusiastic people.' It is worth mentioning here, as it shows his true literary turn as a humourist, and adds greatly to the completeness of his drawings and of his genius, that all the funny, witty, and often most felicitous titles and wordings of

all sorts *were written by himself;* he was most particular about this.

One day a sporting nobleman visited the gallery
with his huntsman, whose naïve and knowing criti-
cisms greatly amused his master. At last, coming to
one of the favourite hunting pictures, he said, ' Ah !
my Lord, nothin' but a party as knows 'osses cud have
draw'd them 'ere 'unters.' The origin and means of
these sketches in oil is curious. Mr. Leech had often
been asked to undertake works of this character, but
he had for so many years been accustomed to draw
with the pencil, and that only on small blocks, that
he had little confidence in his ability to draw on a
large scale. The idea originated with Mr. Mark
Lemon, his friend and colleague, who saw that by a
new invention—a beautiful piece of machinery—the
impression of a block in *Punch*, being first taken on
a sheet of india-rubber, was enlarged ; when, by a
lithographic process, the copy thus got could be
transferred to the stone, and impressions printed
upon a large sheet of canvas. Having thus obtained
an outline groundwork consisting of his own lines
enlarged some eight times the area of the original
block, Leech proceeded to colour these. His knowledge of the manipulation of oil colours was very
slight, and it was under the guidance of his friend
John Everett Millais, that his first attempts were
made, and crude enough they were. He used a

kind of transparent colour which allowed the coarse
lines of the enlargement to show through, so that the
production presented the appearance of indifferent
lithographs, slightly tinted. In a short time, however, he obtained great mastery over oil colour, and
instead of allowing the thick fatty lines of printers'
ink to remain on the canvas, he, by the use of turpen-
tine, removed the ink, particularly with regard to the
lines of the face and figure. These he re-drew with
his own hand in a fine and delicate manner. To
this he added a delicacy of finish, particularly in
flesh colour, which greatly enhanced the value and
beauty of his later works. To any one acquainted
with these sketches, we may mention for illustration
of these remarks, No. 65 in the Catalogue. This
work presents all the incompleteness and crudity
of his early style. The picture represents *Piscator*
seated on a wooden fence on a raw morning in a
pelting shower of rain, the lines necessary to give
the effect of a leaden atmosphere being very numerous and close. The works which illustrated his
later style are best shown in Nos. 36 and 41. In
the framing of these sketches he persisted in leaving
a margin of white canvas somewhat after the manner
of water-colour sketches.

Of all art satirists none have such a pervading
sense and power of girlish and ripe womanly beauty
as Leech. Hogarth alone, as in his Poor Poet's

Wife, comes near him. There is a genuine domes-
ticity about his scenes that could come only from
a man who was much at his own fireside, and in the
nursery when baby was washed. You see he is himself *paterfamilias*, with no Bohemian taint or raffish
turn. What he draws he has seen. What he asks
you to live in and laugh at and with, he has laughed
at and lived in. It is this wholesomeness, and, to
use the right word, this goodness, that makes Leech
more than a drawer of funny pictures, more even
than a great artist.[1] It makes him a teacher and an
example of virtue in its widest sense, from that of
manliness to the sweet devotion of woman, and the
loving, open mouth and eyes of *parvula* on your
knee. How different is the same class of art in
France! you dare not let your wife or girls see their
Leech; he is not for our virgins and boys. Hear
what Thackeray says on this point :—

'Now, while Mr. Leech has been making his com-
ments upon our society and manners, one of the
wittiest and keenest observers has been giving a
description of his own country of France, in a thousand brilliant pages, and it is a task not a little amus-

---

[1] It is honourable to the regular art of this country that
many of its best men early recognised in Leech a true brother.
Millais and Elmore and others were his constant friends; and
we know that more than twelve years ago Sir George Harvey
wished to make Leech and Thackeray honorary members of
The Royal Scottish Academy [1865].

ing and curious for a student of manners to note the difference between the two satirists—perhaps between the societies which they describe.   Leech's England is a country peopled by noble elderly squires, riding large-boned horses, followed across country by lovely beings of the most gorgeous proportions, by respectful retainers, by gallant little boys emulating the courage and pluck of the sire.   The joke is the precocious courage of the child, his gallantry as he charges at his fences, his coolness as he eyes the glass of port or tells grandpapa that he likes his champagne dry.   How does Gavarni represent the family-father, the sire, the old gentleman in *his* country, the civilised country?   Paterfamilias, in a dyed wig and whiskers, is leering by the side of Mademoiselle Coralie on her sofa in the Rue de Bréda ; Paterfamilias, with a mask and a nose half-a-yard long, is hobbling after her at the ball.   The *enfant terrible* is making Papa and Mamma alike ridiculous by showing us Mamma's lover, who is lurking behind the screen.   A thousand volumes are written protesting against the seventh commandment.   The old man is for ever hunting after the young woman, the wife is for ever cheating the husband.   The fun of the old comedy never seems to end in France ; and we have the word of their own satirists, novelists, painters of society, that it is being played from day to day.

' In the works of that barbarian artist Hogarth, the subject which affords such playful sport to the civil-ised Frenchman is stigmatised as a fearful crime, and is visited by a ghastly retribution. The English savage never thinks of such a crime as funny, and a hundred years after Hogarth, our modern "painter of mankind," still retains his barbarous modesty, is tender with children, decorous before women, has never once thought that he had a right or calling to wound the modesty of either.

' Mr. Leech surveys society from the gentleman's point of view. In old days, when Mr. Jerrold lived and wrote for that celebrated periodical, he took the other side : he looked up at the rich and great with a fierce, sarcastic aspect, and a threatening posture ; and his outcry or challenge was—" Ye rich and great, look out ! We, the people, are as good as you. Have a care, ye priests, wallowing on a tithe-pig, and rolling in carriages and four ; ye landlords grinding the poor ; ye vulgar fine ladies bullying innocent governesses, and what not,—we will expose your vulgarity, we will put down your oppression, we will vindicate the nobility of our common nature," and so forth. A great deal is to be said on the Jerrold side ; a great deal was said ; perhaps even a great deal too much. It is not a little curious to speculate upon the works of these two famous contributors of *Punch,* these two "preachers," as the phrase is.

"Woe to you, you tyrant and heartless oppressor of the poor !" calls out Jerrold as Dives's carriage rolls by. "Beware of the time when your bloated coachman shall be hurled from his box, when your gilded flunkey shall be cast to the earth from his perch, and your pampered horses shall run away with you and your vulgar wife and smash you into ruin." The other philosopher looks at Dives and his cavalcade in his own peculiar manner. He admires the horses and copies with the most curious felicity their form and action. The footman's calves and powder, the coachman's red face and floss wig, the over-dressed lady and plethoric gentleman in the carriage, he depicts with the happiest strokes ; and if there is a pretty girl and a rosy child on the back seat, he "takes them up tenderly" and touches them with a hand that has a caress in it. This artist is very tender towards all the little people. It is hard to say whether he loves boys or girls most—those delightful little men on their ponies in the hunting fields, those charming little Lady Adas flirting at the juvenile ball ; or Tom the butcher's boy, on the slide ; or ragged little Emly pulling the go-cart freighted with Elizarann and her doll. Steele, Fielding, Goldsmith, Dickens are similarly tender in their pictures of children. "We may be barbarians, Monsieur——, but even the savages are occasionally kind to their papooses." When are the holidays ?

Mothers of families ought to come to this exhibition and bring the children. Then there are the full-grown young ladies—the very full-grown young ladies —dancing in the ball-room, or reposing by the sea-shore—the men can peep at whole seraglios of these beauties for the moderate charge of one shilling, and bring away their charming likenesses in the illus-trated catalogue (two-and-six). In the " Mermaids' Haunt," for example, there is a siren combing her golden locks, and another dark-eyed witch actually sketching you as you look at her, whom Ulysses could not resist. To walk by the side of the much-sounding sea and come upon such a bevy of beauties as this, what bliss for a man or a painter ! The mermaids in that haunt, haunt the beholder for hours after. Where is the shore on which those creatures were sketched ? The sly catalogue does not tell us.

' The outdoor sketcher will not fail to remark the excellent fidelity with which Mr. Leech draws the back-grounds of his little pictures. The homely landscape, the sea, the winter wood by which the huntsmen ride, the light and clouds, the birds float-ing over head, are indicated by a few strokes which show the artist's untiring watchfulness and love of nature. He is a natural truth-teller, as Hogarth was before him, and indulges in no flights of fancy. He speaks his mind out quite honestly, like a thorough Briton. He loves horses, dogs, river and field sports.

He loves home and children,—that you can see.
He holds Frenchmen in light esteem. A bloated
" Mosoo " walking Leicester Square, with a huge
cigar and a little hat, with " billard " and " esta-
minet " written on his flaccid face—is a favourite
study with him ; the unshaven jowl, the waist tied
with a string, the boots which pad the Quadrant
pavement, this dingy and disreputable being exercises
a fascination over Mr. Punch's favourite artist. We
trace, too, in his work a prejudice against the Hebrew
nation, against the natives of an island much celebrated for its verdure and its wrongs; these are
lamentable prejudices indeed, but what man is without his own ? No man has ever depicted the little
" Snob " with such a delightful touch. Leech
fondles and dandles this creature as he does the
children. To remember one or two of those dear
gents is to laugh. To watch them looking at their
own portraits in this pleasant gallery will be no small
part of the exhibition ; and as we can all go and see
our neighbours caricatured here, it is just possible
that our neighbours may find some smart likenesses
of *their* neighbours in these brilliant, life-like, good-
natured sketches in oil.'[1]

We could not resist giving this long extract. What
perfection of thought and word ! It· is, alas ! a
draught of a wine we can no more get ; the vine is

[1] *Times*, June 21, 1862.

gone. What flavour in his ' dear prisoned spirit of the impassioned grape !' What a *bouquet !* Why is not everything that hand ever wrote, reproduced ? shall we ever again be regaled with such œnanthic acid and ether ?—the volatile essences by which a wine is itself and none other—its flower and bloom ; the reason why Chambertin is not sherry, and Sauterne neither. Our scientific friends will remember that these same delicate acids and oils are compounds of the lightest of all bodies, hydrogen, and the brightest when concentrated in the diamond, carbon ; and these in the same proportion as sugar ! Moreover, this ethereal oil and acid of wine, what we may call its genius, never exceeds a forty-thousandth part of the wine ! the elevating powers of the fragrant Burgundies are supposed to be more due to this essence than to its amount of alcohol. Thackeray, Jeremy Taylor, Charles Lamb, old Fuller, Sydney Smith, Ruskin, each have the felicity of a specific œnanthic acid and oil—a bouquet of his own ; others' wines are fruity or dry or brandied, or ' from the Cape,' or from the gooseberry, as the case may be. For common household use commend us to the stout home-brewed ale from the Swift, Defoe, Cobbett, and Southey taps.

Much has been said about the annoyance which organ-grinding caused to Leech, but there were other things which also gave him great annoyance, and amongst these was his grievance against the wood-engravers.

His drawings on the polished and chalked surface of the wood-block were beautiful to look at. Great admiration has been bestowed upon the delicacy and artistic feeling shown in the wood-blocks as they appeared in *Punch*, but any one who saw these exquisite little gems as they came from his hands would scarcely recognise the same things when they appeared in print in *Punch*. When he had finished one of his blocks, he would show it to his friends and say, 'Look at this, and watch for its appearance in *Punch*.' Sometimes he would point to a landscape, and calling particular attention to it, would say that probably all his fine little touches would be 'cut away,' in a still more literal sense than that in which he uses the word in his address.

When, however, we come to consider the circumstances and pressure under which these blocks were almost always engraved, the wonder will be that they were so perfect. The blocks upon which he drew were composed of small squares, fastened together at the back, so that when the drawing was completed on the block, it was unscrewed, and the various pieces handed over to a number of engravers, each having a square inch or two of landscape, figure, or face, as the case might be, not knowing what proportion of light and shade each piece bore to the whole.

Had these blocks been carefully and thoughtfully engraved by one hand, and then been printed by the hand instead of the steam press, we might have seen some of the *finesse* and beauty which the drawing showed *before* it was ' cut away.'

There was nothing that was so great a mark of the gentleness of his nature as his steady abstinence from personality. His correspondence was large, and a perusal of it only shows how careful he must have been, to have shunned the many traps that were laid for him to make him a partisan in personal quarrels. Some of the most wonderful suggestions were forwarded to him, but he had a most keen scent for everything in the shape of personality.

We need do little more than allude to the singular purity and good taste manifested in everything he drew or wrote. We do not know any finer instance of blamelessness in art or literature, such perfect delicacy and cleanness of mind,—nothing coarse,— nothing having the slightest taint of indecency,—no *double entendre*,—no laughing at virtue,—no glorifying or glozing at vice,—nothing to make any one of his own lovely girls blush, or his own handsome face hide itself. This gentleness and thorough gentlemanliness pervades all his works. They are done by a man you would take into your family and to your heart at once. To go over his five volumes of Pictures of Life and Character is not only a wholesome pleasure

3

and diversion : it is a liberal education. And then he is not the least of a soft or *goody* man, no small sentimentalism or *petit maître* work : he is a man and an Englishman to the backbone ; who rode and fished as if that were his chief business, took his fences fearlessly, quietly, and mercifully, and knew how to run his salmon and land him. He was, what is better still, a public-spirited man ; a keen, hearty, earnest politician, with strong convictions, a Liberal deserving the name. His political pencillings are as full of good, energetic politics, as they are of strong portraiture and drawing. He is almost always on the right side,—sometimes, like his great chief Mr. Punch, not on the popular one.

From the wonderful fidelity with which he rendered the cabmen and *gamins* of London, we might suppose he had them into his room to sit to him as studies. He never did this ; he liked actions better than states. He was perpetually taking notes of all he saw. With this, and with his own vivid memory and bright informing spirit, he did it all. One thing we may be pardoned for alluding to as illustrative of his art. His wife, who was every way worthy of him, and without whom he was scarce ever seen at any place of public amusement, was very beautiful ; and the appearance of those lovely English maidens we all so delight in, with their short foreheads, arch looks, and dark laughing eyes, their innocence and *esprit*, dates from about

his marriage. They are all, as it were, *after* her,—
her sisters ; and as she grew more matronly, she may
still be traced in her mature comeliness and motherly
charms. Much of his sketches and their dramatic
point are personal experience, as in ' Mr. Briggs has
a Slate off his House, and the Consequences.' He
was not, as indeed might be expected, what is called
a funny man. Such a man was Albert Smith, whose
absolute levity and funniness became ponderous,
serious, and dreary, the crackling of thorns under the
pot. Leech had melancholy in his nature, especially
in his latter years, when the strain of incessant production and work made his fine organisation supersensitive and apprehensive of coming evil. It was
about a year before his death, when in the hunting
field, that he first felt that terrible breast-pang, the
last agony of which killed him, as he fell into his
father's arms ; while a child's party, such as he had
often been inspired by, and given to us, was in the
house. Probably he had by some strain, or sudden
muscular exertion, injured the mechanism of his
heart. We all remember the shock of his death :
how every one felt bereaved,—felt poorer,—felt
something gone that nothing could replace,—some
one that no one else could follow.

What we owe to him of wholesome, hearty mirth
and pleasure, and of something better, good as they
are, than either—purity, affection, pluck, humour,

kindliness, good humour, good feeling, good breeding, the love of nature, of one another, of truth—the
joys of children, the loveliness of our homely English
fields, with their sunsets and village spires, their
glimpses into the pure infinite beyond—the sea and
all its fulness, its waves 'curling their monstrous
heads and hanging them,' their crisping smiles on
the sunlit sands—all that variety of nature and of
man which is only less infinite than its Maker; something of this, and of that mysterious quality called
humour, that fragrance and flavour of the soul, which
God has given us to cheer our lot, to help us to
'take heart and hope, and steer right onward,' to
have our joke, that lets us laugh at and make game
of ourselves when we have little else to laugh at or
play with—of that which gives us when we will the
silver lining of the cloud, and paints a rainbow on
the darkened sky out of our own 'troublous tears;'—
something of all these has this great and simple-
hearted, hard-working artist given to us and to our
children, as a joy and a possession for ever. Let us
be grateful to him, let us give him our best honour,
affection, and regard.

Mr. Leech was tall, strongly but delicately made,
graceful, long-limbed, with a grave, handsome face,
a sensitive, gentle mouth, but a mouth that could
be 'set,' deep, penetrating eyes, an open, high,
and broad forehead, finely modelled. He looked

like his works—nimble, vigorous, and gentle; open, and yet reserved; seeing everything, saying not much; capable of heartiest mirth, but generally quiet. Once at one of John Parry's wonderful performances, 'Mrs. Roseleaf's Tea-party,' when the whole house was in roars, Leech's rich laughter was heard topping them all. There are, as far as we know, only two photographs of him; one—very beautiful, like a perfect English gentleman—by Silvy; the other more robust and homely, but very good. by Caldesi. We hope there is a portrait of him by his devoted friend Millais, whose experience and thoughts of his worth as a man and as an artist one would give a good deal to have.

When Thackeray wrote the notice of his sketches in *The Times*, Leech was hugely delighted—rejoiced in it like a child, and said, 'That's like putting £1000 in my pocket. With all the temptations he had to Club life, he never went to the Garrick to spend the evenings, except on the Saturdays, which he never missed. On Sunday afternoons, in summer, Thackeray and he might often be seen regaling themselves with their fellow-creatures in the Zoological Gardens, and making their own queer observations, to which, doubtless, we are indebted for our baby hippopotamus and many another four-footed joke. He never would go to houses where he knew he was asked only to be

seen and trotted out.   He was not a frequenter of
Mrs. Leo Hunter's at-homes.

We now give a few remarks on some of Leech's
typical woodcuts, and we hope they will send everybody to the volumes themselves.   There should
immediately be made, so long as it is possible, a
complete collection of his works, and a noble monument to industry and honest work, as well as genius
and goodness, it would be.   We begin with the
British Lion :—

THE STATE OF THE NATION.—DISRAELI MEASURING
THE BRITISH LION.

[*Punch*, vol. xvii., July 1849.]

This is from a large Cartoon, but we have only
space for the British Lion's head.   He is dressed as a
farm-labourer.   He has his hat and a big stick in his
hand, and his tail innocently draggling under his
smock-frock, which has the usual elaborate needle-
work displayed.   Disraeli, who is taking his measure
for rehabilitating the creature, is about a third shorter,
and we would say six times lighter.

What a leonine simpleton ! What a visage ! How
much is in it, and how much not ! Look at his shirt
collar and chubby cheek ! What hair ! copious and
rank as the son of Manoah's, each particular hair
growing straight out into space, and taking its own
noway particular way ; his honest, simple eyes, well

apart; his snub, infantile nose; his long upper lip, unreclaimed as No-man's-land, or the Libyan desert, unstubbed as 'Thornaby Waäste;' his mouth closed, and down at the corner, partly from stomach in discontent (Giles is always dyspeptic), partly from contempt of the same. He is submitting to be measured and taken advantage of behind his back by his Semitic brother. He will submit to this and much more, but not to more than that. He draws his line like other people, when it occurs to him; and he keeps his line, and breaks yours if you don't look to it.

He may be kicked over, and take it mildly, smiling it may be, as if he ought somehow to take it well, though appearances are against it. You may even knock him down, and he gets up red and flustered, and with his hands among his hair, and his eyes rounder and brighter, and his mouth more linear, his one leg a little behind the other; but if you hit him again, calling him a liar or a coward, or his old woman no better than she should be, then he means mischief, and is at it and you. For he is like Judah, —a true lion's whelp. Let us be thankful he is so gentle, and can be so fierce and staunch.

HEALTHY EXCITEMENT.—HUNTING IN A GALE OF WIND.

Did you ever see such a wind? How it is making game of everything; how everything scuds! Look at his whiskers. Look at the tail of his descending friend's horse. Look at another's percursory 'Lincoln and Bennett' bowling along ! Look at his horse's head —the jaded but game old mare ; the drawing of her is exquisite ; indeed there is no end of praising his horses. They are all different, and a dealer could tell you their ages and price, possibly their pedigree.

There is a large woodcut in the *Illustrated London News* (any one who has it should frame it, and put the best plate-glass over it) ; it is called 'Very Polite. The party on the grey, having invited some strangers to lunch, shows them the nearest way (by half a mile) to his house.' The 'party' is a big English squire— sixteen stone at least—with the handsome, insolent face of many of his tribe, and the nose of William the Conqueror. He has put the grey suddenly and quite close to a hurdle-fence that nobody but such a man would face, and nothing but such blood and bone could take. He is returning from a 'run,' and is either ashamed of his guests, and wants to tail them off, or would like to get home and tell his wife that 'some beggars' are coming to lunch ; or it may be merely of the nature of a sudden lark, for the escape of his own and his grey's unsatisfied 'go.' The grey is over it like a bird. The drawing of this horse is marvellous ; it is an action that could only last a fraction of a second, and yet the artist has taken it. Observe the group in the road of the

astounded 'strangers.' There is the big hulking,
sulky young cornet, 'funking,' as it is technically
called; our friend Tom Noddy behind him, idiotic
and ludicrous as usual, but going to go at it like a
man such as he is,—the wintry elms, the big hedger
at his work on his knees,—all done to the quick. But
the finest bit of all is the eye of the mare. She
knows well it is a short cut home; and her cheery,
fearless, gentle eye is keenly fixed, not on where she
is about to land—that's all right—but on the distance,
probably her own stable belfry. This woodcut is
very valuable, and one of the largest ever done after
him.

REMARKABLE OCCURRENCE.

[Pictures of Life and Character, vol. iii. p. 21.]

How arch! how lovely! how maidenly in this
their 'sweet hour of prime,' the two conspirators are!
What a clever bit of composition! how workmanlike
the rustic seat! how jauntily the approaching young
swells are bearing down upon them, keeping time
with their long legs! you know how they will be
chaffing all through other in a minute; what ringing
laughs!

'AND JOCUND DAY
STANDS TIPTOE ON THE MISTY MOUNTAIN TOPS.'

[Little Tour in Ireland, p. 28.]

And is not she a jocund *morn?* day is too old for
her. She is in 'the first garden of her simpleness'—in

'the innocent brightness of her new-born day. How plumb she stands! How firm these dainty heels!— leaning forward just a little on the wind; her petti- coat, a mere hint of its wee bit of scolloped work, done by herself, doubtless; the billowy gown; the modest little *soupçon* of the white silk stockings, anybody else would have shown none, or too much; the shadow of puffing papa approaching to help her down; the wonderful sense of air and space. The only thing we question is—Would papa's hat's shadow show the rim *across*, instead of only at the sides?

BIT FROM THE MINING DISTRICTS.

FIRST—'*W'nt tak' thy quoat off, then! Oi tell thee oi'm as good a mon as thee!*'

SECOND—'*Thee a mon! Whoy, thou be'est only walkin aboot to save thy funeral expenses.*'

[*Pictures of Life and Character,* vol. ii. p. 19.]

This belongs to a set of drawings made when down in Staffordshire, his wife's county. They are all full of savage strength. They show how little he drew from fancy, and how much from nature, memory and invention proper, which, as does also true imagination, postulate a foundation in materials and fact. A mere Cockney—whose idea of a rough was that of a London ruffian—would have put Staffordshire clothes on the Bill Sykes he may have seen in the flesh or more likely on the stage, and that would be all: Leech gives you the essence, the clothes and the county. Look at these two fellows, brutal as their own bull-dogs and as staunch,—having their own virtues too, in a way,—what a shoulder, what a deltoid and biceps! the upper man developed largely by generations of arm-work, the legs well enough, but not in proportion,—their education having been neglected. Contrast these men with Leech's Highlandmen in *Briggs' Salmon and Grouse Adventures:* there matters are reversed, because so are the conditions of growth. A Staffordshire torso on Rannoch or Liddesdale legs would be an ugly customer. Observe the pipe fallen round from the mouth's action in speaking, and see how the potteries are indicated by the smoking brick cupola.

MR. BRIGGS STRUGGLING INTO HIS NEW HUNTING-BOOTS.

[*Pictures of Life and Character*, vol. iv. p. 90.]

This is delicious! What comic *vis!* Pluck and perspiration! bewilderment and bottom! He'll be at it again presently, give him time. This is only one of the rounds, and the boot-hooks are ready for the next. Look at the state of his back hair, his small, determined eye! the braces burst with the stress! The affair is being done in some remote solitary room. The hat is ready, looking at him, and so are the spurs and the other boot, standing bolt upright and impossible; but he'll do it; apoplexy and asphyxia may be imminent; but doubtless these are the very boots he won the steeplechase in. A

British lion this too, not to be ' done, hating that *bête* of a word 'impossible' as much as Bonaparte did, and as Briggs does him. We have an obscure notion, too, that he has put the wrong foot into the boot; never mind.

The character of *Mr. Briggs*, throughout all predicaments in *Punch*, is, we think, better sustained, more real, more thoroughly respectable and comic, than even Mr Pickwick's. Somehow, though the latter worthy is always very delightful and like himself when he is with us, one doesn't know what becomes of him the rest of the day; and if he was asked to *be*, we fear he couldn't live through an hour, or do anything for himself. He is for the stage. *Briggs* is a man you have seen, he is a man of business, of sense, and energy; a good husband and citizen, a true Briton and Christian, peppery, generous, plucky, obstinate, faithful to his spouse and bill, only he has this craze about hunting and sport in general.

CONNEMARA BAY.
[Little Tour in Ireland, p. 73.]

This is from the Little Tour in Ireland, in which, by the by, is one of the only two drawings he ever made of himself,—at page 141; it is a back view of him, riding with very short stirrups a rakish Irish pony; he is in the Gap of Dunloe, and listening to a barefooted master of blarney. The other likeness is in a two-page Cartoon,—' Mr. Punch's Fancy Ball,

January 1847. In the orchestra are the men on the *Punch* staff at the time. The first on the left is Mayhew, playing the cornet, then Percival Leigh the double bass, Gilbert A'Beckett the violin, Doyle the clarionet, Leech next playing the same—tall, handsome, and nervous—Mark Lemon, the editor, as conductor, appealing to the fell Jerrold to moderate his bitter transports on the drum. Mooning over all is Thackeray—big, vague, childlike—playing on the piccolo; and Tom Taylor earnestly pegging away at the piano. What a change from such a fancy to this sunset and moonrise on the quiet, lonely Connemara Bay,—nothing living is seen but the great winged sea-bird flapping his way home, close to the 'charmed wave.' The whole scene radiant, sacred, and still; ' the gleam, the shadow, and the peace supreme.' The man who could feel this, and make us feel it, had the soul and the hand of a great painter.

A MORAL LESSON FROM THE NURSERY.

ARTHUR. *Do you know, Freddy, that we are only made of dust?*

FREDDY. *Are we? Then I'm sure we ought to be very careful how we pitch into each other so, for fear we might crumble each other all to pieces.*

[*Pictures of Life and Character*, vol. iii. p. 27.]

This speaks for itself. Nobody needs to be told which is Freddy; and you see the book from which Arthur got his views of genesis and the mystery of being; and the motherly, tidy air of the beds!

Freddy's right thumb in his belt ; the artistic use of that mass of white beyond his head ; the drawing of his right sole ; the tremendous bit of theology in that ' only '—do any of us know much more about it now than does Arthur ?—only surely nobody would now say, according to Pet Marjorie's brother, that our Arthur, as he now sits, clean and caller, all tucked up in his night-gown—made of soft cotton, thick and (doubtless) tweeled—and ready for any amount of discussion, is only ' dirt.'[1]

We have said he was greater in humour than in caricature or even satire, and, like all true humour-ists, he had the tragic sense and power—for as is the height so is the depth, as is the mirth so is the melancholy ; Loch Lomond is deepest when Ben

[1] This word, in conjunction with children, brings into our mind a joke which happened to Dr. Norman M'Leod, and which he tells as only he could tell his own stories. He was watching some barelegged Glasgow street children who were busied in a great mud-work in the kennel. ' What's that ? ' said he, stooping down. ' It's a kirk,' said they, never look-ing up. ' Where's the door ? ' ' There's the door,' points a forefinger, that answers young Fleming's account of the consti-tution of man. ' Where's the steeple ? ' ' There's the steeple,' —a defunct spunk, slightly off the perpendicular. ' Where's the poopit ? ' ' There's the poopit,' said the biggest, his finger making a hole in a special bit of clay he had been fondly round-ing in his palms ; ' and where's the minister ? ' ' Oh, ye see, looking as vacant as a congregation in such circumstances should, and as the hole did when he withdrew his finger : ' *Ou're run oot o' dirt ;*' but jumping up, and extinguishing for

dips into it.—Look at this. Mr. Merryman and his dead wife—there is nothing in Hogarth more tragic and more true. It is a travelling circus ; its business at its height ; the dying woman has just made a glorious leap through the papered hoop ; the house is still ringing with the applause ; she fell and was hurt cruelly, but saying nothing, crept into the caravan room ; she has been prematurely delivered, and is now dead ; she had been begging her Bill to come near her, and to hear her last words ; Bill has kissed her, taken her to his heart—and she is gone. Look into this bit of misery and nature ; look at her thin face, white as the waning moon

' Stranded on the pallid shore of morn ;'

the women's awe-stricken, pitiful looks (the great

the time, with his bare foot, the entire back gallery, he exclaims, 'There's Airchie comin', he's got a bit.' Airchie soon converted his dirt into a minister, who was made round, and put into his hole, the gallery repaired, and the 'call' vociferously unanimous and 'sustained.' Wouldn't that jovial piece of professional 'dirt' chew his cud of droll fancies as he walked off, from the fall of man to the Aberdeen Act, and the entire subject of dirt ?

'Where did Adam fall?' said his kindly old minister to 'Wee Peter' at the examination. 'Last nicht, at the closemooth, sir' (Adam, like his old namesake, was in the way of frequenting a certain trot; his was the 'The Lemon Tree'—it was in Aberdeen),—'and he's a' *glaur* yet' (glaur being *Scottice*, wet dirt). 'Ay, ay, my wee man, said the benevolent Calvinist, patting his head, 'he's a' glaur yet,—he's a' glaur yet.'

Gomersal, with his blue-black unwhiskered cheek, his heavy moustache, his business-like, urgent thumb,—even he is being solemnised and hushed); the trunk pulled out for the poor baby's clothes, secretly prepared at bye-hours by the poor mother; the neatly-mended tear in Mary's frock; the coronet, the slippers, the wand with its glittering star; the nearness of the buzzing multitude; the dignity of death over the whole. We do not know who 'S. H. is, who tells, with his strong simplicity, the story of 'The Queen of the Arena'—it is in the first volume of *Once a Week*—but we can say nothing less of it than that it is worthy of this woodcut; it must have been true. Here, too, as in all Leech's works, there is a manly sweetness, an overcoming of evil by good, a gentleness that tames the anguish; you find yourself taking off your shoes, and bow as in the presence of the Supreme,—who gives, who takes away,—who restores the lost.[1]

[1] We remember many years ago, in St. Andrews, on the fair-day in September, standing before a show, where some wonderful tumbling and music and dancing was being done. It was called by way of *The Tempest*, a ballet, and *Miranda* was pirouetting away all glorious with her crown and rouge and tinsel. She was young, with dark, wild, rich eyes and hair, and shapely, tidy limbs. The Master of ceremonies, a big fellow of forty, with an honest, merry face, was urging the young lady to do her best, when suddenly I saw her start, and thought I heard a child's cry in the midst of the rough music. She looked eagerly at the big man, who smiled, made her jump

THE GREAT SOCIAL EVIL.

TIME—MIDNIGHT.　A SKETCH NOT A HUNDRED MILES FROM
THE HAYMARKET.

BELLA—'*Ah! Fanny! how long have you been gay?*'

This, too, tells its own story. It appeared in
1857, and Leech was warned that this was not for
Punch—it was too serious. It certainly is serious
enough. He was thanked privately by many of the
best men and women of England for this terribly
true 'tract for the times.' What deepest misery
and melancholy! the wind and rain, the wet muddled
paint on the cheeks, the weak hopeless mouth, the
thin shoes, frayed with casino work, the beauty, the
desolation and ruin—who is inclined to cast a stone
at these *filles de joie?* who blames them alone?
who does not wonder why such things are? who
would not do them every good if one could—if

higher than ever, at the same time winking to some one within.
Up came the bewitching *Ferdinand*, glorious, too, but old and
ebriose; and, under cover of a fresh round of cheers from the
public, *Miranda* vanished. Presently the cry stopped, and the
big man smiled again, and thumped his drum more fiercely. I
stepped out of the crowd, and getting to the end of the caravan,
peered through a broken panel. There was our gum-flower-
crowned *Miranda* sitting beside a cradle, on an old regimental
drum, with her baby at her breast. Oh! how lovely, how
blessed, how at peace they looked, how all in all to each other!
and the fat handy-pandy patting its plump, snowy, unfailing
friend; it was like Hagar and young Ishmael by themselves
I learned that the big man was her husband, and used her well
in his own gruff way.

4

one only knew how to reach, how to prevent their
ever being what they are?   Here, too, as everywhere,
is his gentleness, his compassion, his sympathy.   It
is as affecting, though not so terrible, as the dying
and the burial scenes in the Harlot's Progress, and
surely it is more humane, more merciful and less
hopeless, than Hogarth's awful story.   He never did
anything of this kind again in *Punch*, except once.
It is given in the second series of *Pictures of Life
and Character*, page 72, and is called, 'Always Gay.'
It is a scene from a Parisian masque ball, and has a
Satanic perfection of wickedness that haunts one,
the woman's mouth, the man's cloven feet, his eye—
as if damned already.

We end as we began, by being thankful for our
gift of laughter, and for our makers of the same, for
the pleasant joke, for the mirth that heals and
heartens, and never wounds, that assuages and
diverts.   This, like all else, is a gift from the
Supreme Giver—to be used as not abused—to be
kept in its proper place, neither despised nor esti-
mated and cultivated overmuch; for it has its perils
as well as its pleasures, and it is not always, as in this
case, on the side of truth and virtue, modesty and
sense.   If you wish to know from a master of the art
what are the dangers of giving one's-self too much up
to the comic view of things, how it demoralises the

whole man, read what we have already earnestly commended to you, Sydney Smith's two lectures, in which there is something quite pathetic in the earnestness with which he speaks of the snares and the degradations that mere wit, comicality, and waggery bring upon the best of men. We end with his concluding words :—

' I have talked of the *danger* of wit and humour : I do not mean by that to enter into commonplace declamation against faculties because they *are* dangerous ;—wit is dangerous, eloquence is dangerous, a talent for observation is dangerous, *every* thing is dangerous that has efficacy and vigour for its characteristics ; nothing is safe but mediocrity. The business is, in conducting the understanding well, to risk something ; to aim at uniting things that are commonly incompatible. The meaning of an extraordinary man is, that he is *eight* men, not one man ; that he has as much wit as if he had no sense, and as much sense as if he had no wit ; that his conduct is as judicious as if he were the dullest of human beings, and his imagination as brilliant as if he were irretrievably ruined. But when wit is combined with sense and information ; when it is softened by benevolence, and restrained by strong principle ; when it is in the hands of a man who can use it and despise it, who can be witty and something much *better* than witty, who loves honour, justice, decency, good-nature, morality, and religion, ten thousand times better than wit ;—wit is *then* a beautiful and delightful part of our nature. There is no more interesting spectacle than to see the effects of wit upon the different characters of men ; than to observe it expanding caution, relaxing dignity, unfreezing coldness,—teaching age, and care, and pain, to smile,—extorting reluctant gleams of pleasure from melancholy, and charming even the pangs of grief. It is pleasant to observe how it penetrates through the coldness and awkwardness of society, gradually bringing men nearer together, and, like the combined force of wine and oil, giving every man a glad heart and a shining countenance. *Genuine and innocent wit and humour like this, is surely the flavour of the mind ! Man could direct his ways by plain reason, and support his life by tasteless food; but God has given us wit, and flavour, and brightness, and laughter, and perfumes, to enliven the days of man's pilgrimage, and to " charm his pained steps over the burning marle." '*

Some time after the publication of the foregoing article, the author received, among various papers and letters relating to the great humourist, the following reminiscences, written by his friend the Rev. S. Reynolds Hole, now Canon of Lincoln,—to whom we owe the letterpress of '*A Little Tour in Ireland,*'

' *A Book on Roses,* ' *The Six of Spades,*' ' *Hints to Preachers,*' and just the other day '*Nice and her Neighbours,*' all full—besides much else that is excellent in sense, knowledge and feeling—of the best of ' heart-easing mirth,'—with the generous purpose of aiding him in a projected Memoir of John Leech ; ill health, however, put a stop to this congenial labour (as well as to much else), and this beautiful tribute of friendship has remained for the last dozen years in an old box among wood-blocks, proof-sheets, sketches, and other *disjecta membra* of ' a book in progress.' As there is small likelihood of the author carrying out his intention, he trusts that the kind friend will forgive the long delay that has intervened, and he is sure that his readers will thank him for giving the sketch now without the encumbrance of a commentary.

DE AMICITIÂ.

' Would you like to meet John Leech ?' said to me a kindly friend and neighbour, in the spring-tide of the year 1858.

There could only be one answer, ' Would a famished pike like to meet a gudgeon?' seeing that it had long been a chief yearning of my heart to know one who had so often brought brightness into it. Accordingly, upon one of the happiest days of the Christian year, upon Easter Monday, I met Leech. How well I remember the anxiety with which I

awaited, in my friend's drawing-room, the entrance of
my hero !   At last, with the gentleness and quietude
which, out of his beautiful humility, graced all he
did, he was with us. Appraising them at their own
valuation, the butler, who subsequently announced
the dinner, was infinitely superior to the guest, and
yet he was the man who, I verily believe, brought
more innocent gladness into our homes, and, far
beyond that, taught men to despise humbug and to
admire honesty, to 'ring out the false, ring in the
true,' more generally, more convincingly, than any
teacher alive. Well, he was very like my idea of him
—only 'more so.' A slim, elegant figure, over six feet
in height, with a grand head, 'on which Nature had
written Gentleman,'—with wonderful genius on his
ample forehead, wonderful penetration, observation,
humour in his blue-grey Irish eyes, and wonderful
sweetness, sympathy, and mirth about his lips, which
seemed to speak in silence. He was, as we gardeners
have it, 'rather short of foliage ;' and a vacant space at
the back of his head no doubt suggested his charming
sketch of the *enfant terrible*, climbing up the visitors'
chair, and proclaiming to his mamma that 'Mr.
Boker had got a double forehead.'[1]   His clothes were
Shakespearean (how Shakespeare would have loved

---

[1] His own little boy, he told me, while under the scissors of
the haircutter, solemnly requested the performer 'not to leave
any on the top, as he wished to be like papa !'

him!), and the apparel proclaimed the man, to whom gaudy or ill-fitting raiment would have been uncomfortable as the shirt of Hercules. Vividly as I recall his advent, I have few distinct recollections of the happy evening which followed. I was too much excited, and interested, and delighted, to make mental notes or reflections. I remember that we were greatly amused by his account of the whisperings which he overheard in the hunting-field that day (he had been out with our host, and his friend Adams, in the Belvoir country), as to the wonderful feats of horsemanship which, 'as the celebrated Mr. Leech,' he was expected to perform—he being the quietest and most retiring of riders, much as he loved the sport, and never going over a fence when he could find a gap or a gate. It seemed, nevertheless, to be the general impression and belief of the yeomen who followed his Grace of Rutland's hounds, that, when a fox was found, the celebrated Mr. Leech would utter a wild Irish yell, clench his teeth, put both spurs into his steed, and bound over Lincolnshire like a mad buck. His complete inaptitude for these gymnastics, and the consequent disappointment and disgust of the agricultural interest, when he made an early deviation from the line of chase in favour of the king's highway, seemed to please him vastly, and there was, I need hardly say, an irresistible influence in Leech's mirth. We went over many other fields besides those of the hunt, and in all he was the pleasant, observant companion, never wishing to lead or to teach, and yet always the first to see the things which were best worth the seeing. Too soon had come to us that night the time for wise men to part, had not that hour brought to me the glad assurance that John Leech and I were to be friends. I knew it thankfully, when I held that wonder-working right hand in mine, and we exchanged invitations, and expressed hopes of reunion—

> ' Love at first sight, first born and heir to all,
>   Made the night thus,'

to be followed by so many happy days, and by so many sweet, though pathetic memories.

II.

Three months after our first meeting, I went to dine with him at his home in Brunswick Square. I was in London, to superintend the final arrangements of the First National Exhibition of Roses (and nothing but roses) which had ever been held in England, having originated the idea and organised the plan, and Leech, knowing this, sent me, together with a charming sketch of a stand-up fight between Venus and Flora, which was to come off at the Rose Show,[1] a summons to his house. As an inducement to come (it

[1] This subsequently appeared in *Punch.*

was as though one offered to a red-hot cabman upon an August day a sovereign if he would kindly swallow a pint of foaming stout) he told me I should meet Thackeray! I began to think that I must have done something unconsciously, in my sleep, or in a mesmeric trance, which had placed the country under obligation. Perhaps there was truth in transmigration, and I was somebody else. Yes, it must be so, and I said to the person whom I saw in the looking-glass, when I was dressed for dinner, and who used to be me, 'Sir, I am going to dine with the great Mr. Leech, to meet the great Mr. Thackeray, and we must part for ever.' Whereupon he winked.

Ah! but, in all seriousness, that was a memorable night, 'a green spot on the path of time,' at which I was introduced by the great artist to the great author. And the latter, instead of eyeing me as he might have done, and as some immense and awful mastiff might have eyed a poor country shepherd-dog, with a look which said, 'If you dare to wag your tail, I'll eat you,' came to me with a genial welcome, because I was the guest of the dearest friend he had,[1] and, ere you could have boiled an egg, we were standing back to back to know which of the twain was the longest.[2] The company

---

[1] Leech had the intense happiness of hearing that when Thackeray was asked to name his dearest friend, he replied, after a few moments' thought, 'John Leech.'

[2] While this measurement was going on, he narrated how he once went with his friend Higgins, 'Jacob Omnium,' to see a

decided that there was no difference, and I remember that my modesty, which there and then fled away for ever, made her last expiring speech, 'Yes the fiddle-cases are of equal size, but in his there's a glorious violoncello, and in mine a dancing-master's kit.' Then Leech's boy came into the room, and the great man left me to greet and to 'tip' his god-son; but he was ever from that time my hearty, hospitable, beloved, and honoured friend.

John Leech's consideration for others was patent wherever he went, but his anxiety for his friends, their enjoyment and amusement, in his own house, was a very winsome sight to see. 1 think that he would have put on his rough dreadnought overcoat, and placed himself in a prostrate position at his front door, if he had thought that any guest would have gone home happier, because he had used him as a mat; and I feel sure, that if each friend had appeared not only, like Briareus, with a hundred hands, but with fifty palates to correspond, he would have rejoiced to find knives, and forks, and food. Far too much of a gentleman to be a gourmand, though he was wont to say that he felt as though he deserved a good dinner when he had done a hard day's work, and that as a matter of economy he was reluctantly

giant, and the man at the door of the exhibition inquired 'whether they were in the business!' (I think Thackeray was 6 ft. 2, Hole 6 ft. 4, and Higgins 6 ft. 6.—J. B.)

compelled to eat and drink of the best, lest he should injure his manipulation, he seemed to think, nevertheless, that his guests were bound to be greedy (it never occurred to him that mutton with a Leech was far better than venison with a lout), and that it was his duty to provide the material. I remember that on one occasion the strawberries were so large, that he put the largest on a plate, and handed it to a servant, with a request that it might be carved on the sideboard.

It was not only in the matter of viands; whenever you were in his house, unless he saw you occupied, he waited upon you, while the world itself waited for him, and expressed its impatience in a smell of corduroy. That perfume, he was wont to affirm, never left his hall, and it proceeded from the raiments of certain small boys, who came continually to his house to convey thence to the wood engraver the boxwood 'blocks' on which he drew.

III.

Only a few days elapsed before he paid me the first of many happy visits. I perplexed myself with the question, how a man, who lived in London amid the wits of the day, could be entertained agreeably in the loneliness and dulness of our country life, but I soon saw that my anxiety was foolish. It was evidently, as he said, a grand enjoyment to him simply to sit under a tree and rest, to hear the throstle instead of the hurdy-gurdy, to see the sun instead of the smoke, and to smell the roses instead of the corduroy. I drove him to see the great oaks of the Shire Wood,—Sherwood Forest, as it is now called,—and he could only sigh his admiration. Presently he opened his pocket sketch-book, and put a point on his pencil, but he turned from one bit of loveliness to another as he sauntered on, and soon he closed his book in a kind of profound but calm resignation. 'Much too beautiful for work,' he said ; 'I can do no work to-day.' So we sat 'mid the bracken and drank in that delicious air, 'quite as pure in flavour, and reasonable in cost, although *not quite* so wholesome, as—the still champagne at the Garrick !'

Next day, I remember, I had a garden-party, to do homage to the king of artists and the queen of flowers. His majesty was delighted with her majesty, and he was perfectly happy in helping us to arrange the profusion of roses and other flowers sent in for table decoration. Some of my guests were, I think, a little disappointed at first to see the man whom they had so long associated and identified with Punch, in the ordinary clothes of society, instead of in gay habiliments, and were vexed to find that he had left his hump and the larger moiety of his nose at home ; but all accounted it an honour to touch that beneficent hand. And nothing could exceed the king's affability—specially to the pretty girls. Some of them wore their sweetest smiles, with an evident expectation of having their portraits taken for the future admiration of the world, and the kindliness with which the great artist noticed and encouraged their little efforts was beautiful to see, save to one young man of a sullen temperament, who, after watching the idol of his heart, 'making up,' as he termed it, to J. L. with all her fascinations, retired into a shrubbery to smoke, and murmured a desire (mercifully qualifying his wrath with humour) to '*punch* that fellow's head!' All others admired, and I shall never forget the perplexity, the mixture of amusement and annoyance upon his countenance, when one of them, with more heart than head, and slightly heightened as with wine, jocund, and boon, began to praise him with a loud enthusiasm, and to address him as 'the delight of the nation.'

That evening he told me, when our guests were fled, our garlands dead, and all but he departed, that he thought of refreshing himself with a fortnight's holiday in Ireland—would I go with him. As Ireland was not then the calm, peaceful, happy, loyal, united country which it now is, or rather, is going to be in a few days, when the Government has made its arrangements, as there were some unpleasantnesses between the landlords and the tenants, together with some little reserve and stiffness between the Catholics and the Protestants, brought on by the intemperate use of whisky and loaded guns, it seemed my duty to go and settle these misunderstandings (as every Englishman so well knows how to do), and, accordingly, I resolved to accompany him; and though next morning my resolution shook in its shoes, when, just as he was leaving me, he said, 'You must write your impressions, and I will illustrate,' I fortified myself with the fact that nobody much heeds the description at a good diorama, and that if I broke down in my small comedy, *his* scenery and dresses would still make it a success; and so with a light heart and a heavy portmanteau I made ready to sail.

IV.

Mr. John Deane, who had been long in Ireland, as one of the Royal Commissioners, in the terrible time of the famine, kindly drew out a route which enabled us to see a great deal in a brief space or time—Dublin, Galway, the wild grandeur of Connemara, the scenery of the Shannon from Athlone to Limerick, the gentle loveliness of Killarney, the miniature prettiness of Glengarriff, 'that beautiful city called Cork,' and its suburbs, in little more than a fortnight. Moreover, we had ample time thoroughly to enjoy that which we saw, not acting on the principle of that Cockney tourist whom dear old Waterton, the naturalist, met in Belgium, and who boasted that he 'had knocked off thirteen churches that morning,' but going leisurely, like large butterflies from flower to flower, and resting on them, till we knew them well. In fact, you cannot hurry in Ireland, there is something in the humid atmosphere and in the habits and demeanour of the people which ignores haste. Ah me, how happy we were! Looking from the steamer at the calm phosphorescent waves (so thankful they were calm, for we were miserable mariners, though Leech had represented himself in a letter as revelling in stormy seas),[1] or gliding along the rails, or riding in cars, or rowing in boats, listening to quaint carmen, oarsmen, and guides, talking and laughing in genial converse with each other, or silent in serene fruition of the exquisite scenery around—silent in perfect sympathy, one of the surest signs, and one of the purest delights of a true friendship! There are so many worthy folks who are afraid you will be dull if they don't go on gently buzzing into your ear, and there are so many unenlightened folks to whom, upon the same kindly principles, we consider it our duty to buz. But in all our easy and placid enjoyment, Leech never forgot his art. There was constantly a lovely bit of expression upon the face of nature, animate or inanimate, or there was something which he had never been able to get quite right, or something

[1] See pen-and-ink sketch of John Leech as the jolly tar, by himself, on next page.

which he wanted for a special purpose, or which
could not fail to be useful, or which would illustrate
our tour. Of course, I was intensely curious upon

'À LA T. P. COOKE.'

the latter point; but the memoranda which he made
from time to time, as we agreed that this or that
were worthy of delineation, were not instructive. Just
a few lines, and dots, and curves. All that he
wanted was there, none the less, and all the truth,
as surely as in shorthand notes. Nothing absurd,
abnormal, incongruous, in any way ridiculous, ever
escaped him, I need hardly say; and a touch of his
elbow, or a turn of his thumb, drew my attention
continually to something amusing in the aspect, or the
remarks of those about us, at the *table-d'hôte*, on the
steamer, or the public car, which else in my obtuseness
I had never relished. On rare, very rare, occasions
it was my privilege to tell or to show him something
which took his fancy, and he would say, in a tone
which told you at once that he really thought he was
asking a favour, 'May I make use of that?' Then
would I draw myself up as a monarch upon his
throne, and, extending my arms in royal clemency,
would make reply, '*You may!*' Thus passed the
pleasant days of that '*Little Tour in Ireland*,' which
his truthful, charming sketches afterwards made so
justly popular. These illustrations are not numerous,
but with them as with all his work, he took anxious
pains. He went a second time over the Channel,
and across Ireland to Galway, that he might finish
to his satisfaction that wonderful picture of the
Claddagh, which makes the frontispiece of the book.

5

It was always his rule, however pressed for time, surrounded with engagements, or enticed by pleasures, never to 'scamp' his work. This is proved by the fact, that in looking through it, you always find some new attractions, some delicate touch, which you had missed before. Sometimes his rapidity of execution was marvellous (I have known him send off from my own house three finished drawings on the wood, designed, traced, and rectified, without much effort, as it seemed, between breakfast and dinner), but there was never haste. How I used to wish that the world could have seen those blocks! They were committed, no doubt, to the most skilful gravers of the day, but the exquisite fineness, clearness, the faultless grace and harmony of the drawing could not be reproduced. If the position of an eyelash was altered, or the curve of a lip was changed, there might be an ample remainder to convey the intention, and to win the admiration of those who never knew their loss, but the perfection of the original was gone. Again and again I have heard him sigh, as he looked over the new number of *Punch;* and as I, seeing nothing but excellence, would ask an explanation, he would point to some almost imperceptible obliquity (not 'a pleasing obliquity,' as Charles Matthew says in the play, when he would compliment his friend with the squint) which vexed his gentle soul.

V.

After our Irish tour, the friendship between us was very brotherly and true, and a continuous intercourse, personal and epistolary, was continued up to his death. The city mouse and the country mouse paid each other many visits, but without any interruption of their mirth. It was a great intellectual treat to me to meet at his house Thackeray and Millais, Holman Hunt and Tenniel, Dasent, Wingrove Cooke, Knox, Mark Lemon and Shirley Brooks, and dear old Percival Leigh; and it was a refreshment to him to have a walk over the stubbles, or a gallop after the hounds, or a day of tranquil rest. The latter was to me the prime happiness of our communion—to sit and converse quietly with the friend I loved best on earth. Next to this, to see him in his house, with his wife and children.

He first saw Mrs. Leech, then Miss Eaton, walking in London, and felt as the opossum, who, on the approach of a great American rifleman, requested him to take no further trouble, for that he was perfectly willing to come down. He followed her home, noted the number, looked out the name, obtained an introduction, married the lady. She was one of those Anglican beauties whom he loved to draw (I could show you faces like hers in *Punch*), a very pleasant and amiable person—a devoted mother and wife.

No one was more amused than she, when Leech 'had just seen the most fascinating creature, most probably a "female marquis," with whom he was devotedly in love, and who, he had occasion to believe, was not indifferent, etc. etc. etc.' *Semper fidelis*, nevertheless, was on John Leech's shield.

His boy, John George Warrington Leech, was in a double sense his son, for he was the main warmth and brightness of his life.[1]   And how the child returned his love !   I have mentioned his ambition for the tonsure, that he might be like his father ; and he was ever trying to imitate him.   He wore a little coat of velvet, made exactly like that in which Leech generally did his work, and he stood before a miniature easel (*æt.* 5), painting the engravings of the *Illustrated London News* with an air of profound interest.   Even then he had, like his father in *his* childhood, a marvellous notion of drawing.   Nor was that his only development in art.   I was in the house when he said to a new nurse-maid, who had just appeared in his nursery, ' Nurse, papa says that I am one of those children that can only be managed by kindness, and I 'll trouble you to fetch some sponge-cakes and oranges !'[2]

[1] He was drowned at South Adelaide in the year 1876.
  'The spoiler came, and all his promise fair
    Hath sought the grave, to sleep for ever there.' [1881.]
[2] I recall another occasion in which this clever little man was master of the position.   My wife's maid had paid a long visit

'Ada, sole daughter of his house and heart,' was a clever and charming girl.

His mother [1] and sisters I met frequently, and with pleasure always, but his father I first saw standing by John Leech's grave. Afterwards I had much interesting correspondence and conversation with him, and learned from him, as well as from my beloved friend himself, certain particulars of the great artist's life, which I will now repeat.

VI.

A man of fine culture, a profound Shakespearean, and a thorough gentleman, John Leech, the elder, an Irishman, was landlord of the London Coffee House on Ludgate Hill, the most important at that time of the large city hotels. Unfortunately for him, fortunately for the world, he did not succeed in this vocation, and was obliged to retire from it. I say happily for the world, because the son was stimulated to the exercise of the genius which has so enriched that world.

to the nursery, for a chat with his lady-in-waiting, and when he began some display of disobedience, she said, 'Really, Master Leech, if you won't be good, I must tell your mamma.' 'And I shall tell her,' he rejoined, 'if you do, what a time you've been idling here.'

[1] Mrs. Leech could claim consanguinity with the great scholar and master of Trinity College, Cambridge, Richard Bentley.

The son was born on the 29th of August, in the year 1817.

So meanly did he think of this sphere of existence, that when he had only been three years in it he tried hard to leave it. ‘He had a sudden and most severe inflammatory attack’ (his father writes to me), ‘and only the skill of Sir Charles Mansfield Clarke and Dr. James Nicholls, humanly speaking, brought him out of it. He used to resist *à l'outrance* the application of remedies suggested by these great physicians, and on one occasion, when he was to be bled by cupping, he baffled the whole domestic force brought against him, until, hearing of his mother's sorrowful disappointment, he jumped up, Sir Charles used to say, like a Spartan, and bade them, *do it.*’

He was only seven when he went to Charterhouse, but ‘I thought,’ writes his father, ‘that I was not wrong in sending him thus early, as Dr. Russell, the head master, had a son of the same age in the school, and John was in the same form with him.’

This early departure from his home was, of course, a sore trial to his fond mother's heart. It had cost her many a pang to part with him ; but as she was a lady of good sense, as well as of gentle heart, she resolved to abstain from visiting him at his boarding-house. She knew it was right that he should be left to take his chance with the others, and she had sufficient strength of mind not to sacrifice his future welfare to the indulgence of her own affection. See him, however, she would, but in such a way that the child should not see her. She therefore hired a room in one of the houses which commanded a view of the Carthusian playing-ground; and here she would sit behind a blind day after day, happy and content so that she could get a glimpse of her child. Sometimes she would see him strolling about with his arm round the neck of one of his little companions as the manner of schoolboys is; sometimes he was playing and jumping about with childish glee; but still the mother kept her watch. And some thirty-six years afterwards, John Leech showed to his friend, whose words I have been quoting (see *Once a Week*, vol. iii. p. 101), the window at which she sat. In this same article, there is, moreover, a charming illustration of a boy, like himself, surveying from 'The Coach Tree' at Charterhouse one of His Majesty's mails below.

What sort of boy was he? A friend of mine and schoolmate of his (Mr. Nethercote of Northampton-shire) thus answers the question:—'All I recollect of John Leech as a Charterhouse boy is a nice-looking, genial lad, liked by every one in the school for his good temper and winning manner.

'As far as I remember, he did not take part in athletic sports, such as cricket, tennis, hocky, racing, etc.'

It is easy to account for his absence from the
rougher sports of the play-ground, because his arm
was broken in early boyhood by a fall from his pony,
and was for a long time weak in consequence, but
he was always fond of sports and manly exercises,
and preferred the lessons of Angelo the fencing-
master, to those of Mr. Burgess the drawing-master,
despite that early excellence with the pencil, which
developed itself as soon as he took pencil in hand.
Before he mounted the Coach Tree, he had made
some marvellous sketches of the four-in-hand, and
'to play at coaches' was his favourite childish game.
A pile of boxes and portmanteaus represented the
coach, Master Leech, perched atop, the coachman,
and a brace of chairs for wheelers, with a couple of
sisters for leaders, supplied the 'spanking team.' On
one occasion there was dole in Astolat, and dismay
in the house of Leech, for the eldest daughter was
going to her first ball, and as the time drew near the
dress of the debutante could nowhere be found.
Ultimately it was discovered in its box, but the box
had been converted into the hind boot of Master
Leech's coach, and was all but hidden from view.

His future profession was also prefigured in his
nursery amusements, and the residence of 'John
Leech, surgeon,' was represented by a doll-house,
upon which he wrote his name and avocation.
Perhaps one of the prettiest sketches he ever drew

was a mimic scene of a visit from the doctor, which appeared in a number of *Punch's Pocket Book*, under the title of 'a Bad Case for Influenza.' The neck-tie of the physician, with the sweet little legs below, the invalid doll, the wee sister holding the doctor's (rocking) horse, are exquisite.

I don't know whether his youngest sister wrote the song, 'I'd like to be a Bird,' but she was discovered one day, placed under the seat of a cane chair, weighted with a heap of heavy books, lest the little birdie should escape, which he was feeding with crumbs, administered between the bars of her cage.

That when at school, being on one occasion 'stood up' with his playmate, Merewether, son of the sergeant, he summoned courage to plead aloud for pardon, 'Please, sir, may Merewether and me get down?' The answer was, 'Merewether may, but Me mayn't.'

He left Charterhouse in the year 1833, and entered the medical profession under the auspices of Mr. Stanley, surgeon of St. Bartholomew's Hospital, who expressed to his father the admiration of his anatomical drawings.

Mr. Leech, the elder, writes to me that his first intention was to apprentice his son to Sir George Ballingall of Edinburgh, but the embarrassment of his affairs prevented the arrangement, and the young student went, no long time after, to reside with a Mr.

Whittle, whose eccentricities have been set forth by
Albert Smith in his 'Adventures of Mr. Ledbury and
his friend Jack Johnson,' first published in *Bentley's
Miscellany.* Leech frequently referred to 'Rawkins'
as being the facsimile of Whittle, a man of giant size,
but tapering off sadly in the leg department, very
fond of 'doing statues,' dying gladiator, Hercules,
and a *pose plastique*, which he beautifully described
as 'Thingamyjig defying the Lightning,' the name of
Ajax having escaped his memory. He was also very
fond of animals, guinea-pigs, rabbits, ferrets, and
birds, the back premises being a regular menagerie,
and the roof an aviary. Here Leech made the
acquaintance of those ornithological and canine
enthusiasts, bird-fanciers and dog-dealers, whose
countenances, contour, and costume he could always
reproduce at will.

In a complicated case of organic disease, or in
one which required delicate surgical manipulation,
Mr. Whittle, as represented by Leech 'returning
from the masquerade as Hercules,' was not the best
man in London. The *Pil. Hum.*, of which Albert
Smith writes, was extensively given to his patients.
It meant *Pilula Humbugensis*, and was made of
liquorice powder and yellow soap. Thus was Mr.
Whittle continually (as Pitt said of Addington, when
he was soft-sawdering the country members), 'an
apothecary, gulling of simples.'

At St. Bartholomew's and elsewhere, John had at this early period of his life made friendships, which he always prized, with Albert Smith, with Percival Leigh (the author of the *Comic English Grammar, Pips' Diary*, etc.), for whom he had a most affectionate regard, with Mr. Adams who was, I think, reading law, and who being well-to-do, and having a carriage and horses, delighted young Leech by driving him about town, as afterwards, when Mr. Adams lived in Hertfordshire, by mounting him with the hounds. The young gentlemen occasionally 'heard the chimes at midnight, Master Shallow,' and enjoyed together a large amount of harmless fun. On one occasion when they were representing with great success before His Majesty's lieges a select company of glee-singers, and were liberally rewarded with small coin and copper, 'I crossed the street' (said J. L. to me), 'to a very attentive listener, and held out my cap. But he quietly produced a small fiddle from behind his back, and silently pleaded exemption from my claims, on the score of "being in the trade."'

Mr. 'Rawkins' married the widow of a publican, and his former pupils derived intense gratification from his last new cartoon, which they went often to see,—Hercules in his shirt-sleeves (the shirt not by Deianira), peacefully drawing beer.

John Leech seems to have gradually given up his medical studies, and to have resolved to live by his art. Well, if he had persevered in them until he had become the founder of a new College of Surgeons, not he and all his coadjutors could have brought the comfort and refreshment into sick-rooms and hospitals which that one pencil has bestowed. But he had a hard battle to fight. He had to carry about sketches, and blocks, and stones, from publisher to publisher. When he drew that picture of Social Miseries, in which the little maid-of-all-work says to her master, 'Oh, if you please, sir, here's that dark gentleman called again; I told him you wasn't at home, but he says he'll just step up, and he's a-comin' upstairs,' it is to be feared that the scene was suggested by experience rather than fancy. How by degrees he achieved greatness, and therewith a large income, is recorded in his works, and may be read by all.

VII.

From success to success, from rude sketches in *Bell's Life* until his masterly political cartoons and his wonderful little pictures of daily life were appreciated and expected throughout the civilised world, *but he was always overworked*. A passionate love of his art, and a desire to increase his income, not for himself but that he might be generous to others, these were the perpetually motive powers which robbed him of his rest. They acquired new force, as he acquired new fame; and as his great powers developed themselves more and more, and higher rewards were offered, he increased, when he should have relaxed, his efforts. The enlargement of his drawings by a mechanical contrivance (of which I possess some of the earliest results, in illustrations of our Little Tour in Ireland), to be afterwards coloured by hand, brought him a new class of works in those 'Sketches in Oil,' which were exhibited in London and purchased at such high prices. To be a painter was his grand ambition, and I remember that I rebuked him, when he said, 'that he would rather have painted a great picture, than all he had ever done,' and expressed my belief that his pencil had done more good to his generation than all the brushes of the Royal Academy.

'Work, work, work' (as his friend Hood sang), new projects, new applications, daily! The brain busy when the hand was unoccupied; the mind abstracted and employed, when the man was supposed to be taking holiday—even when at his meals.[1] Then the shadow of a coming danger fell upon the hearts which loved him best. 'Can't you take him back with you into the country?' Thackeray said to me

---

[1] My neighbour, Lord Ossington, then Speaker, told me that he met Leech on the rail, and expressed to him the hope that he enjoyed in his work some of the gratification which it brought to others. The answer was, 'I seem to myself to be a man who has undertaken to walk a thousand miles in a thousand hours.'

almost angrily; never thinking, in his unselfishness and tender forethought for his friend, that he himself was as much in need of rest; but I strove and pleaded in vain. 'There was a great opportunity; he had brilliant offers; he would certainly come, shortly.'

Then the great man, who had been to him as a brother, the schoolmate of his boyhood, the chief friend of his manhood, Thackeray, died. He told Millais of his presentiment, that he also should die suddenly and soon. His nervous system became more and more unstrung; in London, the street music produced an intolerable irritation; in the country, the sound of a scythe at work under his bedroom, made him not only restless but wretched; yet he went working on.

At last the brave heart broke. 'Please God, Annie, I'll make a fortune for us yet,' he said to his wife on the morning of the 29th of October 1864; and, a few hours afterwards, that same voice whispered into the same loving ear, 'I'm going.'

> 'I go,' he said; and as he spoke, she found
> The hand grow cold, and fluttering was the sound—
> Then gazed affrighted, but she caught a last.
> A dying, look of love, and all was past.

I did not know of my friend's death until the 31st, when, with a grief which here will never leave me, I read it in the *Times* Very. very sadly I thought next morning, as I went to my daily service, that we should no more take sweet counsel together, and go up to the house of God in company. And then the great solace came, came in these glorious words, which I read to my little flock, in the first lesson of All Saints' Day : 'But the souls of the righteous are in the hand of God, and there shall no torment touch them. In the sight of the unwise, they seemed to die ; and their departure is taken for misery, and their going from us to be utter destruction : *but they are in Peace.*'

A JACOBITE FAMILY.

A JACOBITE FAMILY.

DID you ever, when journeying along a road at night, look in curiously at some cottage window, and, like a happier Enoch Arden, watch unseen the bright life within, and all the *naïve* ongoings of the household?

Such a glimpse of the inner life of a Jacobite family in the latter half of last century we have had the privilege of enjoying, and we wish we could tell our readers half as vividly what it has told to us. We shall try.

On the river Don, in Aberdeenshire—best known to the world by its Auld Brig, which Lord Byron, photography, and its own exceeding beauty have made famous—is the house of Stoneywood, four miles from the sea. It was for many generations the property of the Lords Frazer of Muchalls, now Castle Frazer, one of the noblest of the many noble castles in that region, where some now nameless architect has left so many memorials of the stately life of their strong-brained masters, and of his own quite singular genius for design.

Stoneywood was purchased near the close of the

sixteenth century, from the Lord Frazer of that time, by John Moir of Ellon, who had sold his own estate, as tradition tells, in the following way:—Bailie Gordon, a wealthy Edinburgh merchant, made a bargain with the Laird of Ellon, when in his cups, to sell his estate at a price greatly under its value. The country folk, who lamented the passing away of the old family, and resented the trick of the bailie, relieved themselves by pronouncing their heaviest malediction, and prophesying some near and terrible judgment. Strangely enough, the curse, in the *post hoc* sense, was not causeless. A short time after the purchase an awful calamity befell Mr. Gordon's family.

Its story has been told by a master pen, that which gave us *Matthew Wald* and *Adam Blair*, and the murderer *M'Kean*. We give it for the benefit of the young generation, which, we fear, is neglecting the great writers of the past in the wild relish and exuberance of the too copious present. It will be an evil day when the world only reads what was written yesterday, and will be forgotten to-morrow.

Gabriel's Road [in Edinburgh] derives its name from a horrible murder committed there a great number of years ago.

'Gabriel was a preacher or licentiate of the Kirk, employed as domestic tutor in a gentleman's family in Edinburgh, where he had for pupils two fine boys of eight or ten years of age. The tutor entertained, it seems, some partiality for the Abigail of the children's mother, and it so happened, that one of his pupils observed him kiss the girl one day in passing through an anteroom, where she was sitting. The little fellow carried this interesting piece of intelligence to his brother, and both of them mentioned it by way of a good joke to their mother the same evening. Whether the lady had dropped some hint of what she had heard to her maid, or whether she had done so to the preacher himself, I have not learned; but so it was, that he found he had been discovered, and by what means also. The idea of having been detected in such a trivial trespass was enough to poison for ever the spirit of this juvenile Presbyterian—his whole soul became filled with the blackest demons of rage, and he resolved to sacrifice to his indignation the instruments of what he conceived to be so deadly a disgrace. It was Sunday, and after going to the church as usual with his pupils, he led them out to walk in the country— for the ground on which the New Town of Edinburgh now stands, was then considered as *the country* by the people of Edinburgh. After passing calmly, to all appearance, through several of the green fields, which have now become streets and squares, he came to a place more lonely than the rest, and there drawing a large clasp-knife from his pocket, he at once stabbed the elder of his pupils to the heart.

6*

The younger boy gazed on him for a moment, and then fled with shrieks of terror: but the murderer pursued with the bloody knife in his hand, and slew him also as soon as he was overtaken.   The whole of this shocking scene was observed distinctly from the Old Town, by innumerable crowds of people, who were near enough to see every motion of the murderer, and hear the cries of the infants, although the deep ravine between them and the place of blood, was far more than sufficient to prevent any possibility of rescue. The tutor sat down upon the spot, immediately after having concluded his butchery, as if in a stupor of despair and madness, and was only roused to his re-collection by the touch of the hands that seized him.

'It so happened that the magistrates of the city were assembled together in their council-room, waiting till it should be time for them to walk to church in procession (as is their custom), when the crowd drew near with their captive.   The horror of the multitude was communicated to them, along with their intelligence, and they ordered the wretch to be brought at once into their presence.   It is an old law in Scotland, that when a murderer is caught in the very act of guilt (or, as they call it, *red-hand*), he may be immediately executed, without any formality or delay.   Never surely could a more fitting occasion be found for carrying this old law into effect.   Gabriel was hanged within an hour after the deed was done, the red knife being suspended from his neck, and the blood of the innocents scarcely dry upon his fingers.'[1]

The boys were the sons of the new Laird of Ellon. It adds something to the dreadfulness of the story that it was the woman who urged the wretched youth to the deed. We remember well this *Gabriel's Road*, the lane leading up past 'Ambrose's,' the scene of the famous *Noctes*. It is now covered by the New Register Office buildings.

But to return to the ex-Laird of Ellon. Mr. Moir, having lost one estate, forthwith set about acquiring another, and purchased Muchalls, its Lord having got into difficulties. The lady of the Castle, loath, we doubt not, to leave her 'bonnie house,' persuaded Mr. Moir to take instead, the properties of Stoneywood, Watterton, Clinterty, and Greenburn, on Don side, which were afterwards conjoined under the name of the barony of Stoneywood. The grateful Lady of Frazer sent along with the title-deeds a five-guinea gold piece—a talisman which was religiously preserved for many generations.

The family of Stoneywood seem from the earliest record down to their close, to have been devotedly attached to the house of Stuart. In the old house there long hung a portrait of Bishop Juxon, who attended Charles I. on the scaffold, and through this

[1] *Peter's Letters to his Kinsfolk,* vol. ii.

prelate must have come a still more precious relic, long preserved in the family, and which is now before us, the Bible which the doomed King put into the hands of the Bishop on the scaffold, with the word ' Remember,' having beforehand taken off his cloak and presented it and the insignia of the Garter to the same faithful minister and friend ; this is one of our glimpses.[1] We have the sacred and royal book before us now,—a quarto, printed in 1637, bound in blue velvet, and richly embroidered and embossed with gold and silver lace. There is the crown and the Prince of Wales' feathers, showing it had belonged to Charles II. when prince. He must have given it to his hapless father, as the C. P. is changed into C. R. Though faded it looks princely still.

One of the blank leaves, on which was written 'Charles Stuart ano dom. 1648,' was, along with the gold piece, pilfered as follows :—

' Miss Moir, who was rather of an unaccommodating temper, remained alone at Stoneywood for a year longer, and in fact until the sale had been completed, and it became necessary to quit. The retired and solitary life she led during this last period was taken advantage of by a woman in her service, of

---

[1] From Bishop Juxon the Bible passed to his friend Bishop Patrick Scougall of Aberdeen, and was inherited from him, through his daughter, by his descendants and representatives the Moirs of Stoneywood.—[W. F. S.]

the name of Margaret Grant, to commit various thefts, with the assistance of a paramour, who happened unfortunately to be a blacksmith. By his means they got the charter-chest opened, and abstracted thence the prophetic gold piece, gifted by Lady Frazer two hundred years before, and also Bishop Juxon's valuable legacy of King Charles's Bible, presented to him on the scaffold. The gold piece was readily made available, and was, of course, never recovered, but the Bible proved to be a more difficult treasure to deal with, it being generally known in the county to be an heirloom of the Stoneywood family, and accordingly, when she offered it for sale in Aberdeen, she became aware that she was about to be detected. She took the precaution to abscond, and suspecting that mischief might come of so sacrilegious a theft, she came by night to Stoneywood, and deposited the Bible at the foot of a large chestnut-tree which overshaded the entrance of the front court of the house, where it was found next morning. However, it did not return altogether unscathed by its excursion, for a bookseller in Aberdeen, to whom it had been offered for sale, had the cunning, or rather the rascality, to abstract the blank leaf on which the royal martyr's autograph was inscribed, which he managed to paste upon another old Bible, so dexterously as not to be easily discovered, and actually profited by his fraud, in disposing of his counterfeit Bible to the Earl of Fife for a large sum of money, and in whose library it now figures as King Charles's Bible, while the original still remains in the possession of the representative of the family to whom it descended by inheritance, and in its appearance bears ample testimony to its authenticity.'

To go back to Stoneywood. The Laird is now there; his eldest son, James, has married Jane, eldest daughter of Erskine of Pittoderie, and the young bride has got from her mother a green silk purse with a thousand merks in it, and the injunction never to borrow from the purse except in some great extremity, and never to forget to put in from time to time what she could spare, however small, ending with the wish, 'May its sides never meet.' The daughter was worthy of the mother, and became a '*fendy* wife,' as appears by the following picturesque anecdote. Young Moir was going to the neighbouring village of Greenburn to the fair to buy cattle; the green purse was in requisition, and his wife, then nursing her first child, went with him. While he was making his market, she remained outside, and observing a tidy young woman sitting by the roadside, suckling her child, she made up to her and sat down by her side. Waiting, she soon got as hungry for her own baby as doubtless it was for her, so proposed to comfort herself by taking the woman's child.

This was done, the young mother considering it a great honour to have a leddy's milk for her baby. Mrs. Moir, not wishing to be disturbed or recognised, had the woman's cloak thrown over her head, she setting off into the fair to see what her husband was about. She was hardly gone, when a man came suddenly behind Mrs. Moir, and hastily lifting up the corner of the plaid, threw something into her lap, saying, 'Tak' tent o' that!' and was off before Mrs. Moir could see his face. In her lap was the green purse, with all its gear untouched!

Embarrassed with her extempore nursling and cloak, she could not go to her husband, but the young woman returning, she went at once in search; and found him concluding a bargain for some cows. He asked her to wait outside the tent till he settled with the dealer; in they went; presently a cry of consternation; in goes the purse-bearer, counts out the money, tables it, and taking her amazed 'man' by the arm, commanded him to go home.

What a pleasant little tale Boccaccio, or Chaucer, or our own Dunbar would have made of this!

From it you may divine much of the character of this *siccar* wife. Ever afterwards when the Stoneywood couple left home they confided the purse to their body-servant, John Gunn; for in those days no gentleman travelled without his purse of gold: and although we have a shrewd guess that this same John was in the secret of the theft and the recovery of the purse on the fair day, he was as incorruptible ever afterwards as is Mr. Gladstone with our larger purse.

This John Gunn was one of those now extinct functionaries who, like the piper, were the lifelong servants of the house, claiming often some kindred with the chief, and with entire fidelity and indeed abject submission, mingling a familiarity, many amusing instances of which are given in Dean Ramsay's book, and by Miss Stirling Graham. John, though poor, had come of gentle blood, the Gunns of Ross-shire; he went into the army, from which, his Highland pride being wounded by some affront, he deserted, and joined a band of roving gipsies called Cairds.[1]   His great strength and courage

---

[1] We all remember Sir Walter's song; doubtless, like 'ta faliant Fhairshon,' our John Gunn was 'a superior person,' but there must have been much of the same fierce, perilous stuff in him, and the same fine incoherence in his transactions :—

' Donald Caird can lilt and sing,
   Blithely dance the Highland fling ;
   Drink till the gudeman be blind,
   Fleech till the gudewife be kind ;
   Hoop a leglan, clout a pan,
   Or crack a pow wi' ony man ;
   Tell the news in brugh and glen,
   Donald Caird 's come again.

   Donald Caird can wire a maukin,
   Kens the wiles o' dun-deer staukin ;
   Leisters kipper, makes a shift
   To shoot a muir-fowl i' the drift :
   Water bailiffs, rangers, keepers,
   He can wauk when they are sleepers ;
   Not for bountith, or reward,
   Daur they mell wi' Donald Caird.

   Donald Caird can drink a gill,
   Fast as hostler-wife can fill ;
   Ilka ane that sells gude liquor,
   Kens how Donald bends a bicker
   When he 's fou he 's stout and saucy
   Keeps the cantle o' the causey :
   Highland chief and Lowland laird
   Maun gie way to Donald Caird.

   Steek the awmrie, lock the kist,
   Else some gear will sune be mist
   Donald Caird finds orra things
   Where Allan Gregor fand the tings.
   Dunts o' kebbuck, taits o' woo,
   Whiles a hen and whiles a soo ;
   Webs or duds frae hedge or yard—
   'Ware the wuddie, Donald Caird !'

soon made John captain of his band, which for years levied black mail over the county of Aberdeen.

John got tired of his gipsy life, and entered Stoneywood's service, retaining, however, his secret headship of the Cairds, and using this often in Robin Hood fashion, generously, for his friends. So little was this shady side of his life known in the country-side, that his skill in detecting theft and restoring lost property, was looked upon as not 'canny,' and due to 'the second sight.'

On one occasion Mr. Grant, younger of Ballin-dalloch, was dining at Stoneywood. He was an officer in the Dutch Brigade, and had come home to raise men for a company, which only wanted twelve of its complement. He was lamenting this to Mr. Moir, who jocularly remarked, that 'if John Gunn,' who was standing behind his chair, 'canna help ye, deil kens wha can.' Upon which John asked Mr. Grant when he could have his men ready to ship to Holland. 'Immediately,' was the reply. 'Weel a weel, Ballindalloch, tak' yer road at aince for Aberdeen, tak' out a passage for them and twelve mair, and send me word when ye sail, and, if ye keep it to yoursel', ye'll find your ither men a' ready.' Mr. Grant knew his man, and made his arrange-ments. The twelve men made their appearance with John at their head. When they found what was their destination they grumbled, but John, between fleech-

ing and flyting, praised them as a set of strapping
fellows; told them they would soon come back again
with their pockets full of gold. They went and never
returned, finding better quarters abroad, and thus John
got rid of some of his secret confederates that were
getting troublesome.

Another of John's exploits was in a different line.
Mr. Moir had occasion to go to London, taking John
with him of course. He visited his friend the Earl
of Winton, then under sentence of death in the
Tower for his concern in the rebellion of 1715. The
Earl was arranging his affairs, and the family books
and papers had been allowed to be carried into his cell
in a large hamper, which went and came as occasion
needed. John, who was a man of immense size and
strength, undertook, if the Earl put himself, instead
of his charters, into the hamper, to take it under his
arm as usual, and so he did, walking lightly out. Lord
Winton retired to Rome, where he died in 1749.

On 'the rising' in the '45 John joined young Stoneywood, his master's son, but before telling his adventures
in that unhappy time, we must go back a bit.

The grandson of old Stoneywood, James, born in
1710, was now a handsome young man, six feet two
in height, and of a great spirit. As his grandfather
and father were still alive, he entered into foreign
trade; his mother, our keen friend of the green purse,
meantime looking out for a rich marriage for her son,

fixed on Lady Christian, daughter of the Earl of
Buchan, and widow of Fraser of Fraser; but our
young *Tertius* liked not the widow, nor his cousin
of Pittoderie, though her father offered to settle his
estate on him; Lord Forbes's daughter with a tocher
of 40,000 merks was also scorned. And all for the
same and the best reason. He was in love with his
cousin, Margaret Mackenzie of Ardross. It was the
old story,—*liebend und geliebt.* But their 'bright
thing,' though it did not in the end 'come to confusion,' did not for a time 'run smooth.' Thomas,
his brother, a sailor, was likewise bewitched by the
lovely cousin. He was refused, found out the
reason, and in his rage and jealousy intercepted the
letters between the lovers for three long miserable
years, James living all the time at Stoneywood, and
she far away in Ross-shire. The unworthy sailor
made his way to Ardross, asked Margaret and her
sister why they didn't ask for James, and then told
them he was just going to be married to Miss
Erskine of Pittoderie, and to have the estate.
Margaret, thus cruelly struck, said, 'Thomas, ye
know my bindin', I have been aye true; I have
angered my father, and refused a rich and a good
man, and I'll be true till James himsel' is fause,' and
like a frozen lily, erect on its stem, she left them—
to pass her night in tears.

James was as true as his Margaret; and his grand-

father and father agreed to his marriage, under a
singular condition : the bulk of the rents were settled
in annuity on the two seniors, and the estate made
over to the young laird in fee-simple. The seniors
did not long cumber him or the land; they both
died within the year. Straightway James was off to
Ardross to claim his Margaret. He came late at
night, and 'rispit at the ring.' Murdo, the young
laird, rose and let him in, sending a message to his
sister to get a bedroom ready for his cousin Stoneywood. Miss Erskine of Pittoderie was in the house
as it so happened, and old Lady Ardross, in her
ignorance, thinking young Moir was after her,
wrathfully sent word to him that he must not disturb
the family, but might share Murdo's bed. Poor
Margaret said little and slept less, and coming down
before the rest in the early morning to make ready the
breakfast, she found her cousin there alone : they
made good use of their time, we may be sure, and
the cruel mystery about the letters was all cleared up.

James and Thomas never met till they were both
on the verge of the grave ; the old men embraced,
forgiving and forgiven.

The lovers were married at Ardross in September
1740, and they came to Stoneywood, where our
stern old lady gloomed upon them in her displeasure,
and soon left them, to live in Aberdeen, speaking
to her son at church, but never once noticing his

lovely bride. For all this he made far more than up by the tenderest love and service. We quote the touching words of their descendant: 'With the only recollection I have of my grandfather and grandmother in extreme old age, their sedate and primitive appearance, and my veneration for them, makes the perusal of the very playful and affectionate letters which passed betwixt them at this early period of their lives to me most amusing and comic.' But between these times there intervened long years of war, and separation, perils of all kinds, exile, and the death of seven lusty sons in their youth.

We have seen a portrait of Mrs. Moir in her prime, in the possession of her great-grandson; it shows her comely, plump, well-conditioned, restful, debonnair—just the woman for the strenuous, big Stoneywood's heart to safely trust in.

Soon after his marriage, young Stoneywood had a violent fever; the mother and the cold sister came to his bedside, never once letting on that they saw his wife; and Annie Caw, an old servant, many years after, used to say that 'her heart was like to break to see the sweet young leddy stannin' the hale day in silence, pretendin' to look out at the garden, when the big saut draps were rinnin' doon her bonnie cheeks.' The old dame returned to Aberdeen at night without one word or look of sympathy. They

7

had a daughter,—still the old lady was unmitigated, but a son made all sweet.

Then came the stirring, fatal '45. Stoneywood, when laid up with a severe burn of the leg, received an express from the Countess of Errol, desiring his immediate attendance at Slains Castle.[1]   Lame as he was, he mounted his horse and rode to Slains, where the Prince gave him a commission as lieutenant-colonel; he found Gordon of Glenbucket there, having come from France, where he had lived in exile since the '15, his son with him, and though he was blind he joined the cause, so that there were then three generations of John Gordons under the Prince's banner, as sings the Jacobite doggrel :—

> ' Nor, good Glenbucket, loyal throughout thy life,
>   Wert thou ungracious in the manly fight,
>   Thy chief degenerate, thou his terror stood,
>   To vindicate the loyal Gordon's blood.
>   The loyal Gordons they obey the call,
>   Resolvèd with their Prince to fight or fall.'

Stoneywood, from his great strength and courage, and his entire devotedness to the cause, was a man of mark.   Walking down the Broad Street of Aberdeen, he was fired at from a window by one Rigg, a barber. Mr. Moir called up to him to 'come down, and he'd have fair play afore the townsmen,' an invitation *il Barbiere* declined.   Before joining the Prince,

---

[1] It is doubtful if the Prince ever was at Slains.   A commission may have been waiting Stoneywood there.

Stoneywood, with characteristic good sense and forethought, took a step which, if others had done, the forfeiture and ruin of many families would have been spared; he executed a formal Commission of Factory over his whole lands in favour of his wife. On the utter collapse of the enterprise at Culloden, he made his way from Ruthven, near Kingussie, through the wilds of Braemar, and reached his own house—then filled with English troops—at midnight. Leaping over the garden-wall, he tapped at his wife's window, the only room left to her, in which slept the children, and her faithful maid, Anne Caw. She was lying awake,—'a' the lave were sleeping,'—heard the tap, and, though in strange disguise, she at once knew the voice and the build to be her husband's. He had been without sleep for four nights; she got him quietly to bed without waking any one in the room. Think of the faithful young pair, not daring even to speak, for Janet Grant, the wet-nurse, was not to be trusted—a price was on his head!

Stoneywood left late the next evening, intending to cross the Don in his own salmon-boat, but found it drawn up on the other side, by order of Paton of Grandholm, a keen Hanoverian. Stoneywood called to the miller's man to cross with the boat. 'And wha are ye?' 'I'm James Jamieson o' Little Mill,' one of his own farmers. 'Jamieson' was a ready joke on his father's name.

Stoneywood made for Buchan, where he lay for months, being hunted day and night. Here he was joined by our redoubtable friend John Gunn, who, having left his father's service some time before, had gone into his old line, and had been tried before the Circuit Court at Aberdeen, and would have fared ill had Stoneywood not got an acquittal. This made John more attached than ever. He said he would stick to his Colonel, and so he and his gipsy wife did. She continued to carry letters and money between Stoneywood and his wife, by concealing them under the braiding of her abundant black hair. So hot was the pursuit, that Stoneywood had to be conveyed over-night to the house of a solitary cobbler, in the remote muirland. His name was Clarke. Even here he had to make a hole behind the old man's bed, where he hid himself when any one came to the door. It shows the energy of Stoneywood's character, and his light-heartedness, that he set to work under the old cobbler to learn his craft, and to such good purpose, that his master said,—'Jeems, my man, what for did ye no tell me ye had been bred a sutor?' 'And so I was, freend, but to tell ye God's truth, I was an idle loon, gey weel-faured, and ower fond o' the lassies, so I joined the Prince's boys, and ye see what 's come o't!' This greatly pleased old Clarke, and they cobbled and cracked away cheerily for many an hour. So much for brains and will. On one occasion, when hard pressed by their pursuers, Mr. Moir turned his cobbling to good account, by reversing his brother Charles's brogues, turning the heel to the toe, a joke requiring dexterity in the walker as well as in the artist. After many months of this risky life—to which that of a partridge with a poaching weaver from West Linton on the prowl, was a species of tranquillity,—our gallant, strong-hearted friend, hearing that the Prince had escaped, left for Norway in a small sloop from the coast of Buchan, along with Glenbucket and Sir Alexander Bannerman.

It was when living in these wilds that a practical joke of John Gunn's was played off, as follows :—

'After the battle of Culloden, James Moir lurked about in the wildest parts of Aberdeenshire to escape imprisonment. One day the Laird of Stoneywood, with a small party of friends and servants, was on the hill of Bennachie engaged boiling a haggis for their dinner, when they were suddenly aware of a party of soldiers coming up the hill directly towards them. Flight was their only resource, but before leaving the fire John Gunn upset the pot, that their dinner might not be available to their enemies. Instead of bursting on the ground, the haggis rolled unbroken down the hill, towards the English soldiers, one of whom, not knowing what it was, caught it on his bayonet, thereby showering its contents over himself and his comrades, on seeing which termination to the adventure, John Gunn exclaimed, "See there! even the haggis, God bless her, can charge down hill."'

Sir Walter Scott must have heard the story from the same source as ours, and has used it in *Waverley*, as follows, missing of necessity the point of the bayonet and of the joke :—

'The Highlanders displayed great earnestness to proceed instantly to the attack, Evan Dhu urging to Fergus, by way of argument, that "the *sidier roy* was tottering like an egg upon a staff, and that they had a' the vantage of the onset, for even a haggis (God bless her!) could charge down the hill."'

The Duke of Cumberland, on his way north, quartered his men on the Jacobite chiefs. A troop of dragoons was billeted on Stoneywood, where their young English captain fell ill, and was attended during a dangerous illness by the desolate and lovely wife. As soon as he was able, he left with his men for Inverness-shire, expressing his grateful assurance to Mrs. Moir, that to her he owed his life, and that he would never forget her. Some time after, when she was alone, one evening in April, not knowing what to fear or hope about her husband and her prince, a stone, wrapt in white paper, was flung into the darkening room. It was from the young English-man, and told briefly the final disaster at Culloden, adding, 'Stoneywood is safe.' He was then passing south with his men. She never saw him or heard of him again, but we daresay he kept his word : that face was not likely to be forgotten.

Lady Clark gives me the following pleasant joke:— When the Laird was lurking about Stoneywood, as a cobbler, a party of dragoons was sent to search the house for him, and were quartered there for a few days. When the troopers were withdrawn, and moving off, the commanding officer dropped behind, and said in a low voice to the 'Leddie,' 'In case of another visit from us, you had better remove the portrait of *the cobbler* from the dining-room !'

Stoneywood, before leaving his native country, thanked, and as he could, rewarded, his faithful and humble shelterers, saying he would not forget them. And neither he did. Five-and-twenty years afterwards, he visited Bartlett's house, where he lay before he took to the cobbler's. He found he had died. He took the widow and five children to Stoneywood, where they were fed and bred, the boys put to trades, and the girls given away when married, by the noble old Jacobite as a father.

As for John Gunn, his master having gone, he took to his ancient courses, was tried, found guilty this time, and closed his life in Virginia. So ends his lesson. A wild fellow with wild blood, a warm heart, and a shrewd head, such a man as Sir Walter would have made an immortal, as good a match and contrast with the princely Stoneywood, as Richie Moniplies with Nigel Oliphant, Sam Weller and Mr. Pickwick, Sancho and the Don, and those other wonderful complementary pairs, who still, and will for ever, to human nature's delectation, walk the earth.

We need not follow our Ulysses through his life in Denmark and Norway. He carried thither, as Mr. James Jamieson, as into the cobbler's hut, his energy and uprightness, his cheery and unforgetting heart, his strong sense and his strong body. He prospered at Gothenburg, and within a year sent for his Penelope. He went at the King's request to Sweden, was naturalised, and had conferred on him a patent of nobility.

Meantime he was arraigned in his own country before the High Court of Justiciary in Edinburgh, and though he was known by all the country, and had been in most of the actions fought, only two witnesses appeared against him, and their testimony went to prove his having always kept his men from violence and plunder, which drew down from Lord Justice-Clerk Milton[1] the remark, that this was more to the honour of the accused than of the witnesses.

In 1759, Mrs. Moir, out of fifteen children, had

[1] This was not the only instance in which Lord Milton showed his kindly consideration to the Jacobite rebels.

only two sons and two daughters surviving. She came across to Scotland, and settled in Edinburgh for their education. Her husband, broken in health and longing for home, after some difficulty obtained royal permission to return to Stoneywood, which he did in 1762. He died in 1782, aged seventy-two years, leaving his dear Margaret with her two daughters, all his seven sons having gone before him.

Our beautiful old lady lived into this century, dying in 1805, at the age of ninety-six, having retained her cheerfulness and good health, and a most remarkable degree of comeliness, to the last. Her teeth were still fresh and white, and all there, her lips ruddy, her cheeks suffused with as delicate a tint as when she was the rose and the lily of Ardross, gentle in her address, and with the same contented evenness of mind that had accompanied her through all her trials. We cannot picture her better than in her kinsman's loving, skilful words :—

'Accustomed as I was to pass a few hours of every day of my frequent visits to Aberdeen during a good many of the latter years of the worthy old lady's life, the impression can never become obliterated from my recollection, of the neat, orderly chamber in which, at whatever hour I might come, I was sure to see her countenance brighten up with affection, and welcome me with the never-failing invitation to come and kiss her cheek. And there she sat in her arm-chair by the fire, deliberately knitting a white-thread stocking, which, so far as appeared to me, made wondrous slow progress in its manufacture.   Her ancient maid, Miss Anne Caw, who had been seventy years in her service, and shared all the ups and downs, and toils and dangers, of her eventful life, sat in a chair on the opposite side, knitting the counterpart to my grandmother's stocking, and with equal deliberation.   Every now and then the maid was summoned from the kitchen to take up the loops which these purblind old ladies were ever and anon letting down.   A cat (how much their junior I do not know) lay curled up on an old footstool, and various little rickety fly-tables, with mahogany trellis-work around their edge supporting a world of bizarre-looking china-ornaments, stood in different corners of the room.   Every article of furniture had its appointed position, as well as the old ladies them-selves, who sat knitting away till the arrival of two o'clock, their dinner-hour.   The only thing which seemed at all to disturb the habitual placidity of my grandmother, was on being occasionally startled by the noise Miss Caw unwittingly made ; for the latter, being as deaf as a post, was quite unconscious of the disturbance she at times occasioned, when, in her vain attempts to rectify some mishap in her knitting, she so thoroughly entangled her work as to be far beyond the power of her paralytic fingers to extricate, she would touch the bell, as she conceived, with a respectful gentleness, but in fact so as to produce a clatter as if the house had caught fire. My grandmother, too blind to perceive the cause of this startling alarm, would gently remonstrate, "Oh, Annie, Annie, you make such a noise!" to which the ancient virgin, who was somewhat short in temper, seldom hearing what was addressed to her, generally answered quite at cross purposes, and that with a most amusing mixture of respect and testiness, "Yes, meddam, dis yer leddieship never let down a steek!" My grandmother's memory, although rather confused as to the later events of her life, was quite prompt and tenacious in all the details of her early history, particularly the agitating period of 1745, the circumstances of their long exile, and in fact everything seemed clear and distinct down to her husband's death, which was singularly marked as the precise point beyond which she herself even seemed to have no confidence in the accuracy of her recollection. But as the early portion was far the most interesting, it became the unfailing theme on which she seemed to have as much pleasure in dilating as I had in listening to her tales.

'I found it necessary, however, to be cautious of alluding to the present reigning family, which always discomposed her, as to the last she vehemently protested against their title to the throne. I was in the habit, when dining out, of occasionally paying an afternoon visit to her on my way to dinner, which was after tea with her, when she had entered upon the second chapter of her day's employment. For as regularly as the hour of five came round, the card-table was set out, with all its Japan boxes of cards, counters, and Japan saucers for holding the pool, etc., and my grandmother and her old maid sat down to encounter each other at piquette, and so deliberate was the game as to occupy a considerable portion of the afternoon, as the war was not carried on without frequent interlocutory skirmishes, which much prolonged the contest. The one combatant being so blind as to be incapable of ever distinguishing diamonds from hearts, or clubs from spades, while her opponent, who saw sharply enough through a pair of spectacles, so balanced on the tip of her nose, as to be a matter of never-ending wonder to me how they kept their place, was so deaf as to have to guess at the purport of whatever was addressed to her, and as they both blundered each in her own way, it gave rise to *contretemps* of never-ending recurrence, as the property of each trick was disputed. "Oh, Annie, ye are so deaf and so stupid!" "Yes, meddam, it's a sair pity ye are so blind." "Well, well, Annie, I would rather be blind as deaf." "Yes, meddam, it's my trick." But with all her testiness, there never was a more devoted creature to her mistress, and to the Stoneywood family, than that worthy old woman, Miss Caw. She was a meagre, ill-favoured-looking little personage, much bent with old age, dressed in a rusty black silk gown, marvellously short in the skirt, but compensated by a lanky, weasel-shaped waist of disproportionate length, from which was suspended my grandfather's watch, of uncommonly large size, which had been left to her by legacy, and was highly valued, and on the other side her scissors and bunch of keys. These garments were usually surmounted by a small black bonnet, and, trotting about with her high-heeled shoes, which threw the centre of gravity so far forward, her resemblance to a crow, or some curious bird of that class, was irresistibly striking, but having been once considered handsome, she was too jealous of her appearance ever to suffer me to use my pencil on so tempting a subject. She was the sister of a person of some note, Lady Jane Douglas's maid, whose evidence was so influential in the great Douglas Cause, and I think she informed me that her father had once been Provost of Perth, but that their family had after his death got reduced in circumstances. She had passed almost the whole of her life, which was not a short one, in the service of the Stoneywood family. As to my grandmother, she was a perfect picture of an old lady of the last century. Her fair comely countenance was encircled in a pure white

close cap with a quilled border, over which was a
rich black lace cap in the form in which several of
Queen Mary's pictures represent her to have worn,
a grey satin gown with a laced stomacher, and
deeply frilled hanging sleeves that reached the
elbow, and over her arms black lace gloves without
fingers, or rather which left the fingers free for the
ornament of rings, about her shoulders a small black
lace tippet, with high-heeled shoes, and small square
silver buckles; there were also buckles in the
stomacher. From her waistband also was suspended
a portly watch in a shagreen case, and on the
opposite side was a wire-sheath for her knitting.
Such was old Lady Stoneywood.'

And now we must leave our window and our
bright glimpse into the family within, and go our
ways. We might have tarried and seen much else,
very different, but full of interest; we might have
seen by and bye the entrance of that noble, homely
figure, the greatest, the largest nature in Scottish
literature, whose head and face, stoop and smile and
burr we all know, and who has filled, and will
continue to fill, with innocent sunshine the young
(ay, and the old) life of mankind. Sir Walter would
have soon come in, with that manly, honest limp;—
and his earliest and oldest friend would be there with
him, he whose words have just painted for us these
two old companions in their cordial strife, and whose

own evening was as tranquil, as beautiful, and nearly as prolonged, as that of the dear and comely lady of Stoneywood.

As we said before, what material is here for a story ! There is the crafty Bailie and the 'ower canty' Laird of Ellon ; the Sunday tragedy ; the young loves and sorrows of James and Margaret ; the green purse and its gold pieces shining through, and its 'fendy' keeper ; the gallant Stoneywood, six foot two, bending in Slains before his Prince ; John Gunn with his Cairds, and his dark-eyed, rich-haired wife ; the wild havoc of Culloden ; the wandering from Speyside to his own Don ; the tap at the midnight window, heard by the one unsleeping heart ; the brief rapture ; the hunted life in Buchan ; the cobbler with his 'prentice and their cracks ; '*Mons. Jacques Jamieson,*' the honoured merchant and Swedish nobleman ; the vanishing away of his seven sons into the land o' the leal ; Penelope, her Ulysses gone, living on with Annie Caw, waiting sweetly till her time of departure and of reunion came. We are the better of stirring ourselves about these, the unknown and long time dead ; it quickens the capacity of receptive, realising imagination, which all of us have more or less, and this waxes into something like an immediate and primary power, just as all good poetry makes the reader in a certain sense himself a poet, finding him one in little, and leaving him one in much.

So does any such glimpse into our common life, in its truth and depth and power, quicken us throughout, and make us tell living stories to ourselves ; leaves us stronger, sweeter, swifter in mind, readier for all the many things in heaven and on earth we have to do ; for we all have wings, though they are often but in bud, or blighted. Sad is it for a man and for a nation when they are all unused, and therefore shrivel and dwine and die, or leave some sadly ludicrous remembrancer of their absence, as ' of one that once had wings.'

If we grovel and pick up all our daily food at our feet, and never soar, we may grow fat and huge like the Dodo,[1] which was once a true dove, beautiful, hot-blooded, and strong of wing, as becomes Aphro-

---

[1] This is a real bit of natural history, from the Mauritius. The first pigeons there, having plenty on the ground to eat, and no need to fly, and waxing fat like Jeshurun, did not ' plume their feathers, and let grow their wings,' but grovelled, got monstrous, so that their wings, taking the huff, dwarfed into a fluttering stump. Sir T. Herbert thus quaintly describes this embarrassed creature :—' The Dodo, a bird the Dutch call Walghvogel, or Dod Eerson ; her body is round and fat, which occasions the slow pace, so that her corpulence is so great as few of them weigh less than fifty pounds. It is of a melancholy visage, as though sensible of nature's injury, in framing so massive a body to be by directed complimental wings, such, indeed, as are unable to hoist her from the ground, serving only to rank her among birds ; her traine three small plumes, short and unproportionable ; her legs suiting her body ; her pounce sharp ; her appetite strong and greedy ; stones and iron are digested.'—1625. We have in our time seen an occa-

dité's own, but got itself developed into a big goose
of a pigeon, waddling as it went, and proving itself
worthy of its extinction and of its name,—the only
hint of its ancestry being in its bill.

But even the best wings can't act *in vacuo ;* they
must have something to energise upon, and all imagination worth the name must act upon some objective
truth, must achieve for itself, or through others, a
realised ideal or an idealised reality. Beauty and
truth must embrace each other, and goodness bless
them both ;

> ' For Beauty, Good, and Knowledge are three sisters
> That doat upon each other,—friends to man,
> Living together under the same roof,
> And never to be sundered without tears.'

---

sional human Dodo, with its 'complimental wings '—a pure
and advanced Darwinian bird—its earthly appetites strong and
greedy ; 'an ill-favoured head ;' 'great black eyes ;' 'its gape
huge and wide ;' 'slow-paced and stupid ; ' its visage absurd
and melancholy—very.

8

'MYSTIFICATIONS.'

'Health to the auld wife, and weel mat she be,
That busks her fause rock wi' the lint o' the lee (lie),
Whirling her spindle and twisting the twine,
Wynds aye the richt pirn into the richt line.'

'MYSTIFICATIONS.'[1]

THOSE who knew the best of Edinburgh society eight-and-thirty years ago—and when was there ever a better than that best?—must remember the personations of an old Scottish gentlewoman by Miss Stirling Graham, one of which, when Lord Jeffrey was victimised, was famous enough to find its way into *Blackwood*, but in an incorrect form.

Miss Graham's friends have for years urged her to print for them her notes of these pleasant records of the harmless and heart-easing mirth of bygone times; to this she has at last assented, and the result is this entertaining, curious, and beautiful little quarto, in which her friends will recognise the strong understanding and goodness, the wit and invention, and fine *pawky* humour of the much-loved and warm-hearted representative of Viscount Dundee— the terrible Clavers.[2] They will recal that blithe

[1] Edinburgh : printed privately, 1859.

[2] 'DEAR DR. BROWN,—In compliance with your request I send you my genealogy in connection with Claverhouse—the same who was killed at Killiecrankie. John Graham of Claverhouse married the Honourable Jean Cochrane, daughter of William Lord Cochrane, eldest son of the first Earl of Dun-

and winning face, sagacious and sincere, that kindly, cheery voice, that rich and quiet laugh, that mingled sense and sensibility, which all met, and still, to our happiness, meet in her, who, with all her gifts and keen perception of the odd, and power of embodying it, never gratified her consciousness of these powers, or ever played

'Her quips and cranks and wanton wiles,'

so as to give pain to any human being.

The title of this memorial is *Mystifications*, and in the opening letter to her dear kinswoman and life-long friend, Mrs. Gillies, widow of Lord Gillies, she thus tells her story :—

DUNTRUNE, *April* 1859.

MY DEAREST MRS. GILLIES,

To you and the friends who have partaken in these 'Mystifications,' I dedicate this little volume, trusting, that after a silence of forty years, its

donald. Their only son, an infant, died December 1689. David Graham, his brother, fought at Killiecrankie, and was outlawed in 1690—died without issue—when the representation of the family devolved on his cousin, David Graham of Duntrune. Alexander Graham of Duntrune died 1782 ; and on the demise of his last surviving son, Alexander, in 1804, the property was inherited equally by his four surviving sisters, Anne, Amelia, Clementina, and Alison. Amelia was my mother.

'Yours ever,

'CLEM. STIRLING GRAHAM.

'DUNTRUNE, 14*th November* 1860.'

echoes may awaken many agreeable memorials of a society that has nearly passed away.

I have been asked if I had no remorse in ridiculing singularities of character, or practising deceptions;— certainly not.

There was no personal ridicule or mimicry of any living creature, but merely the personation or type of a bygone class, that had survived the fashion of its day.

It was altogether a fanciful existence, developing itself according to circumstances, or for the amusement of a select party, among whom the announcement of a stranger lady, an original, led to no suspicion of deception. No one ever took offence: indeed it generally elicited the finest individual traits of sympathy in the minds of the dupes, especially in the case of Mr. Jeffrey, whose sweet-tempered kindly nature manifested itself throughout the whole of the tiresome interview with the law-loving Lady Pitlyal.

No one enjoyed her eccentricities more than he did, or more readily devised the arrangement of a similar scene for the amusement of our mutual friends.

The cleverest people were the easiest mystified, and when once the deception took place, it mattered not how arrant the nonsense or how exaggerated the costume. Indeed, children and dogs were the only detectives.

I often felt so identified with the character, so charmed with the pleasure manifested by my audience,

*that it became painful to lay aside the veil, and descend
again into the humdrum realities of my own self.*

*These personations never lost me a friend; on the
contrary, they originated friendships that cease only
with life.*

*The Lady Pitlyal's course is run; she bequeaths to
you these reminiscences of beloved friends and pleasant
meetings.*

*And that the blessing of God may descend on 'each
and all of you,' is the fervent prayer of her kinswoman
and executrix,*

   CLEMENTINA STIRLING GRAHAM.

VISIT TO MR. JEFFREY.

AT the theatre one Saturday evening in the year
1821, Mr. Jeffrey—afterwards Lord Jeffrey—requested me to let him see my *old lady*, and on
condition that we should have some one to *take
in*, I promised to introduce her to him very soon.
Accordingly, on the Monday, having ascertained
that he was to dine at home, I set out from Lord
Gillies's in a coach, accompanied by Miss Helen
Carnegie of Craigo, as my daughter, and we stopped
at Mr. Jeffrey's door in George Street between five
and six o'clock. It was a winter evening; and on
the question, 'Is Mr. Jeffrey at home?' being
answered in the affirmative, the two ladies stepped

out, and were ushered into the little parlour, where
he received his visitors.

There was a blazing fire, and wax-lights on the
table ; he had laid down his book, and seemed to be
in the act of joining the ladies in the drawing-room
before dinner.

The Lady Pitlyal was announced, and he stepped
forward a few paces to receive her.

She was a sedate-looking little woman, of an inquisitive, law-loving countenance ; a mouth in which
not a vestige of a tooth was to be seen, and a pair of
old-fashioned spectacles on her nose, that rather ob-
scured a pair of eyes that had not altogether lost their
lustre, and that gave to the voice as much of the
nasal sound as indicated the age of its possessor to
be some years between her grand climacteric and
fourscore. She was dressed in an Irish poplin of
silver grey, a white Cashmere shawl, a mob cap with
a band of thin muslin that fastened it below the chin,
and a small black silk bonnet that shaded her eyes
from any glare of light.

Her right hand was supported by an antique gold-
headed cane, and she leant with the other on the arm
of her daughter.

Miss Ogilvy might be somewhere on the wrong
side of twenty ; how many months or years is of no
particular importance. Her figure, of the middle
size, was robed in a dress of pale blue and short

enough in the skirt to display a very handsome pair of feet and ankles. On her head she wore a white capote, and behind a transparent curtain of pure white blonde glanced two eyes of darkest hazel, while ringlets of bright auburn harmonised with the bloom of the rose that glowed upon her cheeks. Her appearance was *recherché*, and would have been perfectly *lady-like* but for an attempt at style, a mistake which young ladies from the country are very apt to fall into on their first arrival in the metropolis. Mr. Jeffrey bowed, and handed the old lady to a comfortable *chaise longue* on one side of the fire, and sat himself down opposite to her on the other. But in his desire to accommodate the old lady, and in his anxiety to be informed of the purport of the visit, he forgot what was due to the young one, and the heiress of the ancient House of Pitlyal was left standing in the middle of the floor.

She helped herself to a chair, however, and sat down beside her mother. She had been educated in somewhat of the severity of the old school, and during the whole of the consultation she neither spoke nor moved a single muscle of her countenance.

' *Well*,' said Mr. Jeffrey, as he looked at the old lady, in expectation that she would open the subject that had procured him the honour of the visit.

' Weel,' replied her ladyship, ' I am come to tak a word o' the law frae you.

'My husband, the late Ogilvy of Pitlyal, among other property which he left to me, was a house and a yard at the town-end of Kerriemuir, also a kiln and a malt barn.

'The kiln and the barn were rented by a man they ca'd John Playfair, and John Playfair subset them to anither man they ca'd Willy Cruickshank ; and Willy Cruickshank purchased a cargo of damaged lint, and ye widna hinder Willy to dry the lint upon the kiln, and the lint took low and kindled the cupples, and the slates flew aff, and a' the flooring was burnt to the ground, and naething left standin' but the bare wa's.

'Now it wasna insured, and I want to ken wha's to pay the damage, for John Playfair says he has naething *ado wi'* it, and Willy Cruickshank says he has naething *to do it wi'*, and I am determined no' to tak' it off their hand the way it is.'

'Has it been in any of the courts ?'

'Ou ay, it has been in the Shirra Court of Forfar, and Shirra Duff was a gude man, and he kent me, and would ha' gien 't in my favour, but that clattering creature Jamie L'Amy cam' in, and he gave it against me.'

'I have no doubt Mr. L'Amy would give a very fair decision.'

'It wasna a fair decision when he gae it against me.'

'That is what many people think in your circumstances.'

'The minister of Blairgowrie is but a fule body, and advised me no to gae to the law.'

'I think he gave you a very sensible advice.'

'It was onything but that; and mind, if you dinna gie 't in my favour, I 'll no' be sair pleased.'

Mr. Jeffrey smiled, and said he would not promise to do that, and then inquired if she had any papers.

'Ou ay, I have a great bundle of papers, and I 'll come back at any hour you please to appoint, and bring them wi' me.'

'It will not be necessary for you to return yourself —you can send them to me.'

'And wha would you recommend to me for an agent in the business?'

'That I cannot tell; it is not my province to recommend an agent.'

'Then how will Robert Smith of Balharry do?'

'Very well—very good man indeed; and you may bid him send me the papers.'

Meantime her ladyship drew from her pocket a large old-fashioned leather pocket-book with silver clasps, out of which she presented him a letter directed to himself. He did not look into it, but threw it carelessly on the table. She now offered him a pinch of snuff from a massive gold box, and then selected another folded paper from the pocket-book, which she presented to him, saying, 'Here is a prophecy that I would like you to look at and explain to me.'

He begged to be excused, saying, ' I believe your ladyship will find me more skilled in the *law* than the *prophets.*'

She entreated him to look at it ; and on glancing his eyes over it, he remarked, ' that from the words *Tory* and *Whig*, it did not seem to be a very ancient prophecy.'

' May be,' replied her ladyship ; ' but it has been long in our family. I copied these lines out of a muckle book, entitled the *Prophecie of Pitlyal*, just before I came to you, in order to have your opinion on some of the obscure passages of it. And you will do me a great favour if you will read it out loud, and I will tell you what I think of it as you go on.'

Here, then, with a smile at the oddity of the request, and a mixture of impatience in his manner, he read the following lines, while she interrupted him occasionally to remark upon their meaning.

EXTRACT FROM THE PROPHECIE OF PITLYAL.

' 𝔚hen the crown and the head shall disgrace ane anither,
And the Bishops on the Bench shall gae a' wrang thegither;
        𝔚hen 𝔗ory or 𝔚hig,
        𝔉ills the judge's wig ;
        𝔚hen the 𝔏int o' the 𝔐iln
        𝔖hall reek on the kiln ;

O'er the Light of the North,
When the Glamour breaks forth,
And its wild-fire so red
With the daylight is spread;
When woman shrinks not from the ordeal of tryal,
There is triumph and fame to the house of Pitlyal.'

(The Light of the North was Mr. Jeffrey,—the Glamour was herself; but we must give the Lady Pitlyal's own interpretation, as she appeared unconscious of the true meaning.)

' We hae seen the crown and the head,' she said, ' disgrace ane anither no very lang syne, and ye may judge whether the Bishops gaed right or wrang on that occasion ; and the *Tory* and *Whig* may no be very ancient, and yet never be the less true. Then there is the Lint o' the Miln,—we have witnessed that come to pass ; but what the " *Light of the North* " can mean, and the *Glamour*, I canna mak out. The twa hindmost lines seem to me to point at Queen Caroline ; and if it had pleased God to spare my son, I might have guessed he would have made a figure on her trial, and have brought " Triumph and fame to the house of Pitlyal." I begin, however, to think that the prophecie may be fulfilled in the person of my daughter, for which reason I have brought her to Edinburgh to see and get a gude match for her.'

Here Mr. Jeffrey put on a smile half serious half quizzical, and said—

'I suppose it would not be necessary for the gentleman to change his name.'

'It would be weel worth his while, sir; she has a very gude estate, and she's a very bonnie lassie, and she's equally related baith to Airlie and Strathmore; and a' body in our part of the world ca's her the "Rosebud of Pitlyal."'

Mr. Jeffrey smiled as his eyes met the glance of the beautiful flower that was so happily placed before him; but the Rosebud herself returned no sign of intelligence.

A pause in the conversation now ensued, which was interrupted by her ladyship asking Mr. Jeffrey to tell her where she could procure a set of *fause teeth.*

'*What?*' said he, with an expression of astonishment, while the whole frame of the young lady shook with some internal emotion.

'A set of fause teeth,' she repeated, and was again echoed by the interrogation, '*What?*'

A third time she asked the question, and in a more audible key; when he replied with a kind of suppressed laugh, 'There is Mr. Nasmyth, north corner of St. Andrew Square, a very great dentist, and there is Mr. Hutchins, corner of Hanover and George Street.'

She requested he would give her their names on a slip of paper. He rose and walked to the table, wrote down both the directions, which he folded and presented to her.

She now rose to take leave. The bell was rung, and when the servant entered, his master desired him to see if the Lady Pitlyal's carriage was at the door.

He returned to tell there was no carriage waiting, on which her ladyship remarked, 'This comes of *fore-hand payments*—they make *hint-hand wark*. I gae a hackney coachman twa shillings to bring me here, and he's awa' without me.'

There was not a coach within sight, and another had to be sent for from a distant stand of coaches. It was by this time past the hour of dinner, and there seemed no hope of being rid of his visitors.

Her ladyship said she was in no hurry, as they had had tea, and were going to the play, and hoped he would accompany them. He said he had not yet had his dinner.

'What is the play to-night?' said she.

'It is the "Heart of Mid-Lothian,' again, I believe.'

They then talked of the merits of the actors, and she took occasion to tell him that she patronised the *Edinburgh Review*.

'We read your buke, sir.'

'I am certainly very much obliged to you.'

Still no carriage was heard. Another silence

ensued, until it bethought her ladyship to amuse him with the politics of the country.

'We burnt the King's effigy at Blairgowrie.'

'That was bold,' he replied.

'And a pair of dainty muckle horns we gae him.'

'Not very complimentary to the Queen, I should think.'

Here the coach was announced, and by the help of her daughter's arm and her gold-headed cane, she began to move, complaining loudly of a *corny tae*. She was with difficulty got into the coach. The Rosebud stepped lightly after her.

The door was closed, and the order given to drive to Gibb's Hotel, whence they hastened with all speed to Lord Gillies's, where the party waited dinner for them, and hailed the fulfilment of the 'Prophecie of Pitlyal.'

Mr. Jeffrey, in the meantime, impatient for his dinner, joined the ladies in the drawing-room.

'What in the world has detained you?' said Mrs. Jeffrey.

'One of the most tiresome and oddest old women I ever met with. I thought never to have got rid of her;' and beginning to relate some of the conversation that had taken place, it flashed upon him at once that he had been *taken in*.

He ran down-stairs for the letter, hoping it would throw some light upon the subject, but it was only a blank sheet of paper, containing a fee of three guineas.

9

They amused themselves with the relation; but it was not until the day after that he found out from his valued friend, Mrs. George Russell, who the ladies really were. He laughed heartily, and promised to aid them in any other scene they liked to devise; and he returned the fee with the following letter :—

Letter from Mr. Jeffrey to the Lady Pitlyal, returning the fee of three guineas.

'DEAR MADAM,—As I understand that the law-suit about the Malt Kiln is likely to be settled out of Court, I must be permitted to return the fee by which you were pleased to engage my services for that interesting discussion; and hope I shall not be quoted along with the hackney coachman in proof of the danger of *forehand payments*. I hope the dentists have not disgraced my recommendation, and that Miss Ogilvy is likely to fulfil the prophecie, and bring glory and fame to the house of Pitlyal; though I am not a little mortified at having been allowed to see so little of that amiable young lady.

'With best wishes for the speedy cure of your corns, I have the honour to be, dear madam, your very faithful and obedient servant,

'F. JEFFREY.

'92 GEORGE STREET,
 21*st April* 1821.'

SOIRÉE AT MRS. RUSSELL'S.

IT was arranged that there should be an evening party at Mrs. Russell's in honour of the Lady Pitlyal, before the wildfire should have time to spread, in order to give the benefit of an introduction to a few more of the Whig friends. The soiree was accordingly fixed for the Wednesday. We dined at John Clerk's (Lord Eldin's), where were several members of the supper party; and Mr. William Clerk took occasion to inform Miss Dalzell that the lady opposite had a talent for personating character. Mrs. Gillies and I took our departure soon after nine, as we had to stop in York Place to arrange the toilette of the Lady Pitlyal. Her ladyship's dress this evening was abundantly conspicuous, and in the fashion of forty or fifty years back. It consisted of a gown of rich ponceau satin, open in front, and drawn up like the festoon of a window-curtain behind; a long and taper waist, black satin petticoat embroidered with roses of chenille, a muslin apron trimmed with lace, a black lace Teresa, and a stomacher fastened in front with diamond rosettes, a point cap and a green shade, with a veil, and spectacles to protect her eyes. On her feet a pair of embroidered shoes with high heels and large silver buckles.

Miss Helen Carnegy declined personating the

heiress any longer, so it was agreed that the Rosebud should be engaged to a ball at our friend Mr. Baron Clerk's.

We were announced and welcomed by Mrs. Russell, and very soon the Lady Pitlyal became the lion of the evening. Ladies and gentlemen crowded round her. Mr. Jeffrey made his bow, and entered into conversation about the law plea, and expressed disappointment at not having the pleasure of meeting Miss Ogilvy.

Mrs. Simpson of Ogil alluded to their estates being contiguous, spoke of her family, and promised to bring them all to pay a visit at Pitlyal. Lord Gillies was reminded of the time when he was an *ill prettie laddie*, and of breaking the *lozens* of one of her windows, and Mr. Pillans inquired about the state of the roads. Mr. Russell asked if Prince Charles skulked about Pitlyal? 'Ou ay,' she replied, 'he span with the lasses.' He wondered if George the Fourth span with the lasses? As to that she didna ken, but she thought he had managed to spin a ravelled hasp till himsel'.

When Hamilton of Holmhead was presented to her, she accused him of corrupting Lord Newton, who was a sober and peaceable man till he fell in wi' him; and she upbraided him for taking him to dine with Mr. Millar of Ballumbie when he was engaged to be at Pitlyal. He said he never prevented him

dining at Pitlyal. She asked if he remembered
meeting her at Ballumbie; to which he answered,
no; yet he remembered not only the party, but he
could tell every dish that was upon the table, and
one of them was the best shoulder of mutton he ever
saw, and, turning to Lord Gillies, he whispered,
'Surely the auld wife's tellin' a lee.'

Miss Cathcart, Miss Kennedy, Mr. Rutherfurd,—
afterwards Lord Advocate and Lord Rutherfurd,—
and others, were all presented to her in due form,
and when supper was announced, Lord Gillies gave
her his arm down-stairs.

Mr. William Clerk offered his to Mrs. Gillies, that
he might inquire the weight and qualifications of the
heiress, and that they might get a seat near the old
lady. He said he had fancied, on his first entering
the room, that it was some one *dressed up*, but he
now saw she was a very original person, and he
wished to get acquainted with her. Mrs. Gillies
told him the young lady had reddish hair, but he
assured her that was no objection to him, for he had
no dislike to red hair.

She alluded again to some stories of Lord Gillies's
boyhood, and told him she had ploughed up the
Capernaum Park, which he recollected to have been
fine old grass.

Mr. Jeffrey now inquired what the people in her
part of the country thought of the trial of the

Queen. She could not tell him, but she would say
what she herself had remarked on siclike procedings:
'Tak' a wreath of snaw, let it be never so white, and
wash it through clean water, it will no come out so
pure as it gaed in, far less the dirty dubs the poor
Queen has been drawn through.'

Mr. Russell inquired if she possessed any relics of
Prince Charles from the time he used to spin with
the lasses.

'Yes,' she said, 'I have a *flech* that loupit aff him
upon my aunty, the Lady Brax, when she was helping him on wi' his short gown; my aunty rowed it
up in a sheet of white paper, and she keepit it in the
tea canister, and she ca'd it aye the King's Flech,
and the Laird, honest man, when he wanted a cup
of gude tea, sought aye a cup of *Prince's mixture.*'
This produced peals of laughter, and her ladyship
laughed as heartily as any of them. When somewhat composed again, she looked across the table to
Mr. Clerk, and offered to let him see it. 'It is now
set on the pivot of my watch, and a' the warks
gae round the *flech* in place of turning on a
diamond.'

Lord Gillies thought this flight would certainly
betray her, and remarked to Mr. Clerk that the flea
must be painted on the watch, but Mr. Clerk said he
had known of relics being kept of the Prince quite as
extraordinary as a flea; that Mr. Murray of Simprim

had a pocket-handkerchief in which Prince Charles had blown his nose.

The Lady Pitlyal said her daughter did not value these things, and that she was resolved to leave it as a legacy to the Antiquarian Society.

Holmhead was rather amused with her originality, though he had not forgotten the attack. He said he would try if she was a real Jacobite, and he called out, 'Madam, I am going to propose a toast for ye!

'May the Scotch Thistle choke the Hanoverian Horse.'

'I wish I binna among the Whigs,' she said.

'And where wad ye be sae weel?' retorted he.

'They murdered Dundee's son at Glasgow.'

'There was nae great skaith,' he replied; 'but ye maun drink my toast in a glass of this cauld punch, if ye be a true Jacobite.'

'Aweel, aweel,' said Lady Pitlyal, 'as my auld friend Lady Christian Bruce was wont to say, "The best way to get the better of temptation is just to yield to it;"' and as she nodded to the toast and emptied the glass, Holmhead swore exultingly, '*Gad, she's true!*'

Supper passed over, and carriages were announced. The Lady Pitlyal took her leave with Mrs. Gillies.

Next day the town rang with the heiress of Pitlyal. Mr. W. Clerk said he had never met with such an extraordinary old lady, 'for not only is she amusing herself, but my brother John is like to expire when I relate her stories at second hand.'

He talked of nothing else for a week after, but the heiress, and the flea, and the rent-roll, and the old turreted house of Pitlyal, till at last his friends thought it would be right to undeceive him; but that was not so easily done, for when the Lord Chief Commissioner Adam hinted that it might be Miss Stirling, he said that was impossible, for Miss Stirling was sitting by the old lady the whole of the evening.

CRAIGIE.

ANOTHER evening Miss Guthrie requested me to introduce my old lady to Captain Alexander Lindsay, a son of the late Laird of Kinblethmont, and brother to the present Mr. Lindsay Carnegie, and Mr. Sandford, the late Sir Daniel Sandford.

She came as a Mrs. Ramsay Speldin, an old sweetheart of the laird's, and was welcomed by Mrs. Guthrie as a friend of the family. The young people hailed her as a perfectly delightful old lady, and an original of the pure Scottish character, and to the laird she was endeared by a thousand pleasing recollections.

He placed her beside himself on the sofa, and they talked of the days gone by—before the green parks of Craigie were redeemed from the Muir of Gotter-

ston, and ere there was a tree planted between the
auld house of Craigie and the castle of Claypotts.

She spoke of the guid 'auld times, when the laird
of Fintry widna gie his youngest dochter to Aber-
cairney, but tell'd him to tak them as God had gien
them to him, or want.'

'And do you mind,' she continued, 'the grand
ploys we had at the Middleton; and hoo Mrs. Scott
of Gilhorn used to grind lilts out o' an auld kist to
wauken her visitors i' the mornin'?'

'And some o' them didna like it sair, tho' nane o'
them had courage to tell her sae, but Annie Graham
o' Duntrune.

'"Lord forgie ye," said Mrs. Scott, "ye'll no gae
to Heaven, if ye dinna like music." But Annie was
never at a loss for an answer, and she said, "Mrs.
Scott—Heaven's no the place I tak it to be, if there
be auld wives in't playing on hand-organs."'

Many a story did Mrs. Ramsay tell. The party
drew their chairs close to the sofa, and many a joke
she related, till the room rung again with the merriment, and the laird, in ecstasy, caught her round the
waist, exclaiming, 'Oh, ye are a canty wifie.'

The strangers seemed to think so too; they absolutely hung upon her, and she danced reels, first with
the one, and then with the other, till the entrance of
a servant with the newspapers produced a season-
able calm.

They lay, however, untouched upon the table till Mrs. Ramsay requested some one to read over the claims that were putting in for the king's coronation, and see if there was any mention of hers.

'What is your claim?' said Mr. Sandford.

'To pyke the king's teeth,' was the reply.

'You will think it very singular,' said Mr. Guthrie, 'that I never heard of it before; will you tell us how it originated?'

'It was in the time of James the First,' said she. 'That monarch cam to pay a visit to the monks of Arbroath, and they brought him to Ferryden to eat a fish dinner at the house o' ane o' my forefathers. The family name, ye ken, was Speldin, and the dried fish was ca'd after them.

'The king was well satisfied wi' a'thing that was done to honour him. He was a very polished prince, and when he had eaten his dinner he turned round to the lady and sought a preen to pyke his teeth.

'And the lady, she took a fish bane, and wypit it, and gae it to the king; and after he had cleaned his teeth wi' it, he said, "𝔗𝔥𝔢𝔶 '𝔯𝔢 𝔴𝔢𝔢𝔩 𝔭𝔶𝔨𝔦𝔱."

'"And henceforth," continued he, "the Speldins of Ferryden shall pyke the king's teeth at the coronation. And it shall be done wi' a fish bane, and a pearl out o' the Southesk on the end of it. And their crest shall be a lion's head wi' the teeth displayed, and the motto shall be *weel pykit*."'

Mr. Sandford read over the claims, but there was no notice given of the Speldins'.

'We maun just hae patience,' said Mrs. Ramsay, 'and nae doubt it will appear in the next newspaper.'

Some one inquired who was the present representative?

'It's me,' replied Mrs. Ramsay Speldin; 'and I mean to perform the office mysel'. The estate wad hae been mine too, had it existed; but Neptune, ye ken, is an ill neighbour, and the sea has washed it a' awa' but a sand bunker or twa, and the house I bide in at Ferryden.'

At supper every one was eager to have a seat near Mrs. Ramsay Speldin. She had a universal acquaintance, and she even knew Mr. Sandford's mother, when he told her that her name was Catherine Douglas. Mr. Sandford had in his own mind composed a letter to Sir Walter Scott, which was to have been written and despatched on the morrow, giving an account of this fine specimen of the true Scottish character, whom he had met in the county of Angus.

We meant to carry on the deception next morning, but the laird was too happy for concealment. Before the door closed on the goodnight of the ladies, he had disclosed the secret, and before we reached the top of the stairs, the gentlemen were scampering at our heels like a pack of hounds in full cry.

TULLIALLAN.

I went with Lord Gillies and Mrs. Gillies to spend the Christmas holidays at Tulliallan. We met Admiral and Mrs. Fleming, Mr. and Mrs. Keay of Snaigo, Mr. John Murray (afterwards Lord Murray), Mr. and Mrs. Russell, Mr. Thomas Thomson, etc.— a very pleasant party.

Lady Keith wished me to *take in* Count Flahault, but no feasible means could be devised till one day that a robbery had been committed in the neighbourhood. Two boys were accused, named John Murray and Alexander Jamieson; the former had escaped, but the other was taken up, and brought to be examined before the justices of the peace assembled at the castle.

It was suggested that I should come in the form of the mother of one of these lads. Accordingly, a costume was borrowed from the dairymaid, and I was speedily transformed into the character of Mrs. Jamieson, who desired to speak with some of the gentlemen that were taking the precognition.

I cannot say that I felt altogether comfortable when I was ushered into an apartment among a motley group of witnesses, and was desired to wait until I was called up-stairs; but Lady Keith arranged that I should not have long to wait, and desired the servant

to bring Mrs. Jamieson into the corridor. The
drawing-rooms opened to it, and the doors being left
open, the party within could hear all that passed.

Count Flahault and Admiral Fleming came from
the justice-room, and the latter demanded in an angry
tone, 'What is your business?'

'I am the mither of Alexander Jamieson, and am
come to see if you will let off my son.'

'The devil you are,' said the Admiral; 'your son
is a young thief, and deserves to be hanged.'

'I winna say.'

'Because you know very well that you have brought
him very ill up, and I suppose you encourage him to
steal for you.'

'God forgie ye,' said Mrs. Jamieson; 'it's the like
o' you that hae ruined him. He was a gude, weel-
living lad afore ye sent him to Bridewell.'

'What,' said Count Flahault, 'has your son been
in Bridewell?'

No answer.

'I say,' said the Count, 'has your son been in
Bridewell?'

Still no answer.

The Count then repeated slowly and distinctly,—

'Has your son ever been in Bridewell?'

'Yes.'

'For what was he sent to Bridewell?'

'For nae great affair.'

'Tell instantly,' said the Admiral, 'for what he was sent to Bridewell.'

'For nae ither thing, but just because he whuppit a shawl off a stand, and gie'd it till 's sweetheart.'

'Ay,' said the Admiral, 'and pray how long has your son been in Bridewell?—speak out.'

'Sax weeks, and he cam' out a deal waur than he gaed in.'

'I have not the smallest doubt of that,' said the Admiral; 'I believe you speak the truth now;' and returning to the justice-room, he taxed the boy with having been in Bridewell, and received an answer in the affirmative.

The Count then asked what brought her? 'I am come to mak' ye an offer,' replied the persevering Mrs. Jamieson.

'What kind of an offer?' said the Count with a smile between compassion and contempt.

'I ken,' said Mrs. Jamieson, 'you would like very weel to get a haud o' John Murray, and if ye'll let off my son, I'se engage to get John Murray to you this very night.'

'So you know where John Murray is, do you?' and he went back to the justice-room to relate the further particulars.

Lady Keith, by this time, became fearful of mixing up the false witness with the true, and calling to the Count, she said, 'For God's sake, Charles, give that poor woman half-a-crown, and send her away. I cannot bear to see her standing there.'

The Count desired the weeping Mrs. Jamieson to go home—an order which she very slowly set about obeying, hesitating and turning round to plead her cause every now and then.

The Count, however, was resolute, and gently laying a hand on each shoulder, he marched her before him, and opening the outer door, he put half-a-crown into her hand, and pushed her out, she in the meantime upbraiding him with having the heart of Pharaoh, that could turn a poor woman to the door in sic a night.

The Count was delighted with the *dénouement;* but upbraided Lady Keith with hurrying on the conclusion.

'Why did you not let me be more taken in?' he said; 'and why did Mrs. Jamieson conclude the scene so soon?'

'She shall be brought back again,' he said; 'and we shall have a little fun with Keay.'

After dinner, therefore, Mrs. Jamieson's return was announced. She was ordered to the dining-room door, and Mr. Keay was appointed to hear her statement.

She detailed, in the most pathetic terms, how Sandy Jamieson was the support of her old age, and that she came to petition for his being released.

Mr. Keay endeavoured to soothe her, spoke kindly, bade her be comforted, assured her that her son would be taken care of as far as he was concerned, but that he could not release him.

'I ken weel what kind o' care ye will tak o' him,' she said.

'What do you mean, my good woman?' returned Mr. Keay.

'I ken,' said Mrs. Jamieson, 'you're gaen to mak a ploy o' hangin' him the nicht, and ye've got Edinburgh judges in the house, and I saw them scrapin' a tree as I cam up the gait;' and she wept bitterly, and her grief became clamorous, and she would not move until she should see her son.

Mr. Keay recollected having seen two of the foresters in the morning rubbing the lichens off some old oaks on the lawn; but it was impossible to convince Mrs. Jamieson that it could be for any other purpose but that of preparing a gallows for her son. He returned to the dining-room to communicate to the party the state she was in, and the delusion under which she laboured.

'Give her half-a-crown, Keay,' said the Count; 'and do you, Admiral, give her as much, and she'll go home.'

'I would see her hanged first,' replied the Admiral; but Mr. Keay returned to the comfort of the distressed, and taking her kindly by the hand, slipped half-a-crown into it.

'What is that?' said she, throwing down the money; 'it is the price of blood, and it shall never be said that Janet Jamieson sell'd her bairn's blood for half-a-crown.'

'You mistake, my good woman,' said Mr. Keay, 'it is not the price of blood. I assure you your son is quite safe; he is gone to Culross in a cart.'

'To Culross in a cart!' shrieked Mrs. Jamieson. 'I winna stir from this house till ye bring him back again.'

Mr. Keay's patience was now exhausted, and the more especially when he heard shouts of merriment from the dining-room. 'If you don't speedily take yourself off, you will be turned out. Better, therefore, take the half-crown, and trust me there will no harm happen to your son to-night;' saying which he returned into the dining-room, and shut the door upon the distressed mother.

By the time the gentlemen joined the ladies in the drawing-room, a hole had been drilled through each of the half-crowns, and they were suspended round the neck of their new proprietor.

Some months afterwards I happened to go with some strangers to see the new jail in Edinburgh. The prisoners were amusing themselves in their airing ground.

10

'That,' said the jailer, pointing to a young man, 'is the most hardened and incorrigible offender we have.' I inquired his name, and he said it was John Murray.

RAITH.

FROM Tulliallan we removed to Raith to bring in the new year. A very brilliant party was assembled. The gentlemen enjoyed the pleasures of the battue in the mornings, and we sat down to dinner upwards of twenty every day.

The party consisted of Mr. and Mrs. Ferguson, Sir Ronald and Miss Ferguson, Mr. and Mrs. Henry Ferguson (now Sir Henry and Lady Davie), Mr. and Mrs. Michael Angelo Taylor, Lord Gillies and Mrs. Gillies, Mr. and Mrs. Russell, the Marquis of Tweeddale and his brothers, Lords John and Thomas Hay, Lord Maitland, the present Lord Lauderdale, and the Honourable Captain Maitland, Count Flahault, Lord Duncan, the present Lord Camperdown, Mr. John Murray, and though last, not least, the Honourable John Elliot, the very life and soul of the party. He was the universal favourite, and was altogether a delightful person, full of anecdote, and a mimic of the first water.

Sir Ronald gave us personations of a certain Provost, and Mr. Murray gave specimens of all the judges on the bench; and after we had been some days together, Mr. Ferguson announced the expectation of a visit of the Lady Pitlyal, and expressed his regret that I was engaged to a ball at Lord Rosslyn's.

Her ladyship arrived just as dinner was announced, having remained in Kirkcaldy by the advice of her coachman till after dark, 'as he said there was a great gathering of thoughtless young men at Raith, and there was to be a battle wi' the Ephesians, and he thought we had better keep out o' harm's way.'

Lord Gillies offered his arm to the dining-room, and placed her at table between himself and Mr. Elliot.

She expressed great disappointment in not finding Lord Lauderdale of the party. 'I understood he was to be at Raith,' she said, 'and I wanted to consult him on a piece of business of great importance both to myself and the nation.'

Mr. Elliot pressed her to take Maraschino, till Lord Gillies was obliged to tell him he knew the Lady Pitlyal was a very abstemious person, and that she never took anything but a glass of wine at dinner. She spoke to him of the estate of Melgund, and of its having been the residence of Cardinal Bethune.

He believed it was rather a good place, and inquired if she knew it well.

She said she kenned a' the land thereabout, frae the south side of Seidlaw to the north o' the Grampians. And she told him how a living lobster had fallen out of a cadger's creel up about the parish of Lintrathen, and how a Highlandman had picked it up and carried it to the minister, and how the minister put on his spectacles to see what kind of a beast it was, and after lang examination, and mony a reference to the Bible, he pronounced it to be either an *elephant* or a *turtle-dove.*

Mr. Elliot, in his turn, related how a seafaring friend of his, in giving an order for provisioning the ship, said, 'I am resolved to have a *cow, for I am very fond of new-laid eggs.*'

He then told her that a young lady had taken his purse the night before, and he would refer to the Lady Pitlyal what punishment should be awarded.

She said she would give the same judgment that the bellman of Arbroath did on a like occasion, when he happened to be the finder of it himsel'—

> 'John Elliot's lost his purse,
> And his money which is worse;
> Them that's found it let them keep it,
> Them that's tint it let them seek it.'

When dinner was removed, and the domestics were withdrawn, she recurred again to her regret at missing Lord Lauderdale, as it was of great consequence to her to have her bill brought in this session.

Mr. Ferguson begged to know the nature of the bill, as some of the party present might perhaps be of use to her.

She said it concerned a charter which had lately been discovered in the garret of Pitlyal; it was a grant from James the Fifth, that the leeches of the loch of Pitlyal should become a monopoly; and she wished Lord Lauderdale to bring in a bill obliging the king and all the heads of the nation to use the Pitlyal leeches.

Lord Tweeddale said he would be happy to lay it before the Peers, and Sir Ronald was sure his friend Mr. Taylor would bring it into the House of Commons.

Lord Gillies begged she would explain the origin of the charter.

She said the king was on a hunting party in Strathmore, and he was thrown from his horse and ta'en up for dead; that leeches were got from the loch of Pitlyal and applied to his head, and he recovered; and when he came till himsel', he speered at some o' the bystanders what like his head was, and the gudeman of that place said there was a muckle clour upon 't. '*Muckle Clour*,' says the king; 'henceforth this place shall be ca'd Muckle Clour, and the land, gudeman, shall be your ain.'

'The place was since sell'd to an ancestor of Lady Keith's; it is now ca'd Meikleour, ye ken, Count. And the king said, "Ye shall bear the leeches on your shield, and I bind myself and my subjects to make use of them in need."

'The richt o' the leeches wasna disposed o' when Mickleclour was sold; but for mair than a century the charter has been amissing, and leeches have been ta'en out o' ither lochs, and great quantities have been brought over from Holland; and now it will no' be an easy thing to bring back the monopoly.'

Mr. Taylor was doubtful how such a thing could be done; nor could he distinctly see by what right she could expect it.

Mr. Russell thought it might be a right of the same kind that secures thirlage to a mill.

Lord Duncan interrupted the subject of right by stating that he had many times been at Pitlyal, and had heard her ladyship speak a great deal about the loch leeches, but he would like just to be informed how she had been in the practice of catching them.

'Oh, Robert, Robert!' replied her ladyship reproachfully, 'mony ane speers the road they ken. I've seen you aftner than ance wade into the water, and come out wi' them sticking on your legs.'

The cause was triumphant; his lordship was fairly cheered into recollection, but Mr. Taylor could not be made to understand it, and no one could assume sufficient gravity to explain.

As soon as a hearing could be obtained, Count Flahault inquired after the health of the Rosebud.

'She's very weel, and shortly to be married,' replied her ladyship.

'To whom, may I beg leave to ask?'

'To the Prince of Monaco.'

'A friend of mine,' said the Count; but the name was not familiar to any of the rest of the party.

'I'll gie ye a Scotch mark,' she said to Mr. Ferguson; 'it was his father that thought a' the lamps in London had been lighted up in honour of his arrival, and, as he drove through the city, he exclaimed with delight, "I've often heard the English was a polite nation, but this is too much." I believe,' she added, 'my Jean will be a great match for him, for his principality is the very smallest in Italy; it lies, I believe, on the shore of the Mediterranean.'

The Count bit his lip. 'It does,' said he, 'and the gentleman is my particular friend; he is now the ——,' I forget the name.

In the drawing-room, Mr. Elliot hastened to the side of his new friend, and many was the story they successively told.

'You carry the leeches on your shield?' said Mr. Elliot.

'And the lion for the crest. I am the lion,' she replied.

'I was once a hare myself,' returned he; and he began a story he had told the night before—how he had acted the part of a hare to the astonishment of an old gentleman in the neighbourhood of Minto ; before the end of it, however, he caught the expression of the lady's eye, and lifting up the veil which shaded her features, exclaimed—' Now, I have found the Lion of Pitlyal.'

DINNER PARTY AT LORD GILLIES'S.

Sir Walter Scott expressed a wish to see a personation, and Lord Gillies made a party for the purpose, among whom were Sir Walter and Miss Scott, Sir Henry and Lady Jardine, the Lord Chief Commissioner and Miss Adam, Doctor Coventry, the Chief Baron, Sir Samuel Shepherd, and others.

Among other things that afforded subject of conversation was the fancy ball of the night before ; the various dresses and characters were commented on, and among them the inconsistent conduct of a black knight, who had thrown down the gauntlet without waiting to see who would pick it up. The knight was said to be young Mr. T—.

The dinner passed very pleasantly, as all Lord Gillies's dinners do ; and when we returned to the drawing-room I bade good-night to the ladies.

The Misses Carnegy and their old friend Mrs. Arbuthnott of Balwylie came to tea.

With all the ladies, except Lady Jardine and Miss Scott, Mrs. Arbuthnott was intimately acquainted. To them, therefore, she was now, by Mrs. Gillies, particularly introduced.

Lady Jardine whispered to Mrs. Gillies, 'What a beautifully dressed old lady, her clothes are so handsome, and so suitable to her time of life, and at the same time fashionable and lady-like. I wish some old ladies in this town would only take example by it.'

The gown was a dark silk made up to the throat, and with sleeves to the wrist. A pure white gauze handkerchief pinned tight over it, an apron of clear white muslin trimmed with point lace, and a cap of point with bows of white satin ribbon ; a green shade, and French grey kid gloves seamed with black silk.

Mrs. Gillies hoped she was to have the pleasure of seeing the rest of Mrs. Arbuthnott's family. To which she replied that they would all be here, but that they were dining out.

Miss Adam inquired how many of her family had come up with her.

'There is the laird,' she said, 'my eldest son, and the three orphans left to my care by my second son, and there's our right-hand man and governor, James Dalgetty.'

'The young men,' she continued, 'wanted a little amusement, and they cam' up to the Fancy Ball. The laird had to attend a meeting of the Antiquarian

Society, and I thought I might as weel tak' the opportunity to come and see my friends.'

'Your grandsons will be grown out of my acquaintance,' said Miss Adam.

'They're fine handsome young men,' was the reply; 'and Charles, the youngest of them, is the life and spirit of the whole house. He's a jewel of a creature, and the very image of his father.'

'How did they like the ball?' inquired Miss Scott.

'Extraordinary weel, and Charles went in the dress of a black knight.'

'Was it your grandson, then, Mrs. Arbuthnott,' continued Miss Scott, 'that was the black knight? I am delighted to hear you say so. It destroyed the romance of the thing altogether when we were told it was the son of Mr. T—.'

The gentlemen now entered the drawing-room. All who were previously acquainted with Mrs. Arbuthnott expressed their delight at meeting her, and she became in a high degree animated by the sight of so many old friends.

The Lord Chief Commissioner, claiming the privilege of an old sweetheart, sat down beside her on the sofa, and Sir Walter Scott, though a comparatively new acquaintance, placed himself by her on the other side.

'Do you know, papa,' said Miss Scott, 'that Mrs. Arbuthnott's grandson was the black knight?'

'And poor Charles got a sad fright,' continued Mrs. Arbuthnott,—'he did very weel till he threw down the glove, but syne he lost his presence o' mind a'thegither.'

'I am afraid,' said Sir Walter, 'it is no uncommon thing for knights in his situation to lose their presence of mind.'

'Where is the rest of your party, Mrs. Arbuth nott?' now inquired Lord Gillies.

'They'll be here presently, my Lord, but the laird is gone to a meeting of the Antiquarians, and the young men will come as soon as their dinner-party breaks up.' Then turning to Sir Walter, 'I am sure you had our laird in your e'e when you drew the character of Monkbarns.'

'No,' replied Sir Walter, 'but I had in my eye a very old and respected friend of my own, and one with whom, I daresay you, Mrs. Arbuthnott, were acquainted,—the late Mr. George Constable, of Wallace, near Dundee.'

'I kenned him weel,' said Mrs. Arbuthnott, 'and his twa sisters that lived wi' him, Jean and Christian, and I've been in the blue-chamber of his *Hospitium;* but I think,' she continued, 'our laird is the likest to Monkbarns o' the twa. He's at the Antiquarian Society the night presenting a great curiosity that was found in a quarry of mica slate in the hill at the back of Balwylie. He's sair taen up about it, and puzzled to think what substance it may be; but James Dalgetty, wha's never at a loss either for the name or the nature of onything under the sun, says it's just Noah's auld wig that blew aff yon time he put his head out of the window of the ark to look after his corbie messenger.'

James Dalgetty and his opinion gave subject of much merriment to the company, but Dr. Coventry thought there was nothing so very ludicrous in the remark, for in that kind of slate there are frequently substances found resembling hairs.

Lord Gillies presented Dr. Coventry to Mrs. Arbuthnott, as the well-known professor of agriculture, and they entered on a conversation respecting soils. She described those of Balwylie, and the particular properties of the *Sourock Park*, which James Dalgetty curses every time it's spoken about, and says, 'It greets a' winter, and girns a' simmer.'

The Doctor rubbed his hands with delight, and said that was the most perfect description of cold wet land he had ever heard of; and Sir Walter expressed a wish to cultivate the acquaintance of James Dalgetty, and extorted a promise from Mrs. Arbuthnott that she would visit Abbotsford, and bring James with her. 'I have a James Dalgetty of my own,' continued Sir Walter, 'that governs me just as yours does you.'

Lady Ann and Mr. Wharton Duff and their daughter were announced, and introduced to Mrs. Arbuthnott.

Lady Ann was remarkably spirituelle, possessed a great talent for fun and humour, spoke the Scotch fluently, and entered the lists at once with Mrs. Arbuthnott. Many a good story she told—not only witty herself, but, as Falstaff says, she was also the cause of wit in others—and was altogether a very delightful person.

Mrs. Arbuthnott inquired if she had heard what had happened to a laird on Deeside, when he was salmon-fishing short syne?

'What laird?' said Lady Ann.

'One that shall be nameless for the present,' continued Mrs. Arbuthnott; 'but the first bite nearly whummelled him into the water. "Gie him line," cried Willy Bruce the fisher; "that chield maun hae play."

'And sure enough the laird gae him line—three days and twa nights he warstled wi' the beast, and there wasna a bush, nor the stump o' an auld tree, a' the way between the falls of the Feuch and the Linn o' Dee, that he didna mak steppin'-stanes o'. At length the line broke, and down cam the laird. "The devil's got the hook," he cried, and up again he couldna rise.

'A'body wonders if he saw onything, and some

say it was the auld Abbot of Arbroath, that used to dress himsel' in a white coat and a curled wig, to gar folk believe he was the laird o' Seton, when there was ony ploy gaen on that wasna just suitable for a monk's cowl to be seen in.

'He was doomed to haunt the rivers for a thousand years afore he should get into purgatory.

'But Willy Bruce swears it was naething but a muckle salmon that he's kenned in the water these twenty years, and the fishers ca'd him William the Conqueror, because he managed aye to brak their lines; but be that as it may, the laird got sic a fleg that he was carried hame in a ragin' fever, and he's keepit his bed aye sinsyne.'

'I know where you are now,' exclaimed Lady Ann Duff, and she began to relate a pendant to this history about the laird of Abergeldie. But the laughter caused by the downfall of the salmon-fishing laird only received a fresh impulse from this interruption.

Mr. Henry Jardine and his sister were announced: the former recognised a friend beneath the green shade, and his smile was returned by Mrs. Arbuthnott.

He was a friend of Charles's, and had been at Balwylie.

At ten, Sir Walter and Miss Scott took leave, with a promise that they should visit each other, and bending down to the ear of Mrs. Arbuthnott, Sir

Walter addressed her in these words: 'Awa! awa! the deil 's ower grit wi' you.'

And now are we not all the better for this pleasantry? so womanly, so genial, so rich, and so without a sting,—such a true diversion, with none of the sin of effort or of mere cleverness; and how it takes us into the midst of the strong-brained and strong-hearted men and women of that time! what an atmosphere of sense and good breeding and kindliness! And then the Scotch! cropping out everywhere as blithe and expressive and unexpected as a gowan or sweet-briar rose, with an occasional thistle, sturdy, erect, and bristling with *Nemo me.* Besides the deeper and general interest of these *Mystifications*, in their giving, as far as I know, a unique specimen of true personation—distinct from acting—I think it a national good to let our youngsters read, and, as it were, hear the language which our gentry and judges and men of letters spoke not long ago, and into which such books as Dean Ramsay's and this are breathing the breath of its old life. Was there ever anything better or so good, said of a stiff clay, than that it 'girns (grins) a' simmer, and greets (weeps) a' winter'?

When we read over the names we find here, we see the men, we hear them, and feel their living power. There is Lord Newton, huge in body and in mind, capable of any mental and social effort, full of hard reason. William Clerk, only less witty and odd than his great Swiftian brother, Lord Eldin. Lord Rutherfurd then young, but rejoicing as only a strong man does, to run his race, with those great, burning, commanding eyes, and that noble head. Lord Gillies, every inch a man and judge—strong, clear, prompt, inevitable, with a tenderness of heart that only such men can have and give. I remember well his keen, shrewd, handsome, authoritative face, his shapely, well-knit legs in his Hessian boots. There is Harry Cockburn, with those wonderful eyes, melancholy and lonely, brown, and clear, and deep as a muirland tarn, sparkling at times as if the sun shone on them, or oftener as if a star of their own twinkled from out their depths; but their habitual expression pensive to melancholy: what nature and fun and pathos! what a voice, what homely power! and his long country stride, and his leisurely flow of soul, rippling but strong, singing a perpetual and quiet tune, as if listening to himself and turning everything to his humour,—as native, as inimitable, as unmade and exquisite as a roadside flower spring.[1] And there is Jeffrey, whom flattery,

[1] It would be endless to give instances of his peculiar humour. It was mild in tone, and didn't explode so much as expand; but for quiet and intense exaggeration I don't know anything

success, and himself cannot spoil, or taint that sweet, generous nature—keen, instant, unsparing and true as a rapier; the most painstaking and honest-working of all clever men; such eyes! and that mouth, made to speak to and beguile women—mobile and yet firm, arch, and kind, with a beautiful procacity or petulance about it, that you would not like absent in him, or present in any one else. Michael Angelo Taylor, the conjunction of whose names is glory and peculiarity enough. John Archibald Murray, handsome, courtly, bountiful; strong and full of courage when put to it, and not to be trifled with. The Honourable John Elliott, who still is what he was then, 'the life and soul of the party.' Count Flahault bright, *galant*, and gallant, proud of his English, prouder of his French and his whist.

And moving about, the greatest and naturallest of them all, like a Newfoundland dog or his own Maida among his fellows, Sir Walter, the healthiest, manliest of all our men of letters—frank, open, and full of work as the day; with that homely, burly

to equal it. We all remember his 'Edinburgh is as quiet as the grave, or even Peebles.' One day, coming down the Mound from Court, about five P.M., a friend met him, and said, 'You're looking tired; have you been all this time in Court?' 'Yes,' he said querulously; 'it's that man ——.' 'Does he take up your time at that rate?' 'Time! he exhausts Time, and encroaches on Eternity.' There was genius in that word 'encroach.'

frame, that shrewd, *pawky* face, with its grey eyes and heavy eyebrows, its tall, tower-like skull (he used to say his hat *was* small, but then he filled it)—eyes when at rest heavy, filled with latent genius and story, like music slumbering on its instrument; when awake and lighted from within, how alive, how full of fun, making his rich voice, and rich laugh all the richer! He was then at his zenith; he was after that to go down in that miserable fight—fighting as few men ever did against such odds—ruined as such a man could only be ruined, by himself, by his own romantic, fatal weaknesses; we have no nobler piece of virtue in the old Greek sense of manliness, than in his leading on alone his forlorn hope, sticking to his colours to the last, and giving in only when the brain, his weapon, gave way and failed. I remember him about that time: he used to walk up and down Princes Street, as we boys were coming from the High School, generally with some friend, and every now and then he stopped, and resting his lame leg against his stick, laughed right out at some joke of his friend's or his own: he said a good laugh was worth standing for, and besides required it for its completion. How we rejoiced when we took off our bonnets, to get a smile and a nod from him, thinking him as great as Julius Cæsar or Philopœmen, Hector or Agricola, any day. I can fancy I see and hear him as he bends down to 'Mrs. Arbuthnott of

Balwylie,' and says, with his rich *burr* rolling in his mouth, and in her ear, 'Awa! awa! the deil's ower *grit* wi' ye.'[1]

And the ladies, or, as I prefer calling them, the women of these times, how worthy—how, in scientific phrase, complementary of the men!—meeting them in all common interests half way, neither more nor less,—their companions, well read, well bred, free yet refined, full of spirit and sense—with a strong organ of adhesiveness, as our friends the phrenologists would say. I wish we had more, or many of such women now-a-days : women who, with all their gifts and graces, were always womanly in their ways and speech, and as distinct in character each from the other as were the men—as much so as a beech is from a birch, or a lily from a rose. Now our flowers are what are called composite, and too often double, one of the effects of over cultivation. Our men are like larches—if you have seen one you have seen a

---

[1] All the stories about Scott are good. I had one from his attached and grateful friend the late James Russell, that accomplished actor and true gentleman, which is perhaps not generally known.

John Kemble was acting in the Edinburgh Theatre, and being out of sorts, played languidly and ill, when suddenly he blazed out into his full power, and went on magnificently to the close. William Murray said to him afterwards, 'How was it that you began so ill and finished so well?' 'Oh!' said Kemble, 'didn't you see? *Walter* came in;' and he played up to Walter.

thousand, and if you have seen one of his sides, you have seen all the others.

Then, while they were not all oaks or Scotch firs, though some were but ash, elm, crab-tree, or thorn as each might be, they had all characters of their own, so that if nature had been reversed, and their minds had become visible and their bodies unseen, no one would have mistaken Lord Newton for Lord Jeffrey, or either for Sir Walter or ' Holmhead.' If this same Mystification were applied to many of our men and women now, how hard to make out who was who, when everybody *speaks* as well as reads the newspapers, and nothing else.

It is one of my best pleasures to know, besides the author of this volume which I have so ' unconscionably ' rifled, two who were companions of the men of renown, whose names and work are all that now remain to us. The one to whom Miss Graham so affectionately dedicates her book, was then beautiful and good, shrewd and sincere, gracious and full of grace. She is all these still, and more. She has that wise, deep, gentle goodness which comes from time and sorrow, and a long life of love to man and love to God : were she a modern lady, when our women are too much of everything except women, she would have given us something better than the *Cottagers of Glenburnie,* and as good as *The Inheritance.* And her sister, who again keeps house with

her, meaning to end life as they began it, under the
same roof, as natural, as unhurt by the world, by
custom and by praise, as when they were girls in
George Square; had she been a French woman,
which I am thankful she was not, she would have
been a Madame de Staël, with much of her genius
and power, her eloquence and 'large discourse,' her
strength of thought, of feeling, and of expression, her
public heart, without any of her faults or foibles.
She is the only woman I ever knew who is not only
eloquent but an orator. She has the gift of great
speech, can wield a long sentence like a man, and
keep it alive and make it *tell*—make it sting, or flash,
or convince as she desires. With all these great,
and as I may call them public powers, she is, like
her sister, more of a woman than of all these,—
truthful, full of sympathy for suffering, indeed her
feeling for long-continued bodily pain—a by no
means common but very true virtue—I have never
known equalled, having herself been too well quali-
fied to be so; full of public spirit, but fuller of
private worth and heart. To know such women, to
have the privilege of familiar life with them, is of
itself, as Steele said, 'a liberal education.' They
were worthy to be the wives and companions of
Adam Gillies and of Malcolm Laing.

I have seen many deaths, but these come vividly
into my mind.

Mrs. Gillies, after being kept alive for years by keeping her in bed in winter, was dying, and, like her life, her death was gentle. A very short time before it came she took her round, little, embossed gold watch, which she always when awake carried in her shut left hand, with a short black ribbon and its key; collecting her breath and holding out the watch, she said to her sister Mrs. Laing, her life-long companion, 'Take that, Margaret, I am done with Time.'

Another fine old lady was dying, and could not lie down. Not many minutes before the end—sitting up—she had heart disease—she caught sight of her own face in a *console* mirror. She looked steadfastly at herself, then, with a serious smile, gave a nod, as if to say 'good-bye,' and died.

A very old man—thoroughbred—a great salmon fisher—a lover of pleasure and of nicety of body—sent for me in the middle of the night : he was fast dying, and knew it—and, with a strange frown said, Doctor, this is a most disgusting process ; and, looking to a bottle of laudanum on the mantelpiece, said, 'Give me that, and end it.' I said what any one would say. His anger deepened, and settling himself straight, and setting his mouth, he, by what I believe was a supreme act of the will, ceased to live

MISS STIRLING GRAHAM

OF DUNTRUNE.

I played with the bairnies at bowls and at ba',
And left them a' greeting when I cam' awa';
Ay! mithers and bairnies, and lassies and a',
Were a' sobbin' loudly when I cam' awa'.

MISS STIRLING GRAHAM

OF DUNTRUNE.

THIS gifted, excellent, and most delightful old lady, the perfect type of a Scottish gentle-woman, died yesterday afternoon, 23d August 1877, at her beautiful seat Duntrune, in Forfarshire, above Broughty Ferry, overlooking the Tay, with the woods of Ballumbie on one side, and those of Linlathen, her dear friend Mr. Erskine's estate, on the other, and with St. Andrews and the noble tower of St. Rule standing out clear on the sky line to the south. Miss Graham was in her ninety-sixth year, having been born in 1782. Her father, Patrick Stirling of Pittendreich, in the county of Forfar, and a much esteemed merchant in Dundee, married the heiress of Duntrune, and Miss Graham, the eldest of two daughters, a brother having predeceased her, in-herited the property. The other daughter was the wife of Colonel Lacon, and to *her* daughters' unfailing love Miss Graham owed much of the best happiness of her life. Her birthplace was an old house in a narrow back lane, leading off the main thoroughfare of Dundee, which is still, we believe, pointed out to strangers as the place where the authoress of the *Mystifications* first saw the light. Her life may almost be said to have been one long summer day, not without its clouds, but on the whole happy, delightful, and beneficent in no ordinary degree. Few have left the world so regarded with immediate, unmixed, and deserved affection, and fewer still have retained to the last, as she did, the pure fresh unblunted attachments of childhood to their friends. Dying at ninety-five, she was as gay and truthful and artless as a girl, with all the serious and 'thoughtful breath' that becomes a 'traveller between life and death.'

Always full of benevolence and public spirit, one of the earliest manifestations of this was some time ago amusingly told by an old Forfarshire farmer whom a friend of ours happened to fall in with in the neighbourhood of Dundee. When Dr. Jenner's great discovery was first announced it immediately attracted Miss Graham's interest and enthusiasm, and long before the Faculty became alive to its importance she used to ride about on her little white pony vaccinating with a needle every child whose birth she heard of in her neighbourhood. We have been told that in this way she protected from the terrible scourge of the smallpox not less than about 300 infants. Our farmer friend had been one of her early patients. So carefully was it done that it used to be said that none of those operated on by Miss Graham ever took smallpox.

In public affairs it was the same thing—always on the side of the right and the true. She was a life-long Liberal—liberal in all the senses of the word. Though intimate with Sir Walter Scott, who has recorded his admiration of her in one of his diaries, she consorted mainly with the men of the *Edinburgh Review.* Jeffrey, Sydney Smith, Gillies, Cockburn, Rutherfurd, Murray, and all that great race whom we had and have not, were among her friends. It was to her that Sydney Smith made that famous joke, of the day being so hot that 'he wished he could put off his flesh and sit in his bones, and let the wind whistle through them.' In her own county, where everybody knew her and she knew everybody and who their forebears were, she will be long remembered. The love of the people for her and their pride in her were wonderful. Those who were nearest to her—the inmates of her household, her servants, her dependants, her tenants—cherished for her something like adoration—she was so tender-hearted, and, interested in all their interests, so steadfast a friend. So modest was she, so just in her sense of herself, that every one was at ease with her, and felt that whatever she did and said and felt was as real as the material objects about them.

She was always being and doing good in multitudes of unseen ways.

To her intimate friends, it is not for us to say what she was and what her loss is. But even to the outside public she is endeared by her marvellous *Mystifications*, which, as far as we know, are quite unique in literature. We have all heard how, in the pleasantest and most thorough way, she 'took in' Jeffrey, Sir Walter, Sir Daniel Sandford, William Clerk, Count Flahault, and everybody; how with a fine faculty for satire she never pained; with so much sense she was never dull; with so much wit and pleasantry she was never excessive in any way; for her nature was based on love and goodness. Who among us does not remember—though we have hardly the heart now to think of them—the wonderful interview at 92 George Street between Jeffrey and the Lady Pitlyal—the 'pykin' of the king's teeth and the royal patent of 'weel pykit,' the stiff clay land that 'grat a' winter and girned a' simmer,' which threw Dr. Coventry, the agricultural professor, into convulsions of delight? It was a singular gift. Meet Miss Graham in company and you found her quiet, unpretending, sensible, shrewd, kindly— perhaps you did not remark anything extraordinary in her. But let her put on the old lady, and immediately it was as if a warlock's spell had passed over her. Not merely her look but her nature was changed. Her spirit had passed into the character she represented, and jest, quick retort, whimsical fancy, the wildest humour flowed from her lips with a freedom and truth to nature which would have been impossible in her own personality. The *Mystifications* were at first privately printed, and it was with some difficulty she was prevailed on to give them to the public. They soon passed here and in America into permanent favourites. Miss Graham also published in 1829 *The Bee Book*, a translation of M. de Gelieu's work, and fifty years afterwards she republished it, to the great benefit of all bee-keepers.

She retained to the last all her faculties and affections—her memory, her humour, her interest in life, her tender fidelity to friends, her love, we might almost say her happy-heartedness, passion for nature and all things fair. One little scene of her early life we like to recall. She and her next neighbour, the late Mr. Erskine of Linlathen, were always great friends, and some now alive, we believe, can still remember seeing them occasionally riding out together—the two so like in some respects, and so unlike—Il Penseroso and L'Allegra—he discoursing doubtless even then, in those young days, of 'righteousness,' and she listening, but with her eyes wide awake the while, to the outward nature which she loved so well, and with a keen and kindly look to the country folk who passed them on the road.

Until the last few years Miss Graham used to spend her winters in Edinburgh, and her modest house in Forth Street (No. 29), with its bright happy evenings of which she was the heart and life, can never be forgotten by those who survive them. With her have perished a thousand memories of old Edinburgh and Forfarshire society. Some of these are added as an appendix to the last edition of the *Mystifications;* but they want, of course, the life and spirit which, when telling them to her friends, she used to put into many a happy story of these old times.

To those who know the *Mystifications* it is hardly necessary to say that she possessed a true literary faculty. The writing is always clear, simple, unaffected, and in perfect taste. With all her sense of humour there was an underlying seriousness in her character; very touching and tender, for instance, are the dedication of *Mystifications* to Mrs. Gillies, and the lines with which she concludes. 'Few,' she says, writing in December 1868, 'are now alive who shared or assisted in these joyous scenes, and the Mystifier, at an advanced age, waits in humble reliance the certainty of her summons.'

> 'Blessed shades of the past,
> In the future I see ye, so fair !
>   Ties that were nearest,
>   Forms that were dearest,
> The truest and fondest are there.

They are flowerets of earth,
That are blooming in heaven, so fair !
   And the stately tree,
   Spreading wide and free,
The sheaves that were ripened are there.

   The tear-drop that trembled
In Pity's meek eye ; and the prayer,
   Faith of the purest,
   Hope that was surest,
The love all-enduring are there.

   And the loved, the beloved,
Whose life made existence so fair !
   The soft seraph voice
   Bade the lowly rejoice,
Is heard in sweet harmony there.

THACKERAY'S DEATH.

THACKERAY'S DEATH.

THIS great writer—our greatest novelist since Scott (and in some senses greater, because deeper, more to the quick, more *naked* than he), our foremost wit and man of letters since Macaulay—has been taken from us with an awful unexpectedness. He was found dead in bed on the morning of 24th December 1863. This is to us so great a personal as well as public calamity, that we feel little able to order our words aright or to see through our blinding tears.

Mr. Thackeray was so much greater, so much nobler than his works, great and noble as they are, that it is difficult to speak of him without apparent excess. What a loss to the world the disappearance of that large, acute, and fine understanding; that searching, inevitable inner and outer eye; that keen and yet kindly satiric touch; that wonderful humour and play of soul! And then such a mastery of his mother tongue! such a style! such nicety of word and turn! such a flavour of speech! such genuine originality of genius and expression! such an insight

into the hidden springs of human action! such a
dissection of the nerves to their ultimate *fibrillæ!*
such a sense and such a sympathy for the worth
and for the misery of man! such a power of bringing human nature to its essence,—detecting at once
its basic goodness and vileness, its compositeness!
In this subtle, spiritual analysis of men and women,
as we see them and live with them ; in this power of
detecting the enduring passions and desires, the
strengths, the weaknesses, and the deceits of the
race, from under the mask of ordinary worldly and
town life,—making a dandy or a dancing-girl as
real, as 'moving delicate and full of life,' as the most
heroic incarnations of good and evil ; in this vitality
and yet lightness of handling, doing it once and
for ever, and never a touch too little or too much,—
in all these respects he stood and stands alone and
matchless. He had a crystalline translucency of
thought and language ; there was no mistaking or
missing his meaning. It was like the finest etching,
done with a needle and bitten in with the best *aqua-
fortis,*—the *manière* incisive to perfection ; while, when
needed, he could rise to the full diapason of passion
and lofty declamation : and this was not the less
striking from being rare and brief, like a flash of
close lightning with its thunder quick and short.

Besides his wit, his quiet, scrupulous, and unerring
eye, his proper satiric gifts, his amazing faculty of

making his men and women talk each in their own voice and tongue, so that you know them before they are named, Mr. Thackeray had, as the condition under which all these acted, a singularly truthful, strong, and roomy understanding. There was an immense quantity, not less than the finest quality of mind in everything he said. You felt this when with him and when you measured with your eye his enormous brain.

His greatest work, one of the great masterpieces of genius in our, or indeed in any language, without doubt, is *Vanity Fair.*

This set him at once and by a bound in the first rank of fiction. One returns again and again to it, with its freshness, its depth, and terrible truth and power, its easy yet exquisite characterisation, its living talk, its abounding wit and fun.

We remember how, at the dinner given to him many years ago here, the chairman (Lord Neaves), with equal felicity and truth, said that two of Mr. Thackeray's master powers were *satire* and *sympathy*, —for without both of them he would not have been all that he peculiarly was.

It should never be forgotten that his specific gift was creative satire,—not caricature, nor even sarcasm, nor sentiment, nor romance, nor even character as such,—but the delicate satiric treatment of human nature in its most superficial aspects as well as in its inner depths, by a great-hearted, and tender and genuine sympathy, unsparing, truthful, inevitable, but with love and the love of goodness and true loving-kindness over-arching and indeed animating it all. It was well said by Brimley, in his subtle and just estimate of our great author in his Essays, that he could not have painted 'Vanity Fair as he has, unless Eden had been shining in his inner eye.' It was this sense of an all-perfect good, of a strict goodness laid upon each one of us as an unescapable law, it was this glimpse into the Paradise, not lost, of the lovely and the pure, which quickened his fell insight into the vileness, the vanity, the shortcomings, the pitifulness of us all, of himself not less than of any son of time. But as we once heard him say, he was created with a sense of the ugly, of the odd, of the meanly false, the desperately wicked; he laid them bare: them under all disguises he hunted to the death. And is not this something to have done? Something inestimable, though at times dreadful and sharp? It purges the soul by terror and pity.

This, with his truthfulness, his scorn of exaggeration in thought or word, and his wide, deep, living sympathy for the entire round of human wants and miseries, goes far to make his works in the best, because a practical sense, wholesome, moral, honest, and of 'good report.'

It is needless to enumerate his works. We not only all know and possess them,—they *possess us ;*

for are not Becky Sharp, Colonel Newcome, Major Pendennis, the Little Sister and Jeames, the Mulligan, and the terrific Deuceace, more really existing and alive in our minds than many men and women we saw yesterday?

Mr. Thackeray had, we believe, all but if not entirely, finished a novel which was to appear in the *Cornhill* next spring. It will be a sad pleasure to read the last words of the great genius and artist to whom we owe so much of our best entertainment.

He had a genuine gift of drawing. The delicious Book of Snobs is poor without his own woodcuts; and he not only had the eye and the faculty of a draughtsman, he was one of the best of art critics. He had the true instinct and relish, and the nicety and directness, necessary for just as well as high criticism: the white light of his intellect found its way into this as into every region of his work. We should not forget his verses,—he would have laughed if they had been called poems; but they have more imaginative *vis*, more daintiness of phrase, more true sensibility and sense, than much that is called so both by its authors and the public. We all know the abounding fun and drollery of his 'Battle of Limerick,' the sweet humour and rustic Irish loveliness of 'Peg of Limavaddy,' and the glorified cockneyism of 'Jacob Omnium's 'Oss.' 'The Ballad of Eliza Davis,' and the joys and woes of 'Pleaceman X,' we all know;

but not so many know the pathetic depth, the dreamy, unforgetting tenderness, of the 'Ballad of Bouilla-baisse,' 'The White Squall,' and 'The End of the Play,'—the last written, strangely as it now reads, for Christmas 1848, this day fifteen years ago. From it we take the following mournful and exquisite lines :—

> 'I'd say we suffer and we strive,
>   Not less nor more as men than boys ;
> With grizzled beards at forty-five,
>   As erst at twelve in corduroys.
> And if, in time of sacred youth,
>   We learned at home to love and pray,
> Pray Heaven that early Love and Truth
>   May never wholly pass away.
>
> And in the world, as in the school,
>   I'd say, how fate may change and shift ;
> The prize be sometimes with the fool,
>   The race not always to the swift.
> The strong may yield, the good may fall,
>   The great man be a vulgar clown,
> The knave be lifted over all,
>   The kind cast pitilessly down.
>
> .　　.　　.　　.　　.　　.
>
> We bow to Heaven that willed it so,
>   That darkly rules the fate of all,
> That sends the respite or the blow,
>   That's free to give, or to recall.
>
> .　　.　　.　　.　　.　　.
>
> So each shall mourn, in life's advance,
>   Dear hopes, dear friends, untimely killed ;
> Shall grieve for many a forfeit chance
>   And longing passion unfulfilled.

Amen ! whatever fate be sent,
  Pray God the heart may kindly glow,
Although the head with cares be bent,
  And whitened with the winter snow.

Come wealth or want, come good or ill,
  Let young and old accept their part,
And bow before the Awful Will,
  And bear it with an honest heart.

.   .   .   .   .

My song, save this, is little worth ;
  I lay the weary pen aside,
And wish you health, and love, and mirth,
  As fits the solemn Christmas-tide.
As fits the holy Christmas birth,
  Be this, good friends, our carol still—
Be peace on earth, be peace on earth,
  To men of gentle will.'

Gentle and sacred as these words are, they are as
much an essential part of their author's nature as that
superfluity of naughtiness, the Marquis of Steyne, in
Vanity Fair, or the elder and truly infernal Deuceace,
or the drunken and savage parson, in *Philip*. It was
no ordinary instrument which embraced so much,
and no ordinary master who could so sound its
chords.

Mr. Thackeray had a warm heart to Edinburgh.
It was here he took courage from the cordial, appre-
ciative reception he got when he lectured here, and
he always returned to us with renewed relish. Many
of us will now think over with a new and deeper
interest—the interest of the sudden grave and the

irrevocable and imperishable past—on those pleasant times when he read his 'Wit and Humour' and his 'Curate's Walk,' and, with a solemn tenderness, simplicity, and perfectness, such as it is now hopeless ever again to hear, read to us 'The spacious firmament on high,' and Johnson's noble and touching lines on poor Levett.

We know of no death in the world of letters since Macaulay's which will make so many mourners,—for he was a faithful friend. No one, we believe, will ever know the amount of true kindness and help, given often at a time when kindness cost much, to nameless, unheard-of suffering. A man of spotless honour, of the strongest possible home affections, of the most scrupulous truthfulness of observation and of word, we may use for him his own words to his 'faithful old gold pen':—

> 'Nor pass the words as idle phrases by;
> Stranger! I never writ a flattery,
> Nor signed the page that registered a lie.'

He has joined the immortals; for we may say of him, what we can say of few,—he is already and for ever classic. He is beyond the fear of forgetfulness or change, for he has enshrined his genius in a style crystalline, strong, beautiful, and enduring. There was much of many great men in him,—of Montaigne, Le Sage, Swift, and Addison, of Steele and Goldsmith, of Fielding, Molière, and Charles Lamb; but there was more of himself than of all others. As a work of art, his *Esmond* is probably the most consummate : it is a curious *tour de force,*—a miracle not only of story-telling, but of archaic insight and skill.

The foregoing estimate of his genius must stand instead of any special portraiture of the man. Yet, before concluding, we would mention two leading traits of character traceable, to a large extent, in his works, though finding no appropriate place in a literary criticism of them. One was the deep steady melancholy of his nature. He was fond of telling how on one occasion, at Paris, he found himself in a great crowded *salon ;* and looking from the one end across the sea of heads, being in Swift's place of calm in a crowd,[1] he saw at the other end a strange visage, staring at him with an expression of comical woebegoneness. After a little he found that this rueful being was himself in the mirror. He was not, indeed, morose. He was alive to and thankful for every-day blessings, great and small ; for the happiness of home, for friendship, for wit and music, for beauty of all kinds, for the pleasures of the 'faithful old gold pen ;' now running into some felicitous expression, now playing itself into some droll initial letter ; nay, even for the creature comforts. But his persistent state, especially

[1] 'An inch or two above it.'

for the later half of his life, was profoundly *morne*,—there is no other word for it. This arose in part from temperament, from a quick sense of the littleness and wretchedness of mankind. His keen perception of the meanness and vulgarity of the realities around him contrasted with the ideal present to his mind could produce no other effect. This feeling, embittered by disappointment, acting on a harsh and savage nature, ended in the *sæva indignatio* of Swift; acting on the kindly and too sensitive nature of Mr. Thackeray, it led only to compassionate sadness. In part, too, this melancholy was the result of private calamities. He alludes to these often in his writings, and a knowledge that his sorrows were great is necessary to the perfect appreciation of much of his deepest pathos. We allude to them here, painful as the subject is, mainly because they have given rise to stories,—some quite untrue, some even cruelly injurious. The loss of his second child in infancy was always an abiding sorrow,—described in the 'Hoggarty Diamond,' in a passage of surpassing tenderness, too sacred to be severed from its context. A yet keener and more constantly present affliction was the illness of his wife. He married her in Paris when he was 'mewing his mighty youth,' preparing for the great career which awaited him. One likes to think on these early days of happiness, when he could draw and write with that loved companion by his side:

he has himself sketched the picture : 'The humblest painter, be he ever so poor, may have a friend watching at his easel, or a gentle wife sitting by with her work in her lap, and with fond smiles or talk or silence, cheering his labours.' After some years of marriage, Mrs. Thackeray caught a fever, brought on by imprudent exposure at a time when the effects of such ailments are more than usually lasting both on the system and the nerves. She never afterwards recovered so as to be able to be with her husband and children. But she has been from the first intrusted to the good offices of a kind family, tenderly cared for, surrounded with every comfort by his unwearied affection. The beautiful lines in the ballad of the ' Bouillabaisse' are well known :—

> ' Ah me ! how quick the days are flitting !
>   I mind me of a time that 's gone,
> When here I 'd sit as now I 'm sitting,
>   In this same place—but not alone.
> A fair young form was nestled near me,
>   A dear, dear face looked fondly up,
> And sweetly spoke and smiled to cheer me
>   —There 's no one now to share my cup.'

In one of the latest Roundabouts we have this touching confession : 'I own for my part that, in reading pages which this hand penned formerly, I often lose sight of the text under my eyes. It is not the words I see ; but that past day ; that bygone page of life's history ; that tragedy, comedy it may

be, which our little home-company was enacting;
that merry-making which we shared; that funeral
which we followed; that bitter, bitter grief which we
buried.'   But all who knew him know well, and
love to recall, how these sorrows were soothed and
his home made a place of happiness by his two
daughters and his mother, who were his perpetual
companions, delights, and blessings, and whose
feeling of inestimable loss now will be best borne
and comforted by remembering how they were
everything to him, as he was to them.

His sense of a higher Power, his reverence and
godly fear, is felt more than expressed—as indeed it
mainly should always be—in everything he wrote.
It comes out at times quite suddenly, and stops at
once, in its full strength.   We could readily give
many instances of this.   One we give, as it occurs
very early, when he was probably little more than
six-and-twenty; it is from the paper, *Madame Sand
and the New Apocalypse.*   Referring to Henri
Heine's frightful words, '*Dieu qui se meurt,*' '*Dieu
est mort,*' and to the wild godlessness of *Spiridion,*
he thus bursts out: 'O awful, awful name of God!
Light unbearable! Mystery unfathomable! Vastness
immeasurable!   Who are these who come forward
to explain the mystery, and gaze unblinking into
the depths of the light, and measure the immeasurable
vastness to a hair?   O name, that God's people of

old did fear to utter! O light, that God's prophet would have perished had he seen! Who are these that are now so familiar with it?' In ordinary intercourse the same sudden '*Te Deum*' would occur, always brief and intense, like lightning from a cloudless heaven; he seemed almost ashamed,—not of it, but of his giving it expression.

We cannot resist here recalling one Sunday evening in December, when he was walking with two friends along the Dean Road, to the west of Edinburgh—one of the noblest outlets to any city. It was a lovely evening,—such a sunset as one never forgets; a rich dark bar of cloud hovered over the sun, going down behind the Highland hills, lying bathed in amethystine bloom; between this cloud and the hills there was a narrow slip of the pure ether, of a tender cowslip colour, lucid, and as if it were the very body of heaven in its clearness; every object standing out as if etched upon the sky. The north-west end of Corstorphine Hill, with its trees and rocks, lay in the heart of this pure radiance, and there a wooden crane, used in the quarry below, was so placed as to assume the figure of a cross; there it was, unmistakeable, lifted up against the crystalline sky. All three gazed at it silently. As they gazed, he gave utterance in a tremulous, gentle, and rapid voice, to what all were feeling, in the word 'CALVARY!' The friends walked on in silence, and then turned to other things. All that evening he was very gentle and serious, speaking, as he seldom did, of divine things, —of death, of sin, of eternity, of salvation; expressing his simple faith in God and in his Saviour.

There is a passage at the close of the 'Roundabout Paper,' No. XXIII., *De Finibus,* in which a sense of the ebb of life is very marked: the whole paper is like a soliloquy. It opens with a drawing of Mr. Punch,[1] with unusually mild eye, retiring for the night; he is putting out his high-heeled shoes, and before disappearing gives a wistful look into the passage, as if bidding it and all else good-night. He will be in bed, his candle out, and in darkness in five minutes, and his shoes found next morning at his door, the little potentate all the while in his final sleep. The whole paper is worth the most careful study; it reveals not a little of his real nature, and unfolds very curiously the secret of his work, the vitality, and abiding power of his own creations: how he 'invented a certain *Costigan,* out of scraps, heel-taps, odds and ends of characters,' and met the original the other day, without surprise, in a tavern parlour. The following is beautiful: 'Years ago I had a quarrel with a certain well-known person (I believed a statement regarding him which his friends imparted to me, and which turned out to be quite

[1] See note on page 194.

incorrect). To his dying day that quarrel was never quite made up. I said to his brother, "Why is your brother's soul still dark against me? *It is I who ought to be angry and unforgiving, for I was in the wrong!*" *Odisse quem læseris* was never better contravened. But what we chiefly refer to now is the profound pensiveness of the following strain, as if written with a presentiment of what was not then very far off: 'Another Finis written; another milestone on this journey from birth to the next world. Sure it is a subject for solemn cogitation. Shall we continue this story-telling business, and be voluble to the end of our age?' 'Will it not be presently time, O prattler, to hold your tongue?' And thus he ends:—

'Oh, the sad old pages, the dull old pages; oh, the cares, the *ennui*, the squabbles, the repetitions, the old conversations over and over again! But now and again a kind thought is recalled, and now and again a dear memory. Yet a few chapters more, and then the last; after which, behold Finis itself comes to an end, and the Infinite begins.'

He sent the proof of this paper to his 'dear neighbours,' in Onslow Square (Sir Theodore and Lady Martin), to whom he owed so much almost daily pleasure, with his corrections, the whole of the last paragraph in manuscript, and above a first sketch of it also in MS., which is fuller and more

13

impassioned.   His fear of 'enthusiastic writing' had led him, we think, to sacrifice something of the sacred power of his first words, which we give with its interlineations :—

'Another Finis, another slice of life which *Tempus edax* has devoured! And I may have to write the word once or twice perhaps, and then an end of Ends.   ~~Finite is over, and Infinite beginning~~.   Oh the troubles, the cares, the *ennui*, the ~~complications~~, disputes, the repetitions, the old conversations over and over again, and here and there and oh the delightful passages, the dear, the brief, the forever remembered! ~~And then~~ A few chapters more, and then the last, and then behold Finis itself coming to an end and the Infinite beginning!'

How like music this,—like one trying the same air in different ways; as it were, searching out and sounding all its depths.   'The dear, the brief, the for ever remembered;' these are like a bar out of Beethoven, deep and melancholy as the sea! He had been suffering on Sunday from an old and cruel enemy.   He fixed with his friend and surgeon to come again on Tuesday; but with that dread of anticipated pain, which is a common condition of sensibility and genius, he put him off with a note from 'yours unfaithfully, W. M. T.' He went out on Wednesday for a little, and came home at ten.

He went to his room, suffering much, but declining his man's offer to sit with him. He hated to make others suffer. He was heard moving, as if in pain, about twelve, on the eve of

> ' That the happy morn,
> Wherein the Son of Heaven's eternal King,
> Of wedded maid, and virgin-mother born,
> Our great redemption from above did bring.'

Then all was quiet, and then he must have died—in a moment. Next morning his man went in, and opening the windows found his master dead, his arms behind his head, as if he had tried to take one more breath. We think of him as of our Chalmers; found dead in like manner; the same childlike, unspoiled open face; the same gentle mouth; the same spaciousness and softness of nature; the same look of power. What a thing to think of,—his lying there alone in the dark, in the midst of his own mighty London; his mother and his daughters asleep, and, it may be, dreaming of his goodness. God help them, and us all! What would become of us, stumbling along this our path of life, if we could not, at our utmost need, stay ourselves on Him?

Long years of sorrow, labour, and pain had killed him before his time. It was found after death how little life he had to live. He looked always fresh with that abounding, silvery hair, and his young, almost infantine face, but he was worn to a shadow, and his hands wasted as if by eighty years. With him it is the end of Ends; finite is over, and infinite begun. What we all felt and feel can never be so well expressed as in his own words of sorrow for the early death of Charles Buller:—

> ' Who knows the inscrutable design?
>   Blessed be He who took and gave!
> Why should your mother, Charles, not mine,
>   Be weeping at her darling's grave?
> We bow to Heaven that willed it so,
>   That darkly rules the fate of all,
> That sends the respite or the blow,
>   That 's free to give, or to recall.'

NOTE.

Mr. Thackeray's connection with *Punch* began very early in the history of that periodical, and he continued a constant contributor at least up to 1850. The acquisition was an invaluable one to *Mr. Punch.* Without undue disparagement of that august dignitary, it may now be said that at first he was too exclusively metropolitan in his tone, too much devoted to 'natural histories' of medical students and London idlers,— in fact, somewhat Cockney. Mr. Thackeray at once stamped it with a different tone; made its satire universal, adapted its fun to the appreciation of cultivated men. On the other hand, the connection with *Punch* must have been of the utmost value to Mr. Thackeray. He had the widest range, could write without restraint, and without the finish and completeness necessary in more formal publications. The unrestrained practice in *Punch*, besides the improvement in style and in modes of thought which practice always gives, probably had no small share in teaching him wherein his real strength lay. For it is worthy of notice in Mr. Thackeray's literary career that this knowledge did not come easily or soon, but only after hard

work and much experience. His early writings both in *Fraser*
and *Punch* were as if groping. In these periodicals his happier
efforts come last, and after many preludes,—some of them
broken off abruptly. 'Catherine' is lost in 'George de
Barnwell;' 'Yellowplush' and 'Fitz-boodle' are the pre-
ambles to 'Barry Lyndon' and 'The Hoggarty Diamond;'
Punch's 'Continental Tour' and the 'Wanderings of the Fat
Contributor' close untimely, and are succeeded by the 'Snob
Papers' and the kindly wisdom of the elder Brown. Fame,
indeed, was not now far off; but ere it could be reached there
remained yet repeated effort and frequent disappointment.
With peculiar pleasure we now recall the fact that these weary
days of struggle and obscurity were cheered in no inconsider-
able degree by the citizens of Edinburgh.

There happened to be placed in the window of an Edinburgh
jeweller a silver statuette of *Mr. Punch*, with his dress *en rigueur*,
his comfortable and tidy paunch, with all its buttons ; his
hunch; his knee-breeches, with their tie ; his compact little
legs, one foot a little forward ; and the intrepid and honest,
kindly little fellow firmly set on his pins, with his customary
look of up to and good for anything. In his hand was his
weapon, a pen ; his skull was an inkhorn, and his cap its lid.
A passer-by—who had long been grateful to our author, as to
a dear unknown and enriching friend, for his writings in *Fraser*
and in *Punch*, and had longed for some way of reaching him,
and telling him how his work was relished and valued—bethought himself of sending this inkstand to Mr. Thackeray.
He went in, and asked its price. 'Ten guineas, sir.' He said
to himself, 'There are many who feel as I do ; why shouldn't
we send him up to him? I'll get eighty several half-crowns,
and that will do it' (he had ascertained that there would be
discount for ready money). With the help of a friend, who
says he awoke to Thackeray, and divined his great future, when
he came, one evening, in *Fraser* for May 1844, on the word
kinopium,[1] the half-crowns were soon forthcoming, and it is

---

[1] Here is the passage. It is from *Little Travels and Roadside
Sketches*. Why are they not republished? We must have his

pleasant to remember, that in the 'octogint' are the names of Lord Jeffrey and Sir William Hamilton, who gave their half-crowns with the heartiest good-will. A short note was written telling the story. The little man in silver was duly packed, and sent with the following inscription round the base :—

.GULIELMO MAKEPEACE THACKERAY.

ARMA VIRUMQUE

GRATI NECNON GRATÆ EDINENSES

LXXX.

D.   D.   D.

To this the following reply was made :—

'13 YOUNG STREET, KENSINGTON SQUARE,
May 11 1848.

'MY DEAR SIR,—The arms and the man arrived in safety yesterday, and I am glad to know the names of two of the eighty Edinburgh friends who have taken such a kind method of showing their good-will towards me. If you are grati I am gratior. Such

---

Opera Omnia. He is on the top of the Richmond omnibus. 'If I were a great prince, and rode outside of coaches (as I should if I were a great prince), I would, whether I smoked or not, have a case of the best Havanas in my pocket, not for my own smoking, but to give them to the snobs on the coach, who smoke the vilest cheroots. They poison the air with the odour of their filthy weeds. A man at all easy in circumstances would spare himself much annoyance by taking the above simple precaution.

'A gentleman sitting behind me tapped me on the back, and asked for a light. He was a footman, or rather valet. He had no livery, but the three friends who accompanied him were tall men in pepper-and-salt undress jackets, with a duke's coronet on their buttons.

'After tapping me on the back, and when he had finished his cheroot, the gentleman produced another wind instrument, which he called a "kinopium," a sort of trumpet, on which he showed a great inclination to play. He began puffing out of the kinopium an abominable air, which he said was the "Duke's March." It was played by the particular request of the pepper-and-salt gentry.

'The noise was so abominable, that even the coachman objected, and said it was not allowed to play on *his* bus. "Very well," said the valet, "*we're only of the Duke of B——'s* establishment, THAT'S ALL."'

tokens of regard & sympathy are very precious to a writer like myself, who have some difficulty still in making people understand what you have been good enough to find out in Edinburgh, that under the mask satirical there walks about a sentimental gentleman who means not unkindly to any mortal person. I can see exactly the same expression under the vizard of my little friend in silver, and hope some day to shake the whole octogint by the hand gratos & gratas, and thank them for their friendliness and regard. I think I had best say no more on the subject, lest I should be tempted into some enthusiastic writing of w^h I am afraid. I assure you these tokens of what I can't help acknowledging as popularity—make me humble as well as grateful—and make me feel an almost awful sense of the responsibility w^h falls upon a man in such a station. Is it deserved or undeserved? Who is this that sets up to preach to mankind, and to laugh at many things w^h men reverence? I hope I may be able to tell the truth always, & to see it aright, according to the eyes w^h God Almighty gives me. And if, in the exercise of my calling I get friends, and find encouragement and sympathy, I need not tell you how much I feel and am thankful for this support. Indeed I can't reply lightly upon this subject or feel otherwise than very grave when people begin to praise me as you do. Wishing you and my Edinburgh friends all health and happiness, believe me, my dear Sir, most faithfully yours, W. M. THACKERAY.'

How like the man is this gentle and serious letter, written these long years ago! He tells us frankly his 'calling :' he is a preacher to mankind. He 'laughs,' he does not sneer. He asks home questions at himself as well as the world : 'Who is this?' Then his feeling 'not otherwise than very grave' when people begin to praise, is true conscientiousness. This servant of his Master hoped to be able 'to tell the truth always, and to see it aright, according to the eyes which God Almighty gives me.' His picture by himself will be received as correct *now*, 'a sentimental gentleman who means not unkindly to any mortal person,'—sentimental in its good old sense, and a gentleman in heart and speech. And that little touch about enthusiastic writing, proving all the more that the enthusiasm itself was there.

MARJORIE FLEMING.

MARJORIE FLEMING.

ONE November afternoon in 1810—the year in
which *Waverley* was resumed and laid aside
again, to be finished off, its last two volumes in three
weeks, and made immortal in 1814, and when its
author, by the death of Lord Melville, narrowly
escaped getting a civil appointment in India—three
men, evidently lawyers, might have been seen escap-
ing like schoolboys from the Parliament House,
and speeding arm-in-arm down Bank Street and the
Mound, in the teeth of a surly blast of sleet.

The three friends sought the *bield* of the low wall
old Edinburgh boys remember well, and sometimes
miss now, as they struggle with the stout west wind.

The three were curiously unlike each other. One,
'a little man of feeble make, who would be unhappy
if his pony got beyond a foot pace,' slight, with
'small, elegant features, hectic cheek, and soft hazel
eyes, the index of the quick, sensitive spirit within,
as if he had the warm heart of a woman, her genuine
enthusiasm, and some of her weaknesses.' Another,
as unlike a woman as a man can be ; homely, almost

common, in look and figure; his hat and his coat, and indeed his entire covering, worn to the quick, but all of the best material; what redeemed him from vulgarity and meanness, were his eyes, deep set, heavily thatched, keen, hungry, shrewd, with a slumbering glow far in, as if they could be dangerous; a man to care nothing for at first glance, but somehow, to give a second and not-forgetting look at. The third was the biggest of the three, and though lame, nimble, and all rough and alive with power; had you met him anywhere else, you would say he was a Liddesdale store-farmer, come of gentle blood; 'a stout, blunt carle,' as he says of himself, with the swing and stride and the eye of a man of the hills— a large, sunny, out-of-door air all about him. On his broad and somewhat stooping shoulders, was set that head which, with Shakespeare's and Bonaparte's, is the best known in all the world.

He was in high spirits, keeping his companions and himself in roars of laughter, and every now and then seizing them, and stopping, that they might take their fill of the fun; there they stood shaking with laughter, 'not an inch of their body free' from its grip. At George Street they parted, one to Rose Court, behind St. Andrew's Church, one to Albany Street, the other, our big and limping friend, to Castle Street.

We need hardly give their names. The first was

William Erskine, afterwards Lord Kinnedder, chased
out of the world by a calumny, killed by its foul
breath—

> ' And at the touch of wrong, without a strife,
> Slipped in a moment out of life.'

There is nothing in literature more beautiful or more
pathetic than Scott's love and sorrow for this friend
of his youth.

The second was William Clerk, the Darsie Latimer
of *Redgauntlet;* ' a man,' as Scott says, ' of the most
acute intellects and powerful apprehension,' but of
more powerful indolence, so as to leave the world
with little more than the report of what he might
have been,—a humorist as genuine, though not quite
so savagely Swiftian as his brother Lord Eldin,
neither of whom had much of that commonest and
best of all the humours, called good.

The third we all know. What has he not done
for every one of us? Who else ever, except Shakespeare, so diverted mankind, entertained and entertains a world so liberally, so wholesomely? We are
fain to say, not even Shakespeare, for his is something
deeper than diversion, something higher than pleasure, and yet who would care to split this hair?

Had any one watched him closely before and
after the parting, what a change he would see!
The bright, broad laugh, the shrewd, jovial word,
the man of the Parliament House and of the world;

and next step, moody, the light of his eye withdrawn, as if seeing things that were invisible; his
shut mouth, like a child's, so impressionable, so
innocent, so sad; he was now all within, as before
he was all without; hence his brooding look. As
the snow blattered in his face, he muttered, 'How
it raves and drifts! On-ding o' snaw—ay, that's the
word—on-ding—' He was now at his own door,
'Castle Street, No. 39.' He opened the door, and
went straight to his den; that wondrous workshop,
where, in one year, 1823, when he was fifty-two, he
wrote *Peveril of the Peak*, *Quentin Durward*, and
St. Ronan's Well, besides much else. We once took
the foremost of our novelists, the greatest, we would
say, since Scott, into this room, and could not but
mark the solemnising effect of sitting where the great
magician sat so often and so long, and looking out
upon that little shabby bit of sky and that back
green, where faithful Camp lies.[1]

He sat down in his large, green morocco elbow-
chair, drew himself close to his table, and glowered

---

[1] This favourite dog 'died about January 1809, and was
buried in a fine moonlight night in the little garden behind
the house in Castle Street. My wife tells me she remembers
the whole family in tears about the grave as her father himself
smoothed the turf above Camp, with the saddest face she had
ever seen. He had been engaged to dine abroad that day, but
apologised, on account of the death of "a dear old friend."'—
Lockhart's *Life of Scott.*

and gloomed at his writing apparatus, a very handsome old box, richly carved, lined with crimson
velvet, and containing ink-bottles, taper-stand, etc.,
in silver, the whole in such order, that it might have
come from the silversmith's window half an hour
before. He took out his paper, then starting up
angrily, said, '"Go spin, you jade, go spin." No,
d— it, it won't do,—

> " My spinnin' wheel is auld and stiff,
>   The rock o't wunna stand, sir,
> To keep the temper-pin in tiff
>   Employs ower aft my hand, sir."

I am off the fang.[1] I can make nothing of *Waverley*
to-day; I'll awa' to Marjorie. Come wi' me, Maida,
you thief.' The great creature rose slowly, and the
pair were off, Scott taking a *maud* (a plaid) with him.
'White as a frosted plum-cake, by jingo!' said he,
when he got to the street. Maida gambolled and
whisked among the snow, and his master strode
across to Young Street, and through it to 1 North
Charlotte Street, to the house of his dear friend,
Mrs. William Keith of Corstorphine Hill, niece of
Mrs. Keith of Ravelston, of whom he said at her
death, eight years after, 'Much tradition, and that of
the best, has died with this excellent old lady, one
of the few persons whose spirits and *cleanliness* and

---

[1] Applied to a pump when it is dry, and its valve has lost
its 'fang;' from the German, *fangen*, to hold.

freshness of mind and body made old age lovely and desirable.'

Sir Walter was in that house almost every day, and had a key, so in he and the hound went, shaking themselves in the lobby. 'Marjorie! Marjorie!' shouted her friend, 'where are ye, my bonnie wee croodlin doo?' In a moment a bright, eager child of seven was in his arms, and he was kissing her all over. Out came Mrs. Keith. 'Come yer ways in, Wattie.' 'No, not now. I am going to take Marjorie wi' me, and you may come to your tea in Duncan Roy's sedan, and bring the bairn home in your lap.' 'Tak' Marjorie, and it *on-ding o' snaw!*' said Mrs. Keith. He said to himself, 'On-ding— that's odd—that is the very word.' 'Hoot, awa! look here,' and he displayed the corner of his plaid, made to hold lambs—(the true shepherd's plaid, consisting of two breadths sewed together, and uncut at one end, making a poke or *cul dé sac*). 'Tak' yer lamb,' said she, laughing at the contrivance, and so the Pet was first well happit up, and then put, laughing silently, into the plaid-neuk, and the shepherd strode off with his lamb,—Maida gambolling through the snow, and running races in his mirth.

Didn't he face 'the angry airt,' and make her bield his bosom, and into his own room with her, and lock the door, and out with the warm, rosy, little wifie, who took it all with great composure! There the

two remained for three or more hours, making the
house ring with their laughter; you can fancy the
big man's and Maidie's laugh. Having made the
fire cheery, he set her down in his ample chair, and
standing sheepishly before her, began to say his
lesson, which happened to be—'Ziccoty, diccoty,
dock, the mouse ran up the clock, the clock struck
wan, down the mouse ran, ziccoty, diccoty, dock.'
This done repeatedly till she was pleased, she gave
him his new lesson, gravely and slowly, timing it
upon her small fingers,—he saying it after her,—

> 'Wonery, twoery, tickery, seven ;
> Alibi, crackaby, ten, and eleven ;
> Pin, pan, musky, dan ;
> Tweedle-um, twoddle-um,
> Twenty-wan ; eerie, orie, ourie,
> You, are, out.'

He pretended to great difficulty, and she rebuked
him with most comical gravity, treating him as a
child. He used to say that when he came to Alibi
Crackaby he broke down, and Pin-Pan, Musky-Dan,
Tweedle-um Twoddle-um made him roar with laughter. He said *Musky-Dan* especially was beyond
endurance, bringing up an Irishman and his hat
fresh from the Spice Islands and odoriferous Ind ;
she getting quite bitter in her displeasure at his ill
behaviour and stupidness.

Then he would read ballads to her in his own
glorious way, the two getting wild with excitement

14

over *Gil Morrice* or the *Baron of Smailholm ;* and he would take her on his knee, and make her repeat Constance's speeches in *King John,* till he swayed to and fro sobbing his fill. Fancy the gifted little creature, like one possessed, repeating—

> ' For I am sick, and capable of fears,
> Oppressed with wrong, and therefore full of fears ;
> A widow, husbandless, subject to fears ;
> A woman, naturally born to fears.'

> ' If thou that bidst me be content, wert grim,
> Ugly and slanderous to thy mother's womb,
> Lame, foolish, crooked, swart, prodigious—.'

Or, drawing herself up ' to the height of her great argument '—

> ' I will instruct my sorrows to be proud,
> For grief is proud, and makes his owner stout.
> Here I and sorrow sit.'

Scott used to say that he was amazed at her power over him, saying to Mrs. Keith, ' She 's the most extraordinary creature I ever met with, and her repeating of Shakespeare overpowers me as nothing else does.'

Thanks to the unforgetting sister of this dear child, who has much of the sensibility and fun of her who has been in her small grave these fifty and more years, we have now before us the letters and journals of Pet Marjorie—before us lies and gleams her rich brown hair, bright and sunny as if yesterday's, with the words on the paper, ' Cut out in her last illness,' and two pictures of her by her beloved Isabella,

whom she worshipped; there are the faded old
scraps of paper, hoarded still, over which her warm
breath and her warm little heart had poured themselves; there is the old water-mark, 'Lingard, 1808.'
The two portraits are very like each other, but
plainly done at different times; it is a chubby,
healthy face, deep-set, brooding eyes, as eager to tell
what is going on within, as to gather in all the glories
from without; quick with the wonder and the pride
of life; they are eyes that would not be soon satisfied
with seeing; eyes that would devour their object,
and yet childlike and fearless; and that is a mouth
that will not be soon satisfied with love; it has a
curious likeness to Scott's own, which has always
appeared to us his sweetest, most mobile, and speaking feature.

There she is, looking straight at us as she did at
him—fearless and full of love, passionate, wild,
wilful, fancy's child. One cannot look at it without
thinking of Wordsworth's lines on poor Hartley
Coleridge :—

> 'O blessed vision, happy child !
> Thou art so exquisitely wild,
> I thought of thee with many fears,
> Of what might be thy lot in future years.
> I thought of times when Pain might be thy guest,
> Lord of thy house and hospitality ;
> And Grief, uneasy lover ! ne'er at rest,
> But when she sat within the touch of thee.

Oh, too industrious folly !
Oh, vain and causeless melancholy !
Nature will either end thee quite,
Or, lengthening out thy season of delight,
Preserve for thee by individual right,
A young lamb's heart among the full-grown flock.'

And we can imagine Scott, when holding his warm plump little playfellow in his arms, repeating that stately friend's lines :—

'Loving she is, and tractable, though wild,
And Innocence hath privilege in her,
To dignify arch looks and laughing eyes,
And feats of cunning ; and the pretty round
Of trespasses, affected to provoke
Mock chastisement and partnership in play.
And as a fagot sparkles on the hearth,
Not less if unattended and alone,
Than when both young and old sit gathered round,
And take delight in its activity,
Even so this happy creature of herself
Is all-sufficient ; solitude to her
Is blithe society ; she fills the air
With gladness and involuntary songs.'

But we will let her disclose herself. We need hardly say that all this is true, and that these letters are as really Marjorie's as was this light brown hair ; indeed you could as easily fabricate the one as the other.

There was an old servant—Jeanie Robertson— who was forty years in her grandfather's family. Marjorie Fleming, or as she is called in the letters,

and by Sir Walter, Maidie, was the last child she
kept. Jeanie's wages never exceeded £3 a year,
and when she left his service, she had saved £40.
She was devotedly attached to Maidie, rather despis-
ing and ill-using her sister Isabella—a beautiful and
gentle child. This partiality made Maidie apt at
times to domineer over Isabella. 'I mention this'
(writes her surviving sister) 'for the purpose of telling
you an instance of Maidie's generous justice. When
only five years old—when walking in Raith grounds,
the two children had run on before, and old Jeanie
remembered they might come too near a dangerous
mill-lade. She called to them to turn back. Maidie
heeded her not, rushed all the faster on, and fell, and
would have been lost, had her sister not pulled her
back, saving her life, but tearing her clothes. Jeanie
flew on Isabella to "give it her" for spoiling her
favourite's dress; Maidie rushed in between crying
out, "Pay (whip) Maidjie as much as you like, and
I'll not say one word; but touch Isy, and I'll roar
like a bull!" Years after Maidie was resting in her
grave, my mother used to take me to the place, and
told the story always in the exact same words.'
This Jeanie must have been a character. She took
great pride in exhibiting Maidie's brother William's
Calvinistic acquirements when nineteen months old,
to the officers of a militia regiment then quartered in
Kirkcaldy. This performance was so amusing that

it was often repeated, and the little theologian was presented by them with a cap and feathers. Jeanie's glory was 'putting him through the carritch' (catechism) in broad Scotch, beginning at the beginning with 'Wha made ye, ma bonnie man?' For the correctness of this and three next replies, Jeanie had no anxiety, but the tone changed to menace, and the closed *nieve* (fist) was shaken in the child's face as she demanded, 'Of what are you made?' 'DIRT' was the answer uniformly given. 'Wull ye never learn to say *dust*, ye thrawn deevil?' with a cuff from the opened hand, was the as inevitable rejoinder.

Here is Maidie's first letter before she was six: the spelling unaltered, and there are no 'commoes.'

'MY DEAR ISA,—I now sit down to answer all your kind and beloved letters which you was so good as to write to me. This is the first time I ever wrote a letter in my Life. There are a great many Girls in the Square and they cry just like a pig when we are under the painfull necessity of putting it to Death. Miss Potune a Lady of my acquaintance praises me dreadfully. I repeated something out of Dean Swift, and she said I was fit for the stage, and you may think I was primmed up with majestick Pride, but upon my word I felt myselfe turn a little birsay— birsay is a word which is a word that William composed which is as you may suppose a little enraged. This horrid fat simpliton says that my Aunt is beauti full which is intirely impossible for that is not her nature.'

What a peppery little pen we wield! What could that have been out of the sardonic Dean? what other child of that age would have used 'beloved' as she does? This power of affection, this faculty of *be*loving, and wild hunger to be beloved, comes out more and more. She perilled her all upon it, and it may have been as well—we know indeed that it was far better—for her that this wealth of love was so soon withdrawn to its one only infinite Giver and Receiver. This must have been the law of her earthly life. Love was, indeed 'her Lord and King;' and it was perhaps well for her that she found so soon that her and our only Lord and King, Himself is Love.

Here are bits from her Diary at Braehead :—' The day of my existence here has been delightful and enchanting. On Saturday I expected no less than three well made Bucks the names of whom is here advertised. Mr. Geo. Crakey (Craigie), and Wm. Keith and Jn. Keith—the first is the funniest of every one of them. Mr. Crakey and I walked to Crakyhall (Craigiehall) hand in hand in Innocence and matitation (meditation) sweet thinking on the kind love which flows in our tender hearted mind which is overflowing with majestic pleasure no one was ever so polite to me in the hole state of my existence.

Mr. Craky you must know is a great Buck and pretty good-looking.

'I am at Ravelston enjoying nature's fresh air. The birds are singing sweetly—the calf doth frisk and nature shows her glorious face.'

Here is a confession :—'I confess I have been very more like a little young divil than a creature for when Isabella went up stairs to teach me religion and my multiplication and to be good and all my other lessons I stamped with my foot and threw my new hat which she had made on the ground and was sulky and was dreadfully passionate, but she never whiped me but said Marjory go into another room and think what a great crime you are committing letting your temper git the better of you. But I went so sulkily that the Devil got the better of me but she never never never whips me so that I think I would be the better of it and the next time that I behave ill I think she should do it for she never never does it. . . . Isabella has given me praise for checking my temper for I was sulky even when she was kneeling an hole hour teaching me to write.'

Our poor little wifie, *she* has no doubts of the personality of the Devil! 'Yesterday I behave extremely ill in God's most holy church for I would never attend myself nor let Isabella attend which was a great crime for she often often tells me that when to or three are geathered together God is in the midst of them, and it was the very same Divil that tempted Job that tempted me I am sure; but he resisted Satan though he had boils and many many other misfortunes which I have escaped. . . . I am now going to tell you the horible and wretched plaege (plague) that my multiplication gives me you can't conceive it the most Devilish thing is 8 times 8 and 7 times 7 it is what nature itself cant endure.'

This is delicious; and what harm is there in her 'Devilish?' it is strong language merely; even old Rowland Hill used to say 'he grudged the Devil those rough and ready words.' 'I walked to that delightful place Crakyhall with a delightful young man beloved by all his friends espacially by me his loveress, but I must not talk any more about him for Isa said it is not proper for to speak of gentalmen but I will never forget him ! . . . I am very very glad that satan has not given me boils and many other misfortunes—In the holy bible these words are written that the Devil goes like a roaring lyon in search of his pray but the lord lets us escape from him but we' (*pauvre petite !*) 'do not strive with this awfull Spirit. . . . To-day I pronunced a word which should never come out of a lady's lips it was that I called John a Impudent Bitch. I will tell you what I think made me in so bad a humor is I got one or two of that bad bad sina (senna) tea to-day,'—a better excuse for bad humour and bad language than most.

She has been reading the Book of Esther : ' It was a dreadful thing that Haman was hanged on the very gallows which he had prepared for Mordeca to hang him and his ten sons thereon and it was very wrong and cruel to hang his sons for they did not commit the crime; *but then Jesus was not then come to teach us to be merciful.*' This is wise and beautiful—has upon it the very dew of youth and of holiness. Out of the mouths of babes and sucklings He perfects His praise.

' This is Saturday and I am very glad of it because I have play half the Day and I get money too but alas I owe Isabella 4 pence for if I am finned 2 pence whenever I bite my nails. Isabella is teaching me to make simme colings nots of interrigations peorids commoes, etc. . . . As this is Sunday I will meditate upon Senciable and Religious subjects. First I should be very thankful I am not a begger.'

This amount of meditation and thankfulness seems to have been all she was able for.

' I am going to-morrow to a delightful place, Brae-head by name, belonging to Mrs. Crraford, where there is ducks cocks hens bubblyjocks 2 dogs 2 cats and swine which is delightful. I think it is shocking to think that the dog and cat should bear them' (this is a meditation physiological), 'and they are drowned after all. I would rather have a man-dog than a woman-dog, because they do not bear like women-dogs ; it is a hard case—it is shocking. I cam here

to enjoy natures delightful breath it is sweeter than
a fial (phial) of rose oil.'

Braehead is the farm the historical Jock Howison
asked and got from our gay James the Fifth, 'the
gudeman o' Ballengiech,' as a reward for the services
of his flail when the King had the worst of it at
Cramond Brig with the gipsies. The farm is unchanged in size from that time, and still in the
unbroken line of the ready and victorious thrasher.
Braehead is held on the condition of the possessor
being ready to present the King with a ewer and
basin to wash his hands, Jock having done this for
his unknown king after the *splore*, and when George
the Fourth came to Edinburgh this ceremony was
performed in silver at Holyrood. It is a lovely neuk
this Braehead, preserved almost as it was 200 years
ago. 'Lot and his wife' mentioned by Maidie—
two quaintly cropped yew-trees—still thrive, the burn
runs as it did in her time, and sings the same quiet
tune—as much the same and as different as *Now*
and *Then*. The house full of old family relics and
pictures, the sun shining on them through the small
deep windows with their plate glass; and there,
blinking at the sun, and chattering contentedly, is a
parrot, that might, for its looks of eld, have been in
the ark, and domineered over and *deaved* the dove.
Everything about the place is old and fresh.

This is beautiful:—'I am very sorry to say that I

forgot God—that is to say I forgot to pray to-day and Isabella told me that I should be thankful that God did not forget me—if he did, O what become of me if I was in danger and God not friends with me— I must go to unquenchable fire and if I was tempted to sin—how could I resist it O no I will never do it again—no no—if I can help it.' (Canny wee wifie!) 'My religion is greatly falling off because I dont pray with so much attention when I am saying my prayers, and my charecter is lost among the Braehead people. I hope I will be religious again—but as for regaining my charecter I despare for it.' (Poor little 'habit and repute!')

Her temper, her passion, and her 'badness' are almost daily confessed and deplored :—' I will never again trust to my own power, for I see that I cannot be good without God's assistance—I will not trust in my own selfe, and Isa's health will be quite ruined by me—it will indeed.' 'Isa has giving me advice, which is, that when I feal Satan beginning to tempt me, that I flea him and he would flea me.' 'Remorse is the worst thing to bear, and I am afraid that I will fall a marter to it.'

Poor dear little sinner!—Here comes the world again :—' In my travels I met with a handsome lad named Charles Balfour Esq., and from him I got ofers of marage—offers of marage, did I say? Nay plenty heard me.' A fine scent for 'breach of promise!'

This is abrupt and strong :—'The Divil is curced and all works. 'Tis a fine work *Newton on the profecies.* I wonder if there is another book of poems comes near the Bible. The Divil always girns at the sight of the Bible.' 'Miss Portune' (her 'simpliton' friend) 'is very fat; she pretends to be very learned. She says she saw a stone that dropt from the skies; but she is a good Christian.' Here come her views on church government :—'An Annibabtist is a thing I am not a member of—I am a Pisplekan (Episcopalian) just now, and' (Oh you little Laodicean and Latitudinarian !) 'a Prisbeteran at Kirkcaldy !'—(*Blandula ! Vagula ! cœlum et animum mutas quæ trans mare* (i.e. *trans Bodotriam*)-*curris !*)—'my native town.' 'Sentiment is not what I am acquainted with as yet, though I wish it, and should like to practise it' (!) 'I wish I had a great, great deal of gratitude in my heart, in all my body.' 'There is a new novel published, named *Self-Control*' (Mrs. Brunton's)—'a very good maxim forsooth !' This is shocking : 'Yesterday a marrade man, named Mr. John Balfour, Esq., offered to kiss me, and offered to marry me, though the man' (a fine directness this !) 'was espused, and his wife was present and said he must ask her permission; but he did not. I think he was ashamed and confounded before 3 gentelman—Mr. Jobson and 2 Mr. Kings.' 'Mr. Banester's' (Bannister's) 'Budjet is to-night; I hope it will be a good one. A great many authors have expressed themselves too sentimentally.' You are right, Marjorie. 'A Mr. Burns writes a beautiful song on Mr. Cunhaming, whose wife desarted him— truly it is a most beautiful one.' 'I like to read the Fabulous historys, about the histerys of Robin, Dickey, flapsay, and Peccay, and it is very amusing, for some were good birds and others bad, but Peccay was the most dutiful and obedient to her parients. 'Thomson is a beautiful author, and Pope, but nothing to Shakespear, of which I have a little knolege. *Macbeth* is a pretty composition, but awful one.' 'The *Newgate Calender* is very instructive' (!) 'A sailor called here to say farewell; it must be dreadful to leave his native country when he might get a wife; or perhaps me, for I love him very much. But O I forgot, Isabella forbid me to speak about love.' This antiphlogistic regimen and lesson is ill to learn by our Maidie, for here she sins again :— 'Love is a very papithatick thing' (it is almost a pity to correct this into pathetic), 'as well as troublesome and tiresome—but O Isabella forbid me to speak of it.' Here are her reflections on a pine-apple :—'I think the price of a pine-apple is very dear: it is a whole bright goulden guinea, that might have sustained a poor family.' Here is a new vernal simile :—'The hedges are sprouting like chicks from the eggs when they are newly hatched or, as the vulgar say, *clacked.*' 'Doctor Swift's works are very funny; I got some of them by heart.' 'Moreheads sermons are I hear much praised, but I never read sermons of any kind; but I read novelettes and my Bible, and I never forget it, or my prayers.' Bravo, Marjorie!

She seems now, when still about six, to have broken out into song :—

'EPHIBOL (EPIGRAM OR EPITAPH—WHO KNOWS WHICH?) ON MY DEAR LOVE ISABELLA.

> Here lies sweet Isabell in bed,
> With a night-cap on her head;
> Her skin is soft, her face is fair,
> And she has very pretty hair;
> She and I in bed lies nice,
> And undisturbed by rats or mice;
> She is disgusted with Mr. Worgan,
> Though he plays upon the organ.
> Her nails are neat, her teeth are white,
> Her eyes are very, very bright;
> In a conspicuous town she lives,
> And to the poor her money gives :
> Here ends sweet Isabella's story,
> And may it be much to her glory.

Here are some bits at random :—

> 'Of summer I am very fond,
> And love to bathe into a pond;
> The look of sunshine dies away,
> And will not let me out to play;
> I love the morning's sun to spy
> Glittering through the casement's eye,

> The rays of light are very sweet,
>   And puts away the taste of meat;
> The balmy breeze comes down from heaven,
>   And makes us like for to be living.'

'The casawary is an curious bird, and so is the gigantic crane, and the pelican of the wilderness, whose mouth holds a bucket of fish and water. Fighting is what ladies is not qualyfied for, they would not make a good figure in battle or in a duel. Alas! we females are of little use to our country. The history of all the malcontents as ever was hanged is amusing.' Still harping on the Newgate Calendar!

'Braehead is extremely pleasant to me by the companie of swine, geese, cocks, etc., and they are the delight of my soul.'

'I am going to tell you of a melancholy story. A young turkie of 2 or 3 months old, would you believe it, the father broke its leg, and he killed another! I think he ought to be transported or hanged.'

'Queen Street is a very gay one, and so is Princes Street, for all the lads and lasses, besides bucks and beggars, parade there.'

'I should like to see a play very much, for I never saw one in all my life, and don't believe I ever shall; but I hope I can be content without going to one. I can be quite happy without my desire being granted.'

'Some days ago Isabella had a terrible fit of the

toothake, and she walked with a long night-shift at
dead of night like a ghost, and I thought she was one.
She prayed for nature's sweet restorer—balmy sleep
—but did not get it—a ghostly figure indeed she was,
enough to make a saint tremble. It made me quiver
and shake from top to toe. Superstition is a very
mean thing, and should be despised and shunned.'

Here is her weakness and her strength again :—
' In the love-novels all the heroines are very desperate.
Isabella will not allow me to speak about lovers and
heroins, and 'tis too refined for my taste.' ' Miss
Egward's (Edgeworth's) tails are very good, particularly some that are very much adapted for youth (!)
as Laz Laurance and Tarelton, False Keys, etc. etc.'

' Tom Jones and Grey's Elegey in a country
churchyard are both excellent, and much spoke of by
both sex, particularly by the men.' Are our Marjories
now-a-days better or worse because they cannot read
Tom Jones unharmed ? More better than worse ;
but who among them can repeat Gray's Lines on
a distant prospect of Eton College as could our
Maidie ?

Here is some more of her prattle :—' I went into
Isabella's bed to make her smile like the Genius
Demedicus' (the Venus de Medicis) ' or the statute
in an ancient Greece, but she fell asleep in my very
face, at which my anger broke forth, so that I awoke
her from a comfortable nap. All was now hushed

15

up again, but again my anger burst forth at her biding
me get up.'

She begins thus loftily :—

> 'Death the righteous love to see,
> But from it doth the wicked flee.'

Then suddenly breaks off (as if with laughter)—

> 'I am sure they fly as fast as their legs can carry them !'

> 'There is a thing I love to see,
> That is our monkey catch a flee.'

> 'I love in Isa's bed to lie,
> Oh, such a joy and luxury !
> The bottom of the bed I sleep,
> And with great care within I creep ;
> Oft I embrace her feet of lillys,
> But she has goton all the pillys.
> Her neck I never can embrace,
> But I do hug her feet in place.'

How childish and yet how strong and free is her
use of words !—' I lay at the foot of the bed because
Isabella said I disturbed her by continial fighting
and kicking, but I was very dull, and continially at
work reading the Arabian Nights, which I could not
have done if I had slept at the top. I am reading
the Mysteries of Udolpho. I am much interested in
the fate of poor, poor Emily.'

Here is one of her swains—

> 'Very soft and white his cheeks,
> His hair is red, and grey his breeks ;
> His tooth is like the daisy fair,
> His only fault is in his hair.'

This is a higher flight :—

'DEDICATED TO MRS. H. CRAWFORD BY THE AUTHOR, M. F.

> Three turkeys fair their last have breathed,
> And now this world for ever leaved ;
> Their father, and their mother too,
> They sigh and weep as well as you ;
> Indeed, the rats their bones have crunched,
> Into eternity theire laanched.
> A direful death indeed they had,
> As wad put any parent mad ;
> But she was more than usual calm,
> She did not give a single dam.'

This last word is saved from all sin by its tender age, not to speak of the want of the *n*. We fear 'she' is the abandoned mother, in spite of her previous sighs and tears.

'Isabella says when we pray we should pray fervently, and not rattel over a prayer—for that we are kneeling at the footstool of our Lord and Creator. who saves us from eternal damnation, and from unquestionable fire and brimston.'

She has a long poem on Mary Queen of Scots :—

> 'Queen Mary was much loved by all,
> Both by the great and by the small,
> But hark ! her soul to heaven doth rise !
> And I suppose she has gained a prize—
> For I do think she would not go
> Into the *awful* place below ;
> There is a thing that I must tell,
> Elizabeth went to fire and hell ;
> He who would teach her to be civil,
> It must be her great friend the divil !'

She hits off Darnley well :—

> 'A noble's son, a handsome lad,
> By some queer way or other, had
> Got quite the better of her heart,
> With him she always talked apart ;
> Silly he was, but very fair,
> A greater buck was not found there.'

'By some queer way or other;' is not this the general case and the mystery, young ladies and gentlemen? Goethe's doctrine of 'elective affinities' discovered by our Pet Maidie.

SONNET TO A MONKEY.

> 'O lively, O most charming pug
> Thy graceful air, and heavenly mug;
> The beauties of his mind do shine,
> And every bit is shaped and fine.
> Your teeth are whiter than the snow,
> Your a great buck, your a great beau;
> Your eyes are of so nice a shape,
> More like a Christian's than an ape;
> Your cheek is like the rose's blume,
> Your hair is like the raven's plume;
> His nose's cast is of the Roman,
> He is a very pretty woman.
> I could not get a rhyme for Roman,
> So was obliged to call him woman.'

This last joke is good. She repeats it when writing of James the Second being killed at Roxburgh :—

> 'He was killed by a cannon splinter,
> Quite in the middle of the winter ;
> Perhaps it was not at that time.
> But I can get no other rhyme !'

Here is one of her last letters, dated Kirkcaldy, 12th October 1811. You can see how her nature is deepening and enriching :—'MY DEAR MOTHER,— You will think that I entirely forget you but I assure you that you are greatly mistaken. I think of you always and often sigh to think of the distance between us two loving creatures of nature. We have regular hours for all our occupations first at 7 o'clock we go to the dancing and come home at 8 we then read our Bible and get our repeating and then play till ten then we get our music till 11 when we get our writing and accounts we sew from 12 till 1 after which I get my gramer and then work till five. At 7 we come and knit till 8 when we dont go to the dancing. This is an exact description. I must take a hasty farewell to her whom I love, reverence and doat on and who I hope thinks the same of

'MARJORY FLEMING.

'*P.S.*—An old pack of cards (!) would be very exeptible.'

This other is a month earlier :—' MY DEAR LITTLE MAMA,—I was truly happy to hear that you were all well. We are surrounded with measles at present on every side, for the Herons got it, and Isabella Heron was near Death's Door, and one night her father lifted her out of bed, and she fell down as they thought lifeless. Mr. Heron said, " That lassie's deed

noo"—"I'm no deed yet." She then threw up a
big worm nine inches and a half long. I have begun
dancing, but am not very fond of it, for the boys
strikes and mocks me.—I have been another night
at the dancing; I like it better. I will write to you
as often as I can; but I am afraid not every week.
*I long for you with the longings of a child to embrace
you—to fold you in my arms. I respect you with all
the respect due to a mother. You dont know how I
love you. So I shall remain, your loving child*—
M. FLEMING.'

What rich involution of love in the words marked!
Here are some lines to her beloved Isabella, in July
1811 :—

> ' There is a thing that I do want,
>   With you these beauteous walks to haunt,
>   We would be happy if you would
>   Try to come over if you could.
>   Then I would all quite happy be
>   *Now and for all eternity.*
>   My mother is so very sweet,
>   *And checks my appetite to eat ;*
>   My father shows us what to do :
>   But O I'm sure that I want you.
>   I have no more of poetry ;
>   O Isa do remember me,
>   And try to love your Marjory.'

In a letter from 'Isa' to

> 'Miss Muff Maidie Marjory Fleming,
> favored by Rare Rear-Admiral Fleming,'

she says—' I long much to see you, and talk over all our old stories together, and to hear you read and repeat. I am pining for my old friend Cesario, and poor Lear, and wicked Richard. How is the dear Multiplication table going on? are you still as much attached to 9 times 9 as you used to be?'

But this dainty, bright thing is about to flee—to come 'quick to confusion.' The measles she writes of seized her, and she died on the 19th of December 1811. The day before her death, Sunday, she sat up in bed, worn and thin, her eye gleaming as with the light of a coming world, and with a tremulous old voice repeated the following lines by Burns—heavy with the shadow of death, and lit with the phantasy of the judgment-seat—the publican's prayer in paraphrase:—

> ' Why am I loth to leave this earthly scene?
> 　　Have I so found it full of pleasing charms?
> Some drops of joy, with draughts of ill between,
> 　　Some gleams of sunshine 'mid renewing storms;
> 　　Is it departing pangs my soul alarms?
> Or Death's unlovely, dreary, dark abode?
> 　　For guilt, for GUILT, my terrors are in arms;
> I tremble to approach an angry God,
> And justly smart beneath his sin-avenging rod.
>
> Fain would I say, ' Forgive my foul offence !'
> 　　Fain promise never more to disobey;
> But, should my Author health again dispense,
> 　　Again I might desert fair virtue's way;
> 　　Again in folly's path might go astray;

Again exalt the brute, and sink the man ;
  Then how should I for heavenly mercy pray,
Who act so counter heavenly mercy's plan ?
Who sin so oft have mourned, yet to temptation ran ?

O Thou, great Governor of all below !
  If I might dare a lifted eye to Thee,
Thy nod can make the tempest cease to blow,
  And still the tumult of the raging sea ;
  With that controlling power assist even me
Those headlong furious passions to confine,
  For all unfit I feel my powers to be
To rule their torrent in the allowed line ;
  O, aid me with Thy help, OMNIPOTENCE DIVINE ! '

It is more affecting than we care to say to read
her Mother's and Isabella Keith's letters written
immediately after her death. Old and withered,
tattered and pale they are now : but when you read
them, how quick, how throbbing with life and love !
how rich in that language of affection which only
women, and Shakespeare, and Luther can use—that
power of detaining the soul over the beloved object
and its loss.

'*K. Philip to Constance*—
    You are as fond of grief as of your child.
Const.—Grief fills the room up of my absent child,
    Lies in his bed, walks up and down with me ;
    Puts on his pretty looks, repeats his words,
    Remembers me of all his gracious parts,
    Stuffs out his vacant garments with his form.
    Then I have reason to be fond of grief.'

What variations cannot love play on this one string !

In her first letter to Miss Keith, Mrs. Fleming
says of her dead Maidie :—'Never did I behold so

beautiful-an object. It resembled the finest wax-work. There was in the countenance an expression of sweetness and serenity which seemed to indicate that the pure spirit had anticipated the joys of heaven ere it quitted the mortal frame. To tell you what your Maidie said of you would fill volumes; for you was the constant theme of her discourse, the subject of her thoughts, and ruler of her actions. The last time she mentioned you was a few hours before all sense save that of suffering was suspended, when she said to Dr. Johnstone, "If you will let me out at the New Year, I will be quite contented." I asked what made her so anxious to get out then? " I want to purchase a New Year's gift for Isa Keith with the sixpence you gave me for being patient in the measles; and I would like to choose it myself." I do not remember her speaking afterwards, except to complain of her head, till just before she expired, when she articulated, " O, mother! mother!"'

Do we make too much of this little child, who has been in her grave in Abbotshall Kirkyard these fifty and more years? We may of her cleverness—not of her affectionateness, her nature. What a picture the *animosa infans* gives us of herself, her vivacity, her passionateness, her precocious love-making, her passion for nature, for swine, for all living things, her reading, her turn for expression, her satire, her frankness, her little sins and rages, her great repentances! We don't wonder Walter Scott carried her off in the neuk of his plaid, and played himself with her for hours.

The year before she died, when in Edinburgh, she was at a Twelfth Night supper at Scott's, in Castle Street. The company had all come—all but Marjorie. Scott's familiars, whom we all know, were there—all were come but Marjorie; and all were dull because Scott was dull. 'Where's that bairn? what can have come over her? I'll go myself and see.' And he was getting up and would have gone; when the bell rang, and in came Duncan Roy and his henchman Tougald, with the sedan chair, which was brought right into the lobby, and its top raised. And there, in its darkness and dingy old cloth, sat Maidie in white, her eyes gleaming, and Scott bending over her in ecstasy—'hung over her enamoured.' 'Sit ye there, my dautie, till they all see you;' and forthwith he brought them all. You can fancy the scene. And he lifted her up and marched to his seat with her on his stout shoulder, and set her down beside him; and then began the night, and such a night! Those who knew Scott best said, that night was never equalled; Maidie and he were the stars; and she gave them *Constance's* speeches and *Helvellyn*, the ballad then much in vogue—and all her *répertoire*, Scott showing her off, and being ofttimes rebuked by her for his intentional blunders.

We are indebted for the following—and our readers will be not unwilling to share our obligations—to her sister :—'Her birth was 15th January 1803; her death 19th December 1811. I take this from her Bibles.[1] I believe she was a child of robust health, of much vigour of body, and beautifully formed arms, and until her last illness, never was an hour in bed. She was niece to Mrs. Keith, residing in No. 1 North Charlotte Street, who was *not* Mrs. Murray Keith, although very intimately acquainted with that old lady. My aunt was the daughter of Mr. James Rae, surgeon, and married the younger son of old Keith of Ravelstone. Corstorphine Hill belonged to my aunt's husband; and his eldest son, Sir Alexander Keith, succeeded his uncle to both Ravelstone and Dunnottar. The Keiths were not connected by rela-tionship with the Howisons of Braehead, but my grandfather and grandmother (who was), a daughter of Cant of Thurston and Giles-Grange, were on the most intimate footing with *our* Mrs. Keith's grand-father and grandmother; and so it has been for three generations, and the friendship consummated by my cousin William Keith marrying Isabella Craufurd.

'As to my aunt and Scott, they were on a very intimate footing. He asked my aunt to be god-

---

[1] 'Her Bible is before me; *a pair*, as then called; the faded marks are just as she placed them. There is one at David's lament over Jonathan.'

mother to his eldest daughter Sophia Charlotte. I had a copy of Miss Edgeworth's "Rosamond, and Harry and Lucy," for long, which was "a gift to Marjorie from Walter Scott," probably the first edition of that attractive series, for it wanted "Frank," which is always now published as part of the series, under the title of *Early Lessons*. I regret to say these little volumes have disappeared.

'Sir Walter was no relation of Marjorie's, but of the Keiths, through the Swintons; and, like Marjorie, he stayed much at Ravelstone in his early days, with his grand-aunt Mrs. Keith; and it was while seeing him there as a boy, that another aunt of mine composed, when he was about fourteen, the lines prognosticating his future fame that Lockhart ascribes in his Life to Mrs. Cockburn, authoress of "The Flowers of the Forest":—

> "Go on, dear youth, the glorious path pursue
> Which bounteous Nature kindly smooths for you;
> Go bid the seeds her hands have sown arise,
> By timely culture, to their native skies;
> Go, and employ the poet's heavenly art,
> Not merely to delight, but mend the heart."

Mrs. Keir was my aunt's name, another of Dr. Rae's daughters.' We cannot better end than in words from this same pen:—'I have to ask you to forgive my anxiety in gathering up the fragments of Marjorie's last days, but I have an almost sacred feeling to all that pertains to her. You are quite correct in stating that measles were the cause of her death. My mother was struck by the patient quietness manifested by Marjorie during this illness, unlike her ardent, impulsive nature ; but love and poetic feeling were unquenched. When Dr. Johnstone rewarded her submissiveness with a sixpence, the request speedily followed that she might get out ere New Year's day came. When asked why she was so desirous of getting out, she immediately rejoined, " Oh, I am so anxious to buy something with my sixpence for my dear Isa Keith." Again, when lying very still, her mother asked her if there was anything she wished : " Oh yes ! if you would just leave the room door open a wee bit, and play ' The Land o' the Leal,' and I will lie and *think*, and enjoy myself " (this is just as stated to me by her mother and mine). Well, the happy day came, alike to parents and child, when Marjorie was allowed to come forth from the nursery to the parlour. It was Sabbath evening, and after tea. My father, who idolised this child, and never afterwards in my hearing mentioned her name, took her in his arms ; and while walking her up and down the room, she said, " Father, I will repeat something to you ; what would you like ?" He said, " Just choose yourself, Maidie." She hesitated for a moment between the paraphrase, " Few are thy days, and full of woe," and the lines of Burns already quoted, but decided on the latter, a remarkable choice for a child. The repeating these lines seemed to stir up the depths of feeling in her soul. She asked to be allowed to write a poem; there was a doubt whether it would be right to allow her, in case of hurting her eyes. She pleaded earnestly, "Just this once;" the point was yielded, her slate was given her, and with great rapidity she wrote an address of fourteen lines, "To her loved Cousin on the Author's recovery," her last work on earth :—

> "Oh! Isa, pain did visit me,
> I was at the last extremity;
> How often did I think of you,
> I wished your graceful form to view,
> To clasp you in my weak embrace,
> Indeed I thought I'd run my race :
> Good care, I'm sure, was of me taken,
> But still indeed I was much shaken,
> At last I daily strength did gain,
> And oh! at last, away went pain;
> At length the doctor thought I might
> Stay in the parlor all the night;
> I now continue so to do,
> Farewell to Nancy and to you."

'She went to bed apparently well, awoke in the middle of the night with the old cry of woe to a mother's heart, "My head, my head!" Three days of the dire malady, "water in the head," followed, and the end came.'

'Soft, silken primrose, fading timelessly.'

It is needless, it is impossible, to add anything to

this : the fervour, the sweetness, the flush of poetic ecstasy, the lovely and glowing eye, the perfect nature of that bright and warm intelligence, that darling child,—Lady Nairne's words, and the old tune, stealing up from the depths of the human heart, deep calling unto deep, gentle and strong like the waves of the great sea hushing themselves to sleep in the dark ;—the words of Burns, touching the kindred chord, her last numbers 'wildly sweet' traced, with thin and eager fingers, already touched by the last enemy and friend,—*moriens canit*,—and that love which is so soon to be her everlasting light, is her song's burden to the end.

> 'She set as sets the morning star, which goes
> Not down behind the darkened west, nor hides
> Obscured among the tempests of the sky,
> But melts away into the light of heaven.'

On looking over some old letters of Thackeray's the other day, I found this by Marjorie in her seventh year ; it is copied by her sister ; it is worthy of the rest. The turtles who 'coo for everlasting and fight' are not unknown to us in domestic life :—

'MY DEAR MUD,—I hope you are well ; give my love to Isa, and I will send her something. I've been often at Ravelstone. I've been acquainted with many very genteel girls, and Janetta is a very fine one. Help is been confined another time. My sleeves is tucked up, and it was very disagreeable, my collar, and I abhor it amoniable (abominable!) I saw the most prettyist two tame pidgeons and two very wee small kittens like our cat. I am very much acquainted with a young gentleman called Mordecai, that I'm quite in love with, and another called Capt. Bell, and Jamie Keith, and Willie's my great tormentor. A good-natured girl gave me a song-book, and I'm very happy. I'll go down and be thinking when I'm eating my dinner more to tell you, Mud. Aunt has got two of the most beautifullest turtle doves you ever saw, they coo for everlasting and fight; the hawk is in good spirits, it is a nice beast, the gentlest animal that ever was seen; six canaries, two green linnets, and a thrush. I play in the back green, and bring in worms for the thrush. I get very long tasks, and when I behave I get them short. Orme Keir is the greatest enemy that ever was, and his thinking about business. My aunt lets out the birds to get the air in her room;—the young gentleman I was speaking of, Mordecai, he's very funny; —James Keith hardly ever spoke to me, he said, "Girl, make less noise;" and, when there was a storm of thunder, "take away all your iron;" and once before he said, "Maidgie, go and dance," which I was very proud of. I've forgot to say, but I've four lovers, the other one is Harry Watson, a very delightful boy.[1] Help is very like a tiger when he bites his fleas, a fine, gentle, wise *creetyer*. Willie was at the moors, but he soon came back again, for the moors was like a fish pond. The whole house plagues me about "Come haste to the Wedding," for there is no sense in it; they think, because it is an Merican, Eliza Purves taught me, they plague me about it exceeding much. I'm affronted to say it, it is so awkward. Remember your dear Madgy. *Amen. Finis.*'

[1] This 'very delightful boy' was the venerable founder of the Fine Arts Chair in our University.

MINCHMOOR.

'Sweet smells the birk, green grows, green grows the grass,
Yellow on Yarrow's bank the gowan,
Fair hangs the apple frae the rock,
Sweet the wave of Yarrow flowan.

'Flows Yarrow sweet? as sweet, as sweet flows Tweed,
As green its grass, its gowan yellow,
As sweet smells on its braes the birk,
The apple frae the rock as mellow.'

HAMILTON OF BANGOUR.

*There is moral as well as bodily wholesomeness in a mountain
walk, if the walker has the understanding heart, and eschews* pic-
nics. *It is good for any man to be alone with nature and himself,
or with a friend who knows when silence is more sociable than
talk—*

> ' In the wilderness alone,
> There where nature worships God.'

*It is well to be in places where man is little and God is great—
where what he sees all around him has the same look as it had a
thousand years ago, and will have the same, in all likelihood, when
he has been a thousand years in his grave. It abates and rectifies a
man, if he is worth the process.*

' *It is not favourable to religious feeling to hear only of the actions
and interference of man, and to behold nothing but what human
ingenuity has completed. There is an image of God's greatness
impressed upon the outward face of nature fitted to make us all
pious, and to breathe into our hearts a purifying and salutary fear.*

' *In cities everything is man, and man alone. He seems to move
and govern all, and be the Providence of cities; and there we do not
render unto Cæsar the things which are Cæsar's, and unto God the
things which are God's; but God is forgotten, and Cæsar is supreme
—all is human policy, human foresight, human power; nothing
reminds us of* invisible dominion, and concealed omnipotence—*it
is all earth, and no heaven. One cure of this is prayer and the
solitary place. As the body, harassed with the noxious air of
cities, seeks relief in the freedom and the purity of the fields and
hills, so the mind, wearied by commerce with men, resumes its
vigour in solitude, and repairs its dignity.*'—From Sydney Smith's
Sermon ' On the effects which the tumultuous life passed in great
cities produces upon the moral and religious character.'—1809.

MINCHMOOR.

NOW that everybody is out of town, and every place in the guide-books is as well known as Princes Street or Pall Mall, it is something to discover a hill everybody has not been to the top of, and which is not in *Black*. Such a hill is *Minchmoor*, nearly three times as high as Arthur Seat, and lying between Tweed and Yarrow.

The best way to ascend it is from Traquair. You go up the wild old Selkirk road, which passes almost right over the summit, and by which Montrose and his cavaliers fled from Philiphaugh, where Sir Walter's mother remembered crossing, when a girl, in a coach-and-six, on her way to a ball at Peebles, several footmen marching on either side of the carriage to prop it up or drag it out of the moss *haggs ;* and where, to our amazement, we learned that the Duchess of Buccleuch had lately driven her ponies. Before this we had passed the grey, old-world entrance to Traquair House, and looked down its grassy and untrod avenue to the pallid, forlorn mansion, stricken all o'er with eld, and

noticed the wrought-iron gate embedded in a foot
deep and more of soil, never having opened since
the '45. There are the huge Bradwardine bears
on each side—most grotesque supporters—with a
superfluity of ferocity and canine teeth. The whole
place, like the family whose it has been, seems dying
out—everything subdued to settled desolation. The
old race, the old religion, the gaunt old house, with
its small, deep, comfortless windows, the decaying
trees, the stillness about the doors, the grass over-
running everything, nature reinstating herself in her
quiet way—all this makes the place look as strange
and pitiful among its fellows in the vale as would the
Earl who built it three hundred years ago if we met
him tottering along our way in the faded dress of his
youth; but it looks the Earl's house still, and has a
dignity of its own.

We soon found the Minchmoor road, and took
at once to the hill, the ascent being, as often is
with other ascents in this world, steepest at first.
Nothing could be more beautiful than the view as
we ascended, and got a look of the 'eye sweet'
Tweed hills, and their 'silver stream.' It was one
of the five or six good days of this summer—in early
morning, 'soft' and doubtful; but the mists drawing
up, and now the noble, tawny hills were dappled
with gleams and shadows—

'Sunbeams upon distant hills gliding apace' —

he best sort of day for mountain scenery—that
ripple of light and shadow brings out the forms and
the depths of the hills far better than a cloudless
sky; and the horizon is generally wider.

Before us and far away was the round flat head of
Minchmoor, with a dark, rich bloom on it, from the
thick, short heather—the hills around being green.
Near the top, on the Tweed side, its waters trotting
away cheerily to the glen at Bold, is the famous
Cheese Well—always full, never overflowing. Here
every traveller—Duchess, shepherd, or houseless
mugger—stops, rests, and is thankful; doubtless so
did Montrose, poor fellow, and his young nobles and
their jaded steeds, on their scurry from Lesly and his
Dragoons. It is called the Cheese Well from those
who rest there dropping in bits of their provisions,
as votive offerings to the fairies whose especial
haunt this mountain was. After our rest and drink,
we left the road and made for the top. When there
we were well rewarded. The great round-backed,
kindly, solemn hills of Tweed, Yarrow, and Ettrick
lay all about like sleeping mastiffs—too plain to be
grand, too ample and beautiful to be commonplace.

There, to the north-east, is the place—*William-
hope* ridge—where Sir Walter Scott bade farewell to
his heroic friend Mungo Park. They had come up
from *Ashestiel*, where Scott then lived, and where

'Marmion' was written and its delightful epistles inspired—where he passed the happiest part of his life—leaving it, as Hogg said, 'for gude an' a';' for his fatal 'dreams about his cottage' were now begun. He was to have 'a hundred acres, two spare bed-rooms, with dressing-rooms, each of which will on a pinch have a couch-bed.' We all know what the dream, and the cottage, and the hundred acres came to—the ugly Abbotsford; the over-burdened, shattered brain driven wild, and the end, death, and madness. Well, it was on that ridge that the two friends—each romantic, but in such different ways—parted never to meet again. There is the ditch Park's horse stumbled over and all but fell. 'I am afraid, Mungo, that's a bad omen,' said the Sheriff; to which he answered, with a bright smile on his handsome, fearless face—'*Freits* (omens) follow those who look to them.' With this expression, he struck the spurs into his horse, and Scott never saw him again. He had not long been married to a lovely and much-loved woman, and had been speaking to Scott about his new African scheme, and how he meant to tell his family he had some business in Edinburgh—send them his blessing, and be off—alas! never to return! Scott used to say, when speaking of this parting, 'I stood and looked back, but he did not.' A more memorable place for two such men to part in would not easily be found.

Where we are standing is the spot Scott speaks of when writing to Joanna Baillie about her new tragedies —'Were it possible for me to hasten the treat I expect in such a composition with you, I would promise to read the volume *at the silence of noonday upon the top of Minchmoor.* The hour is allowed by those skilful in demonology, *to be as full of witching* as midnight itself; and I assure you I have felt really oppressed with a sort of fearful loneliness when looking around the naked towering ridges of desolate barrenness, which is all the eye takes in from the top of such a mountain, the patches of cultivation being hidden in the little glens, or only appearing to make one feel how feeble and ineffectual man has been to contend with the genius of the soil. It is in such a scene that the unknown and gifted author of *Albania* places the superstition which consists in hearing the noise of a chase, the baying of the hounds, the throttling sobs of the deer, the wild hollos of the huntsmen, and the "hoof thick beating on the hollow hill." I have often repeated his verses with some sensations of awe in this place.' The lines— and they are noble, and must have sounded wonderful with his voice and look—are as follows. Can no one tell us anything more of their author?—

> 'There oft is heard, at midnight, or at noon,
> Beginning faint, but rising still more loud,
> And nearer, voice of hunters, and of hounds,

And horns hoarse-winded, blowing far and keen ;
Forthwith the hubbub multiplies ; the gale
Labours with wilder shrieks, and rifer din
Of hot pursuit ; the broken cry of deer
Mangled by throttling dogs ; the shouts of men,
And hoofs thick beating on the hollow hill.
Sudden the grazing heifer in the vale
Starts at the noise, and both the herdsman's ears
Tingle with inward dread—aghast he eyes
The mountain's height and all the ridges round,
Yet not one trace of living wight discerns,
Nor knows, o'erawed and trembling as he stands,
To what or whom he owes his idle fear—
To ghost, to witch, to fairy, or to fiend ;
But wonders, and no end of wondering finds.'

We listened for the hunt, but could only hear the wind sobbing from the blind '*Hopes*.'[1]

The view from the top reaches from the huge *Harestane Broadlaw*—nearly as high as Ben Lomond —whose top is as flat as a table, and would make a racecourse of two miles, and where the clouds are still brooding, to the *Cheviot;* and from the *Maiden Paps* in Liddesdale, and that wild huddle of hills at *Moss Paul*, to *Dunse Law*, and the weird *Lammermoors*. There is *Ruberslaw*, always surly and dark. The *Dunion*, beyond which lies Jedburgh. There are the *Eildons*, with their triple heights ; and you can get a glimpse of the upper woods of Abbotsford, and the top of the hill above Cauldshiels Loch, that very spot where the 'wondrous potentate,'—when

[1] The native word for hollows in the hills : thus, Dryhope, Gameshope, Chapelhope, etc.

suffering from languor and pain, and beginning to break down under his prodigious fertility,—composed those touching lines :—

> 'The sun upon the Weirdlaw Hill
>   In Ettrick's vale is sinking sweet ;
> The westland wind is hushed and still ;
>   The lake lies sleeping at my feet.
> Yet not the landscape to mine eye
>   Bears those bright hues that once it bore,
> Though evening, with her richest dye,
>   Flames o'er the hills of Ettrick's shore.
>
> With listless look along the plain
>   I see Tweed's silver current glide,
> And coldly mark the holy fane
>   Of Melrose rise in ruined pride.
> The quiet lake, the balmy air,
>   The hill, the stream, the tower, the tree,
> Are they still such as once they were,
>   Or is the dreary change in me?
>
> Alas ! the warped and broken board,
>   How can it bear the painter's dye !
> The harp of strained and tuneless chord,
>   How to the minstrel's skill reply !
> To aching eyes each landscape lowers,
>   To feverish pulse each gale blows chill ;
> And Araby's or Eden's bowers
>   Were barren as this moorland hill.'

There, too, is *Minto Hill*, as modest and shapely and smooth as Clytie's shoulders, and *Earlston Black Hill*, with Cowdenknowes at its foot; and there, standing stark and upright as a warder, is the stout old *Smailholme Tower*, seen and seeing all around. It is quite curious how unmistakeable and important it looks at what must be twenty and more miles. It is now ninety years since that 'lonely infant, who has sung its awful joys, was found in a thunderstorm, as we all know, lying on the soft grass at the foot of the grey old Strength, clapping his hands at each flash, and shouting, 'Bonny! bonny!'

We now descended into Yarrow, and forgathered with a shepherd who was taking his lambs over to the great Melrose fair. He was a fine specimen of a border herd—young, tall, sagacious, self-contained, and free in speech and air. We got his heart by praising his dog *Jed*, a very fine collie, black and comely, gentle and keen—'Ay, she's a fell yin, she can do a' but speak.' On asking him if the sheep dogs needed much teaching—'Whyles ay and whyles no; her kind (Jed's) needs nane. She sooks 't in wi' her mither's milk.' On asking him if the dogs were ever sold, he said—'Never, but at an orra time. Naebody wad sell a gude dowg, and naebody wad buy an ill ane.' He told us with great feeling, of the death of one of his best dogs by poison. It was plainly still a grief to him. 'What was he poisoned with?' 'Strychnia,' he said as decidedly as might Dr. Christison. 'How do you know?' 'I opened him, puir fallow, and got him analeezed!'

Now we are on Birkindale Brae, and are looking down on the same scene as did

'James Boyd (the Earle of Arran, his brother was he),'

when he crossed Minchmoor on his way to deliver
James the Fifth's message to

> 'Yon outlaw Murray,
> Surely whaur bauldly bideth he.'

> 'Down Birkindale Brae when that he cam
> He saw the feir Foreste wi' his ee.'

How James Boyd fared, and what the outlaw said,
and what James and his nobles said and did, and
how the outlaw at last made peace with his King,
and rose up 'Sheriffe of Ettricke Foreste,' and how
the bold ruffian boasted,

> 'Fair Philiphaugh is mine by right,
>   And Lewinshope still mine shall be;
> Newark, Foulshiels, and Tinnies baith
>   My bow and arrow purchased me.

> And I have native steads to me
>   The Newark Lee and Hangingshaw;
> I have mony steads in the Forest schaw,
>   But them by name I dinna knaw.'

And how King James snubbed

> 'The kene Laird of Buckscleuth,
> A stalwart man and sterne was he.'

When the Laird hinted that,

> 'For a king to gang an Outlaw till,
>   Is beneath his state and dignitie.
> The man that wins yon Forest intill,
>   He lives by reif and felonie.

> Then out and spak the nobil King,
>   And round him cast a wilie ee—

> Now haud thy tongue, Sir Walter Scott,
> Nor speak o' reif nor felonie—
> *For, had every honest man his awin kye,*
> *A richt puir clan thy name wad be!'*

(by the by, why did Professor Aytoun leave out this
excellent hit in his edition?)—all this and much
more may you see if you take up *The Border
Minstrelsy,* and read 'The Sang of the Outlaw
Murray,' with the incomparable notes of Scott. But
we are now well down the hill. There to the left, in
the hollow, is *Permanscore,* where the King and the
outlaw met—

> 'Bid him mete me at Permanscore,
> And bring four in his companie ;
> Five Erles sall cum wi' mysel',
> Gude reason I suld honoured be.'

And there goes our Shepherd with his long swing-
ing stride. As different from his dark, wily companion, the Badenoch drover, as was Harry Wakefield
from Robin Oig ; or as the big, sunny Cheviot is
from the lowering Ruberslaw ; and there is *Jed* trotting meekly behind him—may she escape strychnia,
and, dying at the fireside among the children, be laid
like

> 'Paddy Tims—whose soul at aise is—
> With the point of his nose
> And the tips of his toes
> Turn'd up to the roots of the daisies '—

unanaleezed, save by the slow cunning of the grave.
And may her master get the top price for his lambs !

Do you see to the left that little plantation on the brow of Foulshiels Hill, with the sunlight lying on its upper corner? If you were there you might find among the brackens and foxglove a little headstone with 'I. T.' rudely carved on it. That is *Tibbie Tamson's grave*, known and feared all the country round.

This poor outcast was a Selkirk woman, who, under the stress of spiritual despair—that sense of perdition which, as in Cowper's case, often haunts and overmasters the deepest and gentlest natures, making them think themselves

'Damn'd below Judas, more abhorr'd than he was,'—

committed suicide; and being, with the gloomy, cruel superstition of the time, looked on by her neighbours as accursed of God, she was hurried into a rough white deal coffin, and carted out of the town, the people stoning it all the way till it crossed the Ettrick. Here, on this wild hill-side, it found its rest, being buried where three lairds' lands meet. May we trust that the light of God's reconciled countenance has for all these long years been resting on that once forlorn soul, as His blessed sunshine now lies on her moorland grave! For, 'the mountains shall depart, and the hills be removed; but my kindness shall not depart from thee, neither shall the covenant of my peace be removed, saith the Lord that hath mercy on thee.'

Now, we see down into the Yarrow—there is the famous stream twinkling in the sun. What stream and valley was ever so be-sung! You wonder at first why this has been, but the longer you look the less you wonder. There is a charm about it—it is not easy to say what. The huge sunny hills in which it is embosomed give it a look at once gentle and serious. They are great, and their gentleness makes them greater. Wordsworth has the right words, ' pastoral melancholy ;' and besides, the region is ' not uninformed with phantasy and looks that threaten the profane '—the Flowers of Yarrow, the Douglas Tragedy, the Dowie Dens, Words-worth's Yarrow Unvisited, Visited, and Re-Visited, and, above all, the glamour of Sir Walter, and Park's fatal and heroic story. Where can you find eight more exquisite lines anywhere than Logan's, which we all know by heart :—

> ' His mother from the window looked
>   With all the longing of a mother ;
> His little sister, weeping, walked
>   The greenwood path to meet her brother.
> They sought him east, they sought him west,
>   They sought him all the forest thorough—
> They only saw the cloud of night,
>   They only heard the roar of Yarrow.'

And there is *Newark Tower* among the rich woods ; and *Harehead*, that cosiest, loveliest, and hospitablest of nests. Methinks I hear certain

young voices among the hazels; out they come on
the little haugh by the side of the deep, swirling
stream, *fabulosus* as was ever Hydaspes. There
they go 'running races in their mirth,' and is not
that—*an me ludit amabilis insania?*—the voice of *ma
pauvre petite*—*animosa infans*—the wilful, rich-eyed,
delicious Eppie?

> 'Oh blessed vision, happy child,
> Thou art so exquisitely wild!'

And there is *Black Andro* and *Glowr owr'em* and
Foulshiels, where Park was born and bred; and
there is the deep pool in the Yarrow where Scott
found him plunging one stone after another into the
water, and watching anxiously the bubbles as they
rose to the surface. 'This,' said Scott to him,
'appears but an idle amusement for one who has
seen so much adventure.' 'Not so idle, perhaps, as
you suppose,' answered Mungo; ' this was the way
I used to ascertain the depth of a river in Africa.'
He was then meditating his second journey, but had
said so to no one.

We go down by *Broadmeadows*, now held by that
Yair 'Hoppringle'—who so well governed Scinde—
and into the grounds of Bowhill, and passing *Philiphaugh*, see where stout David Lesly crossed in the
mist at daybreak with his heavy dragoons, many
of them old soldiers of Gustavus, and routed the

gallant Græme; and there is *Slainmen's Lee*, where the royalists lie; and there is *Carterhaugh*, the scene of the strange wild story of *Tamlane* and Lady Janet, when

> ' She prinked hersel' and prinned hersel'
>   By the ae light of the moon,
>   And she 's awa' to Carterhaugh
>   To speak wi' young Tamlane.'

Noel Paton might paint that night, when

> ' 'Twixt the hours of twelve and yin
>   A north wind *tore the bent ;*'

when ' fair Janet ' in her green mantle

> ' —— heard strange elritch sounds
>   Upon the wind that went.'

And straightway

> ' About the dead hour o' the night
>   She heard the bridles ring ;
>
> ' Their oaten pipes blew wondrous shrill,
>   The hemlock small blew clear ;
>   And louder notes from hemlock large
>   And bog reed, struck the ear,'

and then the fairy cavalcade swept past, while Janet, filled with love and fear, looked out for the milk-white steed, and ' gruppit it fast,' and ' pu'd the rider doon,' the young Tamlane, whom, after dipping ' in a stand of milk and then in a stand of water,'

> ' She wrappit ticht in her green mantle,
>   And sae her true love won !'

This ended our walk. We found the carriage at the Philiphaugh home-farm, and we drove home by *Yair* and *Fernilee*, *Ashestiel* and *Elibank*, and passed the bears as ferocious as ever, 'the orange sky of evening' glowing through their wild tusks, the old house looking even older in the fading light. And is not this a walk worth making? One of our number had been at the Land's End and Johnnie Groat's, and now on Minchmoor; and we wondered how many other men had been at all the three, and how many had enjoyed Minchmoor more than he.

But we must end, and how can we do it better, and more to our readers' and our own satisfaction, than by giving them the following unpublished lines by Professor Shairp,[1] which, by means we do not care to mention, are now before us?—

THE BUSH ABOON TRAQUAIR.

> Will ye gang wi' me and fare
> To the bush aboon Traquair?
> Owre the high Minchmuir we'll up and awa',
> This bonny simmer noon,
> While the sun shines fair aboon,
> And the licht sklents saftly doun on holm and ha'.

---

[1] No longer unpublished. The reader will find them, along with much else that is delightful, in *Kilmahoe, a Highland Pastoral, with other Poems.*

17

And what wad ye do there,
At the bush aboon Traquair?
A lang dreich road, ye had better let it be ;
Save some auld scrunts o' birk
I' the hill-side lirk,[1]
There 's nocht i' the warld for man to see.

But the blythe lilt o' that air,
'The Bush aboon Traquair,'
I need nae mair, it 's eneuch for me ;
Owre my cradle its sweet chime
Cam sughin' frae auld time,
Sae tide what may, I 'll awa' and see.

And what saw ye there,
At the bush aboon Traquair?
Or what did ye hear that was worth your heed?
I heard the cushies croon
Thro' the gowden afternoon,
And the Quair burn singing doun to the vale o' Tweed.

And birks saw I three or four,
Wi' grey moss bearded owre,
The last that are left o' the birken shaw,
Whar mony a summer e'en
Fond lovers did convene,
Thae bonny, bonny gloamins that are lang awa'.

Frae mony a but and ben,
By muirland, holm, and glen,
They cam ane hour to spen' on the greenwood swaird ;
But lang ha'e lad an' lass
Been lying 'neth the grass,
The green green grass o' Traquair kirkyard.

---

[1] 'The hills were high on ilka side
And the bucht i' the *lirk o' the hill.*'
Ballad of Cowdenknowes.

They were blest beyond compare,
When they held their trysting there,
Amang thae greenest hills shone on by the sun ;
And then they wan a rest,
The lownest and the best,
I' Traquair kirkyard when a' was dune.

Now the birks to dust may rot,
Names o' luvers be forgot,
Nae lads and lasses there ony mair convene ;
But the blythe lilt o' yon air
Keeps the bush aboon Traquair,
And the luve that ance was there, aye fresh and green.

Have not these the true flavour of that gentle
place and life,—as musical and as melancholy as
their streams and glens, as fragrant as their birks
and *gale ?*[1] They have the unexpectedness of
nature, of genius, and of true song. The 'native
wood-notes wild' of 'the mountain nymph, sweet
Liberty.'

There must surely be more of this 'lilting' in our
minstrel's wallet ; and he may be assured that such
a gift of genuine Scottish feeling and verse will be
welcomed if revealed. It breathes the caller, strong
air of the south country hills, and is a wild 'flower o'
the forest' not likely soon to be 'wede awa.'

'Sweet smells the birk, green grows, green grows the grass,
Yellow on Yarrow's banks the gowan,
Fair hangs the apple frae the rock,
Sweet the wave of Yarrow flowan.

---

[1] The Bog-Myrtle.

Flows Yarrow sweet? as sweet, as sweet flows Tweed,
    As green its grass, its gowan yellow,
As sweet smells on its braes the birk,
    The apple frae the rock as mellow.'

August 1862.

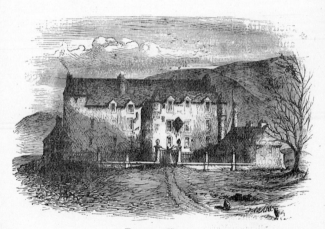

TRAQUAIR HOUSE.

'IN CLEAR DREAM AND
SOLEMN VISION.'

'IN CLEAR DREAM AND
SOLEMN VISION.'

I HAD a friend, and, though he is now elsewhere,
why shouldn't I say I have him still? He was
a man of great powers and of greater gifts. He might
have made himself almost anything a man may be ;
but he died unfulfilled, 'deprived of the residue of
his years ;' and this owing much, among other things,
to an imperfect and damaged organism and an inter-
mittent will. He was an advocate and judge, and
had in him the making of a great lawyer,—good
sense, vast and exact memory, a logical, vigorous
understanding, and readiness, fulness, and felicity of
speech. He had in him, as Jonathan Edwards would
have said, more than the average *quantity* of being ;
and, now that he is gone, I feel what a large space
he filled in my mind. His was a large, multilocular
brain, with room for all sorts of customers. But it
is to his 'study of imagination' I now refer in what
follows.

He was a mighty dreamer, especially in the
diluculum, or 'edge o' dark,' before full awakening ;
and he used to relate to his cronies these Kubla
Khan-like visions with amazing particularity. Many

of us would have it that he made up his dreams, but I had the following proof of the opposite.

Many years ago when we were at college, I had gone up to his lodgings to breakfast with him. I found him sound asleep, his eyes open and fixed as in a mesmeric trance; he was plainly rapt in some internal vision. I stood by him for some seconds, during which his colour and his breathing came and went as if under some deep feeling, first of interest and wonder, finally of horror, from which he awoke into full consciousness, scared and excited, asking me instantly to write. He then, in an anxious, eager voice began thus :—

> "'Tis noon, but desolate and dun
> The —— landscape lies,
> For 'twixt it and the mounting sun
> A cloud came crawling up the skies;
> From the sea it rose all slowly,
> Thin and grey and melancholy,
> And gathered darkness as it went
> Up into the —— firmament.'

Here he stopped, and, with a shrug of regret, said, 'It's gone!' The blanks were two words I could not make out, and which he never could recall. It would be curious if those who may read these lines were to try what adjectives of two syllables they liked best, and send them on to Mr. Macmillan :[1] it would form an odd poetico-statistical inquiry.

[1] This paper was originally published in *Macmillan's Magazine.*

He then gave the following fragments of his vision, which he said was complete, and in verse :—

He found himself in the midst of a vast marshy plain, in utter solitude, nothing around him but the dull, stagnant waters, overrun with dry reeds, through which by fits there stirred a miserable *sough*, leaving the plain oppressed with silence, and the dead, heavy air. On the small bit of ground where he stood was a hut, such as the hunters of water-fowl might frequent in the season ; it was in ruins, everything rude and waste, and through its half-shut, broken door, he was aware of the presence and of the occasional movements of a man, at times as if fiercely struggling in the darkness with some one else. Opposite the door sat and brooded a large white dove,—its lustrous dark eyes fixed on the door,—all its feathers as if 'stirred with prayer,' and uttering a low croodlin sound as in an ecstasy of compassion and entreaty, leaning gently towards its object.

Suddenly, and without noise, an ugly bird, long-legged, lean, mangy, and foul, came poking with measured steps round the end of the hut. It was like the adjutant crane of Eastern cities, and had an evil eye, small and cruel. It walked jauntily past the dove, who took no heed, and stood like a fisher on the edge of the dead and oozy water, his head to one side, and his long sharp beak ready to strike. He stood motionless for an instant ; then, with a jerk, brought up a large, plump, wriggling worm, shining and of the colour of jasper.

He advanced to the dove, who was yearning more and more towards the door. She became agitated, and more earnest than ever, never lifting her eyes from their object, and quivering all over with intensity. The evil bird was now straight in front, and bent over her with the worm. She shut her eyes, shuddered all through; he put his dirty black foot on her snowy back and pressed her down so that she opened her mouth wide, into which the worm was instantly dropped. She reeled over dead, towards the hut, as if the last act of life was to get nearer it.

Up to this moment the struggle inside the hut had gone on, lulling and coming again in gusts, like the wind among the reeds, and the arms of more than one might be seen across the dark ragged doorway, as if in fell agony of strife.

The instant the dove died, all sound and motion ceased within, and the whole region, as my friend said, ' shook throughout.' He was aware that within Judas, ' the son of perdition,' lay alone and dead.

Such was this ' clear dream,' and these are many of the words my friend used. It has always seemed to me full of poetry in *posse*, amorphous and uncrystallised, but the germ there, to which the author of *The Devil's Dream*, Mr. Aird, might have given or if he likes may yet give, 'the accomplishment of verse.'

That lonely and dismal place and day, desolate and overshadowed as in eclipse at noon,—the wretch within and his demon,—the holy, unfailing dove,

'White, radiant, spotless, exquisitely pure,'

in such a place,—the tall, stealthy fellow, with the small cruel eye,—the end,—what was going on elsewhere on that same day,—'the hour and the power of darkness,'—the eternity and the omnipotence of light and love,—'the exceeding bitter cry,'—'the loud voice,' and 'It is finished,'—was there not here something for the highest fantasy, some glimpse of 'the throne and equipage of God's almightiness'?

The above dreamer was the well-known (on his own side of the Tweed) A. S. Logan, Sheriff of Forfarshire. He was the successor, but in no wise the ape, in the true Yorick line,—'infinite jest most excellent fancy,'—of the still famous Peter Robertson, who served himself heir to that grotesque, sardonic wit, John Clerk of Eldin.

Logan differed from each as one wine or one quaint orchid—those flower-jesters which seem always making faces and fun at us and all nature,—from another. He had not the merciless and too often unspeakable Swiftian humour of Lord Eldin, nor the sustained wild burlesque and jocosity of Lord Robertson; but he had more imagination and thought, was more kindly affectioned than either, and his wit was more humorous, his humour more witty. Robertson was a wonderful being : it is not easy to exaggerate his comic powers. A natural son of Falstaff, he had his father's body as well as soul, such a mass of man, such an expanse of countenance,—probably the largest face known among men,—such eyes gleaming and rolling behind his spectacles, from out their huge rotundity, chubby-cheeked, and by way of innocent, like a *Megalopis Garagantua* unweaned,— no more need of stuffing for his father's part than had Stephen Kemble ; while within was no end of the same rich, glorious, overtopping humour ; not so much an occasional *spate* of it, much less a tap, or a pump ; not even a perennial spring ; rather say an artesian well, gushing out for ever by hogsheads, as if glad to escape from its load of superincumbent clay ; or like those fountains of the great oil deep, which are astonishing us all. To set Peter agoing was like tapping the Haggis in that *Nox Ambrosiana,* when Tickler fled to the mantelpiece, and 'The Shepherd' began stripping himself to swim ; the imperial Christopher warding off the tide with his crutch in the manner and with the success of Mrs. Partington,—so rich, so all-encompassing, so 'finely confused' was his flood of Rabelaisian fun. I dare say most of us know the trick played him by his old chum, John Lockhart (what a contrast in mind and body, in eye and voice !) when reviewing his friend's trashy 'Gleams of Thought' in the *Quarterly*, how he made the printer put into the copy for the poet this epitaph,—

> ' Here lies that peerless paper-lord, Lord Peter,
> Who broke the laws of God and man and metre.'

There were eight or ten more lines, but Peter destroyed them in his wrath.

In the region of wild burlesque, where the ridiculous, by its intensity and mass, becomes the sublime, I never met any one to approach 'Peter,' except our amazing Medea-Robson. He could also abate a tiresome prig as effectually as Sydney Smith or Harry Cockburn, though in a different and ruder way. He had *face* for anything; and this is by half (the better half) the secret of success in joking, as it is in more things. Many of us—glum, mute, and inglorious as we are—have jokes, which, if we could but do them justice, and fire them off with a steady hand and eye, would make great havoc; but, like the speeches we all make to ourselves when returning from our Debating Society,— those annihilating replies, those crushing sarcasms,— they are only too late, and a day after the fair. But Lord Peter had no misgivings. When quite a lad, though even then having that spacious expanse of visage, that endless amount of face, capable of any amplitude of stare, like a hillside, and a look of

intentional idiocy and innocence, at once appalling
and touching,—at a dinner-party, the mirth of which
was being killed by some Oxford swell, who was
for ever talking Greek and quoting his authorities,—
Peter who was opposite him, said, with a solemnity
amounting to awe : 'Not to interrupt you, sir ! but
it strikes me that *Dionysius of Halicarnassus* is
against you,' keeping his eyes upon his victim with
the deepest seriousness,—eyes like ordinary eyes
seen close to the big end of an opera-glass of great
magnifying power, opalescent, with fluctuating blinks,
as if seen through water, the lamps as of some huge
sea moon-calf on the gambol through its deep. The
prig reeled, but recovered, and said : 'If I mistake
not, sir, Dionysius of Halicarnassus was dead ninety
or so years before my date.' 'To be sure, he was.
I very much beg your pardon, sir ; I always do make
that mistake ; I meant *Thaddeus of Warsaw !*'

But, indeed, there was the sad thing,—that which
is so touchingly referred to by Sydney Smith in his
lecture on Wit and Humour,—he became the slave
of his own gifts. He gravitated downwards ; and
life and law, friends and everything, existed chiefly
to be joked on. Still, he was a mighty genius in
his own line, and more, as I have said, like Falstaff
than any man out of Shakespeare. There is not
much said or done by that worthy—'that irregular
humorist,' 'that damned *Epicurean* rascal,' 'a

goodly, portly man, i' faith, and a corpulent, of a
cheerful look, a pleasing eye, and a most noble presence'—which Peter might not have said and done,
from the wildest, grossest joke up to 'babbling of
green fields'; for 'Peter' had a gentle, sweet,
though feeblose, and too often falsetto, strain of
poetic feeling and fancy.

In active or receptive imagination, Logan was
infinitely above him; he had far too much of the
true stuff and sense of poetry ever to have written
the 'Gleams of Thought' which their author, and, of
course, no one else, thought not only poetry, but
that of the purest water.

Can an unpoetical man have poetic dreams? I
doubt if he can. Your ordinary man may dream
the oddest, wildest, laughablest, funniest nonsense.
He will not likely dream such a dream as the
one I have recorded. Shakespeare might have dull
dreams, but I question if Mr. Tupper could have
dreamt of a Midsummer Night's Dream, any more
than a man will speak a language in his sleep he
never learned or heard.

If the master of the house is asleep, and some imp
of darkness and misrule sets to playing all sorts of
tricks, turning everything topsy-turvy, ransacking all
manner of hidden places, making every kind of
grotesque conjunction, and running riot in utter
incongruity and drollness, he still must be limited to

what he finds in the house,—to his master's goods and chattels. So, I believe, is it with dreams; the stuff they are made of lies ready-made, is all found on the premises to the imp's hand; it is for him to weave it into what fantastic and goblin tapestry he may. The kaleidoscope can make nothing of anything that is not first put in at the end of the tube, though no mortal can predict what the next shift may be. Charles Lamb was uneasy all the time he was at Keswick visiting Southey; and he escaped to London and 'the sweet security of streets' as fast as the mail could carry him, confessing afterwards that he slept ill 'down there,' and was sure 'those big fellows,' who were always lying all about, Skiddaw and Helvellyn, '*came down much nearer him at night and looked at him !*' So we often feel as if in the night of the body and the soul, when the many-eyed daylight of the pure reason is gone, heights and depths, and many unspeakable things, come into view, looming vaster, and deeper, and nearer in that *camera-obscura*, when the shutters are shut and the inner lights lit, and

> ' When to the sessions of sweet silent thought
> We summon up remembrance of things past,'

and often play such fantastic tricks. But the dreamer is the same *ens rationis*, the same *unus quis*, as the waking man who tells the dream. Philip who

was drunk, and Philip who is sober and remembers
his lapse, is one Philip. So it is only an imaginative
man who can have imaginative dreams. You must
first put in before you can take out. As Samson
long ago put it to the Philistines, 'Out of the eater
came forth meat; out of the strong came forth
sweetness.' No food like lion's marrow; no tenderness like the tenderness of a strong nature. Or
as old Fuller, with a noticeable forecasting of the
modern doctrine of foods, as delivered by Prout and
all the doctors, has it, '*Omne par nutrit suum par;*
the vitals of the body are most strengthened by
feeding on such foods as are likest unto them,'—
a word this of warning as well as good cheer.
He that sows to the flesh, and he who sows to the
spirit, need not doubt what they are severally to
reap. We all, more or less, sow to both; it is
the *plus* that makes the difference between others
and ourselves, and between our former and present
selves.

I might give instances of my friend's wit and
humour; but I could not, in trying to do so, do him
anything but injustice. His jokes were all warm and
at once. He did not load his revolver before going
to dinner, and discharge all its barrels at his friends.
His fun arose out of the sociality of the hour, and
was an integral part of it; and he never repeated his
jokes. He did not pick up his bullet and pocket it

18

and fire it off again. But I remember well his first shot at me,—it was not bad for nineteen. He and I were coming down the Bridges from college, and I saw an unkempt, bareheaded Cowgate boy, fluttering along in full-blown laughter and rags. He had a skull like Sir Walter's, round and high. I said, 'Logan, look at that boy's head,—did you ever see the like of it? it's like a tower.' 'Yes, at any rate a fort-a-lice.'

You know the odd shock of a real joke going off like a pistol or a squib at your ear. It goes through you. That same week another quite as good squib went off in church. A cousin, now long dead, was listening with me to a young preacher-puppy, whose sermon was one tissue of unacknowledged plagiarisms of the most barefaced kind. We were doing little else than nudge each other as one amazing crib succeeded another,—for this ass did know his master's crib. William whispered to me, 'Look at him! I declare his very whiskers are curving into inverted commas;' and it was true, such was the shape of his whiskers, that his face, and especially his grinning and complacent mouth, which they embraced, looked one entire quotation.

Lord Brougham and many others think that dreaming occurs only between sleeping and waking, —the stepping of the soul into or out of the land of forgetfulness,—and that it is momentary in its

essence and action, though often ranging over a
lifetime or more,—

> 'Brief as the lightning in the collied night
> That in a spleen unfolds both heaven and earth.'

There is much in favour of this. One hopes the soul
—*animula, blandula, vagula*—may sometimes sleep
the dreamless sleep of health, as well as its tired
drudge. Dreaming may be a sort of dislocation of
our train of ideas, a sort of jumble as it is shunted
off the main line into its own siding at the station for
the night. The train may stop there and then,
for anything we know; but it may not, for the like
reason the telegraph-office is not open during night.
Ideality, imagination, that sense of the merely beautiful and odd which delights to marry all sorts of
queer couples,—which entertains the rest of the
powers, when they are tired, or at their meals, telling
them and making them stories, out of its own head,
—this family poet, and minstrel, and mime, whom
we all keep, has assuredly its wildest, richest splen-
dours at the breaking up of the company for the
night, or when it arouses them on the morrow, when
it puts out or lets in the lights; for many a dream
awakes us, 'scattering the rear of darkness thin.'

In optics, if you make a hole in the shutter at
noon, or stick a square bit of blackness on the pane,
and make the rays from the hole or around the
square to pass through a prism, then we have, if we

let them fall on whiteness and catch them right,
those colours we all know and rejoice in, that Divine
spectrum,—

> 'Still young and fine,'

as

> 'When Terah, Nahor, Haran, Abram, Lot,
> The youthful world's grey fathers in one knot,
> Did with attentive looks watch every hour
> For thy new light, and trembled at each shower.'

The white light of heaven—*lumen siccum*—opens
itself out as it were, tells its secret, and lies like a
glorious border on the Edge o' Dark (as imaginative
Lancashire calls the twilight, as we Scotsmen call it,
the Gloamin'), making the boundaries between light
and darkness a border of flowers, made out by each.
Is there not something to think of in 'the Father of
lights' thus beautifying the limits of His light, and of
His darkness, which to Him alone is light, so that
here burns a sort of 'dim religious light,'—a sacred
glory,—where we may take off our shoes and rest
and worship? Is not our light rounded with darkness, as our life is with a dream? and, the greater
the area of our light, of our truth, 'won from the vast
and formless Infinite,' the ampler, too, is the outer
ring,—the iridescent edge lying upon the Unknown,
—making a rainbow round the central throne of the
Eternal. And is not the light of knowledge, after
all, the more lovely, the more full of colour, and the
more pleasant to the eye, when lying on and indicat-

ing what is beyond, and past all finding out, making
glorious the skirts of 'the majesty of darkness'? It
is at his rising out of, and his returning into 'old
night,' that the sun is in the full flush of his plighted
clouds, and swims in the depths of his 'daffodil sky,'
making the outgoings of the evening and of the
morning to rejoice before Him and us.

But, thus talking of dreams, I am off into a dream!
A simile is not always even an illustration, much less
an analogy, and more less an argument or proof.
As you see every one likes to tell his own dreams,—
so long as he has them by the tail, which soon slips,
—and few care to listen to them, not even one's wife,
as Sir Walter found to his cost. And so, good-
natured reader, let me end by asking you to take
down the fourth volume of Crabbe's Works, and
turning to page 116, read his 'World of Dreams.'
It is the fashion now-a-days, when he is read at all,
which I fear is seldom,—to call Crabbe coarse, even
dull, a mere sturdy and adroit versifier of prose as
level as his native marshes, without one glimpse of
the vision, one act of the faculty divine. Read these
verses again, and ask yourself, Is this a daguerreo-
typer of the Bœotian crimes and virtues, the sorrows
and the humours, of his dull, rich Essex and its coast?
I wish we had more of this manly imagination; we
have almost too much now of mere wing and colour,
mere flights, mere foliage, and, it may be, blossoms,

—little fruit and timber. The imagination, like a gorgeous sunset or a butterfly's wing, tells no story, has no backbone, is for ever among the clouds and flowers, or down deep in denial and despair. The imagination should inform, and quicken, and flush, and compact, and clarify the entire soul; and it should come home from circling in the azure depths of air, and have its 'seat in reason, and be judicious,' and be a bird rather than a butterfly, or firefly, or huge moth of night.

Many months after this little notice appeared, Mrs. Logan gave me the following fragment found in her husband's desk,—from which it appears he had begun to put his dream into form :—

JUDAS THE BETRAYER—HIS ENDING.

'Tis noon,—yet desolate and dun
   The lonely landscape lies ;
For shortly after day begun,
Betwixt it and the mounting sun,
   A cloud went crawling up the skies.
From the sea it rose all slowly,—
Thin, and grey, and melancholy,—
   But gathered blackness as it went,
Till, when at noon the stately sun
   Paused on his steep descent,
This ghastly cloud had coiled itself
   Before his beamy tent :
Where like a conscious thing it lay,
To shut from men the living day.

And yet all vainly as it seemed ;
  For on each side, beyond its shade,
The sweet, triumphant sunbeams gleamed,
  Rejoicing in the light they made.
On all they shone except that dell,
On which the shadow darkly fell.
' O bear me to yon mountain brow
  That I may look below ;
All that is in that unblest dell
  Full fainly would I know—
Why is the sun to it denied ?
O bear me to yon mountain side.'
We cleave the air, now we are there,
  And what is it you see ?

' A little marsh, whence, low and harsh,
  A strange sound comes to me ;
  I marvel what that sound may be,
For strange it lights upon mine ear ;
My heart it fills with more than fear,
    With something of despair.
This well I know, 'tis not the sound
Of any beast that walks the ground,
    Of any bird that skims the air.'
Right well you guess, for 'tis the wail
Of a lost soul in endless bale,—
The reward of mortal sinning,—
Endless bale, but now beginning ;
Nay, do not turn away your eyes,
  For long before the sun now shining
  Shall be towards yonder world declining,
In that low dell the LORD'S BETRAYER dies.

With fearful horror and surprise,
On that low dell I fixed mine eyes.

The hills came down on every side,
　Leaving a little space between,
The ground of which, scarce five roods wide,
　Was of a cold rank green.
And where it sloped down to the fen,
　Built part of reeds and part of wood,
　A low half-ruined hut there stood,—
For man no home, for beast no den,—
Yet through the openings might be seen
The moving of a form within.

By this the sound had passed away,
And silence like a garment lay
A moment on the little lake,
If such it were, whose surface spake
No tale of wakening breeze or sun,
But choked with reeds all rank and dun ;
Which seemed to me as if they stirred
And shivered, though no wind was heard.
　They gave a shrill and mournful sound,—
'Twas like, and yet unlike, the sighing
You hear in woods when the year is dying,
　And leaves lie thickly on the ground.
As creepingly my ear it sought,
It might be fancy, yet methought
That, of all sounds that live in air,
This sounded likest to despair.

　　　All the while,
Close by the hut a great white dove
　O sight of wonder and of love !)
　Sits with a quiet and brooding air,—
White, and of none other hue.
By its deep yearning eyes of blue,
And by no sign beside, I knew
　It was a guardian spirit of air.
　What doth the lonely creature there ?

(To each man by pitying Heaven
One of these at birth is given ;
   And such their love and constancy,
That through all depths of sin and sadness,
Tempting hope and baffling madness,
   They ever, ever with us be.
Nor, till proud despair we cherish,
Will they leave our souls to perish.)

What doth the lonely creature there?
'Yon spirit quitteth not *his* side
   To whom he hath been given,
Whilst yet his heart has not defied
   The wrath and grace of Heaven,
Nor can his guardian watch be broken
   Till this defiance shall be spoken
     By Judas the Betrayer.'

Hold on thy watch, thou blessed Bird !
   One moment leave it not :
A heart of faith even might be stirred
   To doubt in such a spot.
Of him—the wretched traitor—friend,
   Thou long-forbearing dove !
Let no despairing words offend
   Thy faithfulness and love ;
For in the dark extremes of ill
The tongue will disobey the will,
And words of sin the lips will part,
Whilst holy feelings fill the heart !

It is another bird,—and lo !
   Rounding the corner of the hut,
It cometh silently and slow
   With outstretched head and eyes half shut ;
The feathers do not hide its skin ;
Long is its neck, its legs are thin,—
'Tis plain there is no health within.

It is the bird whose song so harsh,
  But lately sore dismayed me :
Upward it walketh from the marsh,
  It treadeth cunningly.
Too foul it is and melancholy
  To live on the upper ground ;
And I know it for a thing unholy,
  On some bad errand bound.

It rounds the corner of the hut,
  It stops and peers upon the dove :
The unconscious creature sees it not,
  So full are its two eyes with love.
On the dove it peers, and its head the while
  It pusheth out and it draweth in ;
And it smileth, if that a bird may smile,
  At the thought and hope of a joyous sin.
In a moment it thrusts its grisly neck
  With a silent jerk into the lake ;
In a moment it lifteth itself erect,
  And, in its bill, a snake.
The snake is round, and small, and cold,
And as full of venom as it can hold.

With three long steps, all without noise,
  Close to the dove it cometh :
That dreams no ill, for the while its voice
  A sweet low music hummeth.
To the dove's fair neck with a gentle peck
  His long bill he applies :
At the touch and the sound the dove turns round
  With a look of meek surprise,—
'Tis but one look, for swift as thought
That snaky neck is round its throat.

JEEMS THE DOORKEEPER.

JEEMS THE DOORKEEPER.

WHEN my father was in Broughton Place Church, we had a doorkeeper called *Jeems*, and a formidable little man and doorkeeper he was; of unknown age and name, for he existed to us, and indeed still exists to me—though he has been in his grave these sixteen years—as *Jeems*, absolute and *per se*, no more needing a surname than did or do Abraham or Isaac, Samson or Nebuchadnezzar. We young people of the congregation believed that he was out in the '45, and had his drum shot through and quenched at Culloden; and as for any indication on his huge and grey visage, of his ever having been young, he might safely have been *Bottom* the Weaver in 'A Midsummer Night's Dream,' or that excellent, ingenious, and 'wise-hearted' Bezaleel, the son of Uri, whom *Jeems* regarded as one of the greatest of men and of weavers, and whose 'ten curtains of fine twined linen, and blue, and purple, and scarlet, each of them with fifty loops on the edge of the selvedge in the coupling, with their fifty taches of gold,' he, in confidential moments, gave it to be understood were the sacred triumphs of his craft; for, as you may infer, my friend was a man of the treddles and the shuttle, as well as the more renowned grandson of Hur.

Jeems's face was so extensive, and met you so formidably and at once, that it mainly composed his whole; and such a face! Sydney Smith used to say of a certain quarrelsome man, 'His very face is a breach of the peace.' Had he seen our friend's, he would have said he was the imperative mood on two (very small) legs, out on business in a blue great-coat. It was in the nose and the keen small eye that his strength lay. Such a nose of power, so undeniable, I never saw, except in what was said to be a bust from the antique, of Rhadamanthus, the well-known Justice-Clerk of the Pagan Court of Session! Indeed, when I was in the Rector's class, and watched *Jeems* turning interlopers out of the church seats, by merely presenting before them this tremendous organ, it struck me that if Rhadamanthus had still been here, and out of employment, he would have taken kindly to *Jeems's* work,—and that possibly he was that potentate in a U.P. disguise.

Nature having fashioned the huge face, and laid out much material and idea upon it, had finished off the rest of *Jeems* somewhat scrimply, as if she had run out of means; his legs especially were of the shortest, and, as his usual dress was a very long blue greatcoat, made for a much taller man, its tails resting upon the ground, and its large hind buttons in a totally preposterous position, gave him the look of being planted, or rather after the manner of Milton's beasts at the creation, in the act of emerging painfully from his mother earth.

Now, you may think this was a very ludicrous old object. If you had seen him, you would not have said so; and not only was he a man of weight and authority,—he was likewise a genuine, indeed a deeply spiritual Christian, well read in his Bible, in his own heart, and in human nature and life, knowing both its warp and woof; more peremptory in making himself obey his Master, than in getting himself obeyed, and this is saying a good deal; and, like all complete men, he had a genuine love and gift of humour,[1] kindly and uncouth, lurking in those small, deep-set grey eyes, shrewd and keen, which like two sharpest of shooters, enfiladed that massive and redoubtable bulwark, the nose.

One day two strangers made themselves over to *Jeems* to be furnished with seats. Motioning them to follow, he walked majestically to the farthest in

---

[1] On one occasion a descendant of Nabal having put a crown piece into 'the plate' instead of a penny, and starting at its white and precious face, asked to have it back, and was refused —'In once, in for ever.' 'Aweel, aweel,' grunted he, 'I 'll get credit for it in heaven.' 'Na, na,' said *Jeems*, 'ye 'li get credit only for the penny !'

corner, where he had decreed they should sit. The couple found seats near the door, and stepped into them, leaving *Jeems* to march through the passages alone, the whole congregation watching him with relish and alarm. He gets to his destination, opens the door, and stands aside ; nobody appears. He looks sharply round, and then gives a look of wrath 'at lairge.' No one doubted his victory. His nose and eye fell, or seemed to fall on the two culprits, and pulled them out instantly, hurrying them to their appointed place ; *Jeems* snibbed them slowly in, and gave them a parting look they were not likely to misunderstand or forget.

At that time the crowds and the imperfect ventilation made fainting a common occurrence in Broughton Place, especially among '*thae young hizzies*,' as *Jeems* called the servant girls. He generally came to me, 'the young Doctor,' on these occasions with a look of great relish. I had indoctrinated him in the philosophy of *syncopes*, especially as to the propriety of laying the '*hizzies*' quite flat on the floor of the lobby, with the head as low as the rest of the body ; and as many of these cases were owing to what *Jeems* called 'that bitter yerkin' of their boddices, he and I had much satisfaction in relieving them, and giving them a moral lesson, by cutting their stay-laces, which ran before the knife, and cracked 'like a bowstring,' as my coadjutor said.

One day a young lady was our care. She was lying out, and slowly coming-to. *Jeems*, with that huge terrific visage, came round to me with his open *gully* in his hand, whispering, 'Wull oo ripp 'er up noo?' It happened not to be a case for ripping up. The gully was a great sanitary institution, and made a decided inroad upon the *yerking* system—*Jeems* having, thanks to this and Dr. Combe, every year fewer opportunities of displaying and enjoying its powers.

He was sober in other things besides drink, could be generous on occasion, but was careful of his siller; sensitive to fierceness ('we're uncommon *zeelyous* the day,' was a favourite phrase when any church matter was stirring) for the honour of his church and minister, and to his too often worthless neighbours a perpetual moral protest and lesson—a living epistle. He dwelt at the head of Big Lochend's Close in the Canongate, at the top of a long stair—ninety-six steps, as I well know—where he had dwelt, all by himself, for five-and-thirty years, and where, in the midst of all sorts of flittings and changes, not a day opened or closed without the well-known sound of *Jeems* at his prayers,—his 'exercise,'—at 'the Books.' His clear, fearless, honest voice in psalm and chapter, and strong prayer, came sounding through that wide '*land*,' like that of one crying in the wilderness.

Jeems and I got great friends; he called me John,

19

as if he was my grandfather; and though as plain in speech as in feature, he was never rude. I owe him much in many ways. His absolute downrightness and *yaefauldness;* his energetic, unflinching fulfilment of his work; his rugged, sudden tenderness; his look of sturdy age, as the thick silver-white hair lay on his serious and weatherworn face, like moonlight on a stout old tower; his quaint Old Testament exegetics, his lonely and contented life, his simple godliness,—it was no small privilege to see much of all this.

But I must stop. I forget that you didn't know him; that he is not your *Jeems.* If it had been so, you would not soon have wearied of telling or of being told of the life and conversation of this 'fell body.' He was not communicative about his early life. He would sometimes speak to me about '*her*,' as if I knew who and where she was, and always with a gentleness and solemnity unlike his usual gruff ways. I found out that he had been married when young, and that 'she' (he never named her) and their child died on the same day,—the day of its birth. The only indication of married life in his room, was an old and strong cradle, which he had cut down so as to rock no more, and which he made the depository of his books—a queer collection.

I have said that he had what he called, with a

grave smile, *family* worship, morning and evening,
never failing. He not only sang his psalm, but gave
out or chanted *the line* in great style ; and on seeing
me one morning surprised at this, he said, 'Ye see,
John, *oo,*' meaning himself and his wife, 'began that
way.' He had a firm, true voice, and a genuine
though roughish gift of singing, and being methodi-
cal in all things, he did what I never heard of in any
one else,—he had seven fixed tunes, one of which
he sang on its own set day. Sabbath morning it was
French, which he went through with great *birr.*
Monday, *Scarborough*, which, he said, was like my
father cantering. Tuesday, *Coleshill*, that soft, exquisite air,—monotonous, and melancholy, soothing
and vague, like the sea. This day, Tuesday, was
the day of the week on which his wife and child
died, and he always sang more verses then than on
any other. Wednesday was *Irish ;* Thursday, *Old
Hundred ;* Friday, *Bangor ;* and Saturday, *Blackburn*, that humdrummest of tunes, 'as long, and
lank, and lean, as is the ribbed sea-sand.' He could
not defend it, but had some secret reason for sticking to it. As to the evenings, they were just the
same tunes in reversed order, only that on Tuesday
night he sang *Coleshill* again, thus dropping *Blackburn* for evening work. The children could tell the
day of the week by *Jeems's* tune, and would have
been as much astonished at hearing *Bangor* on

Monday, as at finding St. Giles' half-way down the Canongate.

I frequently breakfasted with him. He made capital porridge, and I wish I could get such buttermilk, or at least have such a relish for it, as in those days. Jeems is away—gone over to the majority; and I hope I may never forget to be grateful to the dear and queer old man. I think I see and hear him saying his grace over our bickers with their *brats* on, then taking his two books out of the cradle and reading, not without a certain homely majesty, the first verse of the 99th Psalm,

> ' Th' eternal Lord doth reign as king,
>   Let all the people quake ;
> He sits between the cherubims,
>   Let th' earth be mov'd and shake ;'

then launching out into the noble depths of *Irish.* His chapters were long, and his prayers short, very scriptural, but by no means stereotyped, and wonderfully real, *immediate*, as if he was near Him whom he addressed. Any one hearing the sound and not the words, would say, 'That man is speaking to some one who is with him—who is present,'—as he often said to me, 'There's nae gude dune, John, till ye get to *close grups.*'

Now, I daresay you are marvelling—*first*, Why I brought this grim old Rhadamanthus, Bezaleel, U.P. Naso of a doorkeeper up before you ; and *secondly*,

How I am to get him down decorously in that ancient blue greatcoat, and get at my own proper text.

And first of the *first.* I thought it would do you young men—the hope of the world—no harm to let your affections go out toward this dear, old-world specimen of homespun worth. And as to the *second,* I am going to make it my excuse for what is to come. One day soon after I knew him, when I thought he was in a soft, confidential mood, I said : '*Jeems,* what kind of weaver are you?' '*I'm in the fancical line,* maister John,' said he somewhat stiffly ; 'I like its *leecence.*' So *exit Jeems—impiger, iracundus, acer—torvus visu—placide quiescat !*

Now, my dear friends, I am in the *fancical* line as well as *Jeems,* and in virtue of my *leecence,* I begin my exegetical remarks on the pursuit of truth. By the by, I should have told Sir Henry that it was truth, not knowledge, I was to be after. Now all knowledge should be true, but it isn't ; much of what is called knowledge is very little worth even when true, and much of the best truth is not in a strict sense knowable,—rather it is felt and believed.

Exegetical, you know, is the grand and fashionable word now-a-days for explanatory ; it means bringing out of a passage all that is in it, and nothing more. For my part, being in *Jeems's* line, I am not so particular as to the nothing more. We *fancical* men are much given to make somethings of nothings; indeed, the noble Italians call imagination and poetic fancy *the little more* (*il poco piu*) ; its very function is to embellish and intensify the actual and the common. Now you must not laugh at me, or it, when I announce the passage from which I mean to preach upon the pursuit of truth, and the possession of wisdom :—

> ' On Tintock tap there is a Mist,
> And in the Mist there is a Kist,
> And in the Kist there is a Cap ;
> Tak' up the Cap and sup the drap,
> And set the Cap on Tintock tap. '

As to what Sir Henry[1] would call the context, we are saved all trouble, there being none, the passage being self-contained, and as destitute of relations as Melchisedec.

Tintock, you all know, or should know, is a big porphyritic hill in Lanarkshire, standing alone, and dominating like a king over the Upper Ward. Then we all understand what a *mist* is ; and it is worth remembering that as it is more difficult to penetrate, to illuminate, and to see through mist than darkness, so it is easier to enlighten and overcome ignorance than error, confusion, and mental mist. Then a *kist* is Scotch for chest, and a *cap* the same for cup, and *drap* for drop. Well, then, I draw out of these queer old lines—

---

[1] This was read to Sir Henry W. Moncreiff's Young Men's Association, November 1862.

First, That to gain real knowledge, to get it at first-hand, you must go up the Hill Difficulty—some Tintock, something you see from afar—and you must *climb;* you must energise, as Sir William Hamilton and Dr. Chalmers said and did; you must turn your back upon the plain, and you must mainly go alone, and on your own legs. Two boys may start together on going up Tinto, and meet at the top; but the journeys are separate, each takes his own line.

Secondly, You start for your Tintock top with a given object, to get into the mist and get the drop, and you do this chiefly because you have the truth-hunting instinct; you long to know what is hidden there, for there is a wild and urgent charm in the unknown; and you want to realise for yourself what others, it may have been ages ago, tell they have found there.

Thirdly, There is no road up; no omnibus to the top of Tinto; you must zigzag it in your own way, and as I have already said, most part of it alone.

Fourthly, This climbing, this exaltation, and buckling-to of the mind, of itself does you good; [1] it is capital exercise, and you find out many a thing by the way. Your lungs play freely; your mouth fills with the sweet waters of keen action; the hill

---

[1] 'In this pursuit, whether we take or whether we lose our game, the chase is certainly of service.'—BURKE.

tries your wind and mettle, supples and hardens your joints and limbs ; quickens and rejoices, while it tests your heart.

Fifthly, You have many a fall, many a false step ; you slip back, you tumble into a *moss-hagg ;* you stumble over the baffling stones ; you break your shins and lose your temper, and the finding of it makes you keep it better the next time ; you get more patient, and yet more eager, and not unoften you come to a standstill ; run yourself up against, or to the edge of, some impossible precipice, some insoluble problem, and have to turn for your life ; and you may find yourself overhead in a treacherous *well-ee,* whose soft inviting cushion of green has decoyed many a one before you.

Sixthly, You are for ever mistaking the top ; thinking you are at it, when, behold ! there it is, as if further off than ever, and you may have to humble yourself in a hidden valley before reascending ;· and so on you go, at times flinging yourself down on the elastic heather, stretched panting with your face to the sky, or gazing far away athwart the widening horizon.

Seventhly, As you get up, you may see how the world below lessens and reveals itself, comes up to you as a whole, with its just proportions and relations ; how small the village you live in looks, and the house in which you were born ; how the plan of

the place comes out; there is the quiet churchyard,
and a lamb is nibbling at that infant's grave; there,
close to the little church, your mother rests till the
great day; and there far off you may trace the river
winding through the plain, coming like human-life,
from darkness to darkness,—from its source in some
wild, upland solitude to its eternity, the sea. But
you have rested long enough, so, up and away! take
the hill once again! Every effort is a victory and
joy—new skill and power and relish—takes you
farther from the world below, nearer the clouds and
heavens; and you may note that the more you move
up towards the pure blue depths of the sky—the
more lucid and the more unsearchable—the farther
off, the more withdrawn into their own clear affinity
do they seem. Well, then, you get to the upper
story, and you find it less difficult, less steep than
lower down; often so plain and level, that you can
run off in an ecstasy to the crowning cairn, to the
sacred mist—within whose cloudy shrine rests the
unknown secret; some great truth of God and of
your own soul; something that is not to be gotten
for gold down on the plain, but may be taken here;
something that no man can give or take away;
something that you must work for and learn yourself, and which, once yours, is safe beyond the
chances of time.

Eightly, You enter that luminous cloud, stooping

and as a little child—as, indeed, all the best king-
doms are entered—and pressing on, you come in the
shadowy light to the long-dreamt-of ark,—the chest.
It is shut, it is locked; but if you are the man I take
you to be, you have the key, put it gently in, steadily,
and home.   But what is the key?   It is the love of
truth; neither more nor less; no other key opens it;
no false one, however cunning, can pick that lock;
no assault of hammer, however stout, can force it
open.   But with its own key, a little child may open
it, often does open it, it goes so sweetly, so with a
will.   You lift the lid; you are all alone; the cloud
is round you with a sort of tender light of its own,
shutting out the outer world, filling you with an *eerie*
joy, as if alone and yet not alone.   You see the cup
within, and in it the one crystalline, unimaginable,
inestimable drop; glowing and tremulous, as if alive.
You take up the cup, you sup the drop; it enters
into, and becomes of the essence of yourself; and
so, in humble gratitude and love, 'in sober certainty
of waking bliss,' you gently replace the cup.   It will
gather again,—it is for ever ever gathering; no man,
woman, or child ever opened that chest, and found
no drop in the cup.   It might not be the very drop
expected; it will serve their purpose none the worse,
often much the better.

And now, bending down, you shut the lid, which
you hear locking itself afresh against all but the

sacred key. You leave the now hallowed mist. You look out on the old familiar world again, which somehow looks both new and old. You descend, making your observations over again, throwing the light of the present on the past; and past and present set against the boundless future. You hear coming up to you the homely sounds—the sheep-dog's bark, 'the cock's shrill clarion'—from the farm at the hill-foot; you hear the ring of the blacksmith's *study*, you see the smoke of his forge; your mother's grave has the long shadows of evening lying across it, the sunlight falling on the letters of her name, and on the number of her years; the lamb is asleep in the bield of the infant's grave. Speedily you are at your own door. You enter with wearied feet, and thankful heart; you shut the door, and you kneel down and pray to your Father in heaven, the Father of lights, your reconciled Father, the God and Father of our Lord and Saviour Jesus Christ, and our God and Father in and through Him. And as you lie down on your own delightful bed before you fall asleep, you think over again your ascent of the Hill Difficulty,—its baffling heights, its reaches of dreary moorland, its shifting gravel, its precipices, its quag-mires, its little wells of living waters near the top, and all its 'dread magnificence;' its calm, restful summit, the hush of silence there, the all-aloneness of the place and hour; its peace, its sacredness, its divineness. You see again the mist, the ark, the cup, the gleaming drop, and recalling the sight of the world below, the earth and all its fulness, you say to yourself,—

> ' These are Thy glorious works, Parent of good,
>   Almighty ! Thine this universal frame,
>   Thus wondrous fair ; Thyself, how wondrous then !
>   Unspeakable ! who sitt'st above these heavens.'

And finding the burden too heavy even for these glorious lines, you take refuge in the Psalms—

> ' Praise ye the Lord.
> Praise ye the Lord from the heavens : praise him in the
>   heights.
> Praise him in the firmament of his power.
> Praise ye him, all his angels : praise ye him, all his hosts.
> Praise ye him, sun and moon : praise him, all ye stars of
>   light.
> Praise the Lord from the earth, ye dragons, and all deeps ;
> Fire and hail ; snow and vapour ; stormy wind fulfilling his
>   word :
> Mountains, and all hills ; fruitful trees, and all cedars ;
> Beasts, and all cattle ; creeping things, and flying fowl :
> Kings of the earth, and all people ; princes and all judges of
>   the earth ;
> Both young men and maidens ; old men and children :
> Let them praise the name of the Lord :
> For his name alone is excellent ; his glory is above the
>   earth and heaven.
> Let every thing that hath breath praise the Lord.
> BLESS THE LORD, O my soul !'

I need hardly draw the moral of this, our somewhat *fancical* exercitation and exegesis. You can all make it out, such as it is. It is the toil, and the joy, and the victory in the search of truth ; not the taking on trust, or learning by rote, not by heart, what other men count or call true; but the vital appropriation, the assimilation of truth to ourselves, and of ourselves to truth. All truth is of value, but one truth differs from another in weight and in brightness, in worth ; and you need not me to tell you that spiritual and eternal truth, the truth as it is in Jesus, is the best. And don't think that your own hand has gotten you the victory, and that you had no unseen, and it may be unfelt and unacknowledged hand guiding you up the hill. Unless the Lord had been at and on your side, all your labour would have been in vain, and worse. No two things are more inscrutable or less uncertain than man's spontaneity and man's helplessness,—Freedom and Grace as the two poles. It is His doing that you are led to the right hill and the right road, for there are other Tintocks, with other kists, and other drops. Work out, therefore, your own knowledge with fear and trembling, for it is God that worketh in you both to will and to do, and to know of His good pleasure. There is no explaining and there is no disbelieving this.

And now, before bidding you good-bye, did you ever think of the spiritual meaning of the pillar of cloud by day, and the pillar of fire by night, as connected with our knowledge and our ignorance, our light

and darkness, our gladness and our sorrow? The
everyday use of this divine alternation to the wandering children of Israel, is plain enough.   Darkness is
best seen against light, and light against darkness;
and its use in a deeper sense of keeping for ever
before them the immediate presence of God in the
midst of them, is not less plain; but I sometimes
think, that we who also are still in the wilderness,
and coming up from our Egypt and its fleshpots, and
on our way let us hope, through God's grace, to the
celestial Canaan, may draw from these old-world
signs and wonders, that, in the mid-day of knowledge,
with daylight all about us, there is, if one could but
look for it, that perpetual pillar of cloud—that sacred
darkness which haunts all human knowledge, often
the most at its highest noon; that 'look that threatens
the profane;' that something, and above all, that
sense of *Some One,*—that Holy One, who inhabits
eternity and its praises, who makes darkness His
secret place, His pavilion round about, darkness and
thick clouds of the sky.

And again, that in the deepest, thickest night of
doubt, of fear, of sorrow, of despair; that then, and
all the most then—if we will but look in the right
airt, and with the seeing eye and the understanding
heart—there may be seen that Pillar of fire, of light
and of heat, to guide and quicken and cheer; knowledge and love, that everlasting love which we know

to be the Lord's. And how much better off are we than the chosen people; their pillars were on earth, divine in their essence but subject doubtless to earthly perturbations and interferences; but our guiding light is in the heavens, towards which may we take earnest heed that we are journeying.

> 'Once on the raging seas I rode,
>   The storm was loud, the night was dark ;
> The ocean yawned, and rudely blowed
>   The wind that toss'd my foundering bark.
>
> Deep horror then my vitals froze,
>   Death-struck, I ceased the tide to stem,
> When suddenly a star arose,
>   It was the Star of Bethlehem !
>
> It was my guide, my light, my all,
>   It bade my dark foreboding cease ;
> And through the storm and danger's thrall
>   It led me to the port in peace.
>
> Now safely moored, my perils o'er,
>   I 'll sing first in night's diadem,
> For ever and for evermore
>   The Star, the Star of Bethlehem !'

SIR E. LANDSEER'S PICTURE

'THERE'S LIFE IN THE OLD DOG YET.'

ETC. ETC.

SIR E. LANDSEER'S PICTURE

'THERE'S LIFE IN THE OLD DOG YET.'

1851.

WE have had several of Landseer's best pictures lately, but we are not likely soon to cry, 'Hold, enough!' The natural eye and heart is not easily wearied by nature and her true interpreters, be they poets, philosophers, or painters; the great point is to get nature, and then render her aright. It is, by the way, a new element in the fine arts, this setting famous pictures on their travels, and is on the whole a good one. We cheerfully adopt the peripatetic or to-and-fro doctrine thus far. A brisk circulation is the great thing in the body, natural, social, and commercial,—keep things going, large and quick returns; and it is one proof of a higher organisation, or, to use the cant phrase, 'development' of the body politic, as it is of the individual animal, when there is a heart, and when it sends its life-giving stream swiftly round. Caterpillars, and dead, degraded, and somnolent nations have a local half-and-half sort of circulation, they want the one grand central organ; but lest our readers should mistake us, we don't think this organ in our body politic is London, though Wordsworth calls it this 'mighty heart,'—it is the grand amount of the intelligence, refinement, and goodness of the whole people. We therefore do not despair of having a visit of the Venus de Medici or of the Dying Gladiator, or even the entire Tribune of Florence, with its riches; and getting tickets from Mr. Hill or Mr. Crichton, that they are on view, and thus seeing in our own 'Auld Reekie' what has so long 'entranced the world.' This picture of Sir Edwin's is remarkable in several respects: it is very large; it is twenty years old; it gives us a curious means of judging of his young and his present style, and seeing how he is the same and yet different; it has the grand English qualification of being worth £5000, or £200 a year at 4 per cent.; and best of all, it is a truly great and honest picture. By honest, we mean that the painter does his part in truth and honour, no blinking of difficulties, no filling up out of the lumber-room of other people's odds and ends, called his imagination; his is the truthful loving study of nature. This picture bears this out in every part, and it is worth remarking that being of so large a size, he had the ready temptation to 'generalise' and paint for effect. But he loved nature and honesty and himself too well to do this, and he has had his reward. Look at his last picture at Mr. Hill's, the 'Random Shot,' that dead mother and her suckling calf, on the cold mountain-top, and you will see the recompence of true work at the beginning of life and of art. There he has reached the domain of the 'shaping spirit of imagination;' he has got the flower in summer because he planted the seed in spring, and cherished the plant.

We will not describe this picture; it does that for itself. The entire 'scene' strikes us as wonderfully real. That wild place, out of the reach probably for ages of anything but a bird, a moonbeam, or a lightning stroke, is filled at once to our eyes with the interest of death, life, human sympathy, and the grandeur of nature. You hear the gruff honest fellow, with his handsome face, his iron grey hair, wet with exertion and his speaking hand, shouting out (in Gaelic from his mouth, and in the universal language from his eyes), 'There's life in the old Dog yet,' and you know by his curved lip, his loud look, his anxious eye, and trumpet hand, how far above him is his audience, and the thorough-bred deerhound, happy and contented even in its suffering, for he has got his gentle head on the breast of his master, who is his god. Let our readers mark the blush of its skin through the hair, as indicating the fierce race, and how its tail is drawn in by pain and terror; but there is no end of admiring. It is humanely and beautifully managed, that the other two are quite dead and at rest; it is a true touch of nature to leave the light springing deerhound alone alive of the three. We need hardly speak of the miraculous antlers.

Of course we know, by an act of our understanding, that in Mr. Crichton's room, in the heart of Edinburgh, and within that gilded frame, they must be 'painted' horns; but who does not 'feel' them to be veritable hartshorn? The colour of the whole is deep and rich, perhaps a little too rich, in the figures; but it is finely harmonised. The management of the 'reds' is a study to artists. The great subdued mass on the plaid, the smaller on the tartan stockings, the dead dog's open mouth and gums, the stag's tongue, and the small, intense, living tongue of the deerhound, the stony, obdurate look of the granite blocks, the wild confusion and the verdure, those soothing bits of nature's life-giving touch, working her will sweetly in the midst of desolation, the receding distance, with its mists and ghostly waterfalls, giving to the ear the idea of continual, vague murmuring, the rack of clouds drifting across, —the rope telling the story—all this who else could do so well? It is a great beauty in Landseer, as it is in Rubens, that landscape, dogs, men, flowers, everything is 'his own,' seen with his own eye, rendered by his own hand. It would be well that our young dashing artists, who are for bold-handling execution, would take a lesson from this picture.

Landseer must have been young when he painted this, and yet how 'conscientious' (we say this seriously) the whole performance, how thoroughly honest, and paid in full. Let our young friends take a note of this. The only thing in this picture left to what some of them would call their fancy, is wrong. It is the twist of the double rope; the twist is going the same way in the up and down rope.

The etching by Ryall is first-rate; it looks like an original sketch by the artist himself, so bold and free and subtle his handling, so up to the full idea.

We would despair of him making the remaining work equal had we not before us his Columbus, by Wilkie. We can most cordially recommend this engraving. There is a common, and, we may be allowed to call it, a somewhat vulgar and 'lassieish' objection to Landseer's subjects, that they are painful, as in the case of such representations as those of the 'Otter Hunt,' where that indomitable wretch, 'game' to the last, is held up transfixed and writhing under the adoring and praying eyes, and shaggy muzzles and legs, of up-looking little sturdy ruffians, the terriers and otter hounds, there is too much that is painful; but in such a picture as this of the 'Old Dog' we think the prevailing feeling is, and should be, pleasurable, and that humane and hearty sympathy which is one of the best results of painting, or of anything else.

Young ladies of a tender turn, and who weep their fine eyes and handkerchiefs ugly and sad with sympathetic tears for distressed lovers—in a book (they do very different when they meet them in real life, except they be themselves in the case)—would say on seeing this picture, Oh! shocking! What a horrid sight! Blood and tongues! What a horrid man Landseer must be! Let us analyse the dear creature's horror. It is *her own pain chiefly* that is horrid, it is not her feeling for the animals. It is the same sort of dislike to the sight that a bad smell causes to the nose, it has little better in it than this. A moderate measure of pain,—a real moral sympathy with the lower animals, and a feeling of uneasiness on account of their sufferings,—a going-out towards them, to love and be good to them, is a useful lesson for us all. Art is not a mere toy to be joked with and laughed at,—it is a deep and too little read passage in the nature and in the mind of man, and, with all reverence, it is one of the true manifestations of Him who made, and governs, and blesses us all.

HALLE'S RECITAL.

January 20, 1863.

IF it be a great pleasure to see others pleased, and a greater to be the pleaser, then must this gifted and accomplished artist have been very happy during his two hours on Saturday afternoon. Here was he, all by himself, sitting down at his piano, as if he were at his own fireside, and having his 'At Home' with some fifteen hundred happy people, to each one of whom the hours seemed all too short.

We seldom see, or rather feel (for we were all so much engaged that there was little seeing and less looking, even the perennial cough was checked, to the near suffocation of some self-sacrificing people whom we heard in by-corners tampering with apoplexy and asphyxia), so many people having so much of the same enjoyment all at once, and yet each ear making its own of all it heard, telling its own secret story to itself.

What it was to see Taglioni make music to the eye, gliding about like a shadow, or bounding like a pard, or merely walking; or to see Ducrow in his 'Dumb Man of Manchester,' making his every action speak; what it was to hear Grisi sing, or William Murray or his sister act—the same quiet mastery of expression, the same perfection of feeling and making to feel, the same power of making little into much, and much into more; so it is to come under the charm of this pure, consummate musician. You think of him at first simply as the cause of what he achieves; you find yourself as little thinking of him —of the means of what is to you the pleasant end— as he himself plainly is—each, giver and receivers, are taken up with the idea and its expression, he giving it out, they taking it in; or rather it is so perfectly expressed that you reach it as it were immediately, and get to its life and soul at once, and straight. Much of this arises from his quiet, simple, sensible face and manner. He knows that he is a means to an end—not an end in himself, as too many of our performers are,—and he gets the best reward in being ultimately himself an end as well, and all the better. You think him not the less clever, not the less executive, brilliant, subtle, penetrating, delicate, firm, and up to 'impossible passages,'—in a word, not the less expressive, that he never says to you, 'Now, listen, how clever, how delicious, how miraculous I am!' And it is this possession of his theme, and his self-possession in the best sense, that makes one great secret of his playing; it is not less unaffected and to the point (only much more delightful) than the talk of your man of business. Then think of the rest and satisfying play of the mind, of the diversion in its true meaning, of the many jaded minds, and heavy and weary hearts, and it may be vexed ears, of our busy men and women. Music can soothe other than savage beasts; and next to active exercise—to a ride across the Pentlands or a walk across Corstorphine Hill, and in some deeper and gentler ways, better even than these, though both are best—is the passing two hours of a Saturday, after the week's toil and worry.

its wear and tear, in hearing pure good masterpieces purely expressed. We are all the better of heartily admiring the same thing, the same thought, and the same giver or transmitter of the thought. Therefore it is that we miss the old Saturday subscription concerts, where the great classics were worthily rendered. Who can forget Mozart's 'Jupiter,' or the overture to 'Der Freischütz,' or the delicious, innocent, Elysian 'Surprise' of Haydn—as if it had wandered out of Paradise ; or the many-voiced sonatas of Beethoven —deep, mobile, unfathomable, melancholy as the sea ; or the quartettes with violins and violoncello, rising each above the other like larks singing at 'Heaven's gate,' or like transcendental nightingales in a sweet strife—

> 'That crowds, and hurries, and precipitates
> With fast thick warble [their] delicious notes.
> . . . . . .
> They answer and provoke each other's song,
> With skirmish and capricious passagings,
> And murmurs musical and swift jug jug,
> And one low piping sound more sweet than all.'

Why should not we have these pleasures back again? I daresay we might if we all asked them loud enough.

Beethoven's *Grand Sonata in D* was the first and largest recital; and is it not a great achievement this sitting down without anything but memory, and what a memory ! his fingers, and his genius, his tact and taste, and for anything we see, telling us his own present *Presto* and *Largo è Mesto*, his special at the moment *Minuetto Allegro* and his last *Rondo Allegro*—taking us into his confidence, and getting ours for the asking. As is often the case, we speak in profoundest ignorance of the science or the art beyond being the delighted subjects of their emotional effects. Beethoven begins with a trouble, a wandering and groping in the dark, a strange emergence of order out of chaos, a wild rich confusion and misrule. Wilful and passionate, often harsh, and as it were thick with gloom; then comes as if 'it stole upon the air,' the burden of the theme, the still sad music—*Largo è Mesto*—so human, so sorrowful, and yet the sorrow overcome, not by gladness but by something better, like the sea after a dark night of tempest falling asleep in the young light of morning, and 'whispering how meek and gentle it can be.'

This likeness to the sea, its immensity, its uncertainty, its wild strong glory and play, its peace, its solitude, its unsearchableness, its prevailing sadness, comes more into our minds with this great and deep master's works than with any other. If we think of Handel, his is 'the sea of glass,' and the overarching 'body of heaven in its clearness,' the 'harpers harping on their harps,' the far-off 'sound of many waters,' echoing to 'the utmost bounds of the everlasting hills,' 'the voice of a great multitude and of many thunderings,' the 'sevenfold chorus of halle-

lujahs and harping symphonies,' 'the throne and
equipage of God's Almightiness.' But it seems to
us that with the restless, capacious, unsatisfied and
satisfying German,—so full of passion and tenderness,
so full of the utterance of

'The still, sad music of humanity,'—

the sea, we all know, and love, and fear is the likely
symbol.

Sebastian Bach's perfect Gavotte and Musette
were given to perfection, his purity, his crystalline
depth, his inveteracy, his working out absolutely
and exquisitely his germinal idea,—nothing could be
better. Somehow we did not much care for, and
do not much remember *Mendelssohn's* Presto Scher-
zando; it was too fanciful, too soon, shall we say,
after the great old Sebastian? but we confess to not
always liking, and sometimes not taking in, the main
purpose of his music. Doubtless, we are in a pitiful
minority as to this. Compared with the greatest
masters, we feel him at times difficult, capricious, and
thin. *Weber's Invitation à la Valse* was—as everybody's heart and feet, especially the young ones'
feet, beat time to it in their minds—simply delicious
from beginning to end. We confess to having been
quite beside ourselves, indeed finding ourselves away
altogether; and in the full blaze of one of those ball-
rooms which we can all dance our fill in, and choose
our partners, and get no mischief—and behold!—

> ‘ Yestreen when to the stented string
> The dance gaed through the lichted ha’.’

We saw with our own eyes that splendid young
fellow—a prince of course—with his dark hair and
eyes, with that well-known glow in them finding *her*
out at once in that shadowy recess, where her mother
had left her for a moment, there he is bending down
and asking her to tread a measure. Of course,
he was Lochinvar, only much handsomer, gentler,
altogether an unspeakabler being than that hasty
young reiver who was so hard hunted across Can-
nobie-lee. She—

> ‘ Her eyes like stars of twilight fair,
> Like twilight, too, her dusky hair ;
> But all things else about her drawn
> From Maytime and the cheerful dawn,’—

looks still more down, flushes doubtless, and quietly,
in the shadow,—says ‘ No ’ and means ‘ Yes,’—says
‘ Yes ’ and fully means it, and they are off ! All this
small whispered love-making and dainty device, this
coaxing and being coaxed, is in the (all too short for
us, but not for them) prelude to the waltz, the real
business of the piece and evening. And then such
a waltz for waltzing ! Such precision and decision !
whisking them round, moulding them into twin orbs,
hurrying them past and away from everything and
every one but themselves. Now they all but disappear,
and are far away, almost out of sight and hearing, round

they come! here again! happier than ever, he firmer,
perfecter, abler, she playing with those little feet the
nicest second in the world. Well, the waltz ends,
and they and you have their fill, and they sit down
in the same shadowy nook, happy and out of breath,
and begin again the same 'murmurs made to bless,'
only lower, more serious and more silent; and for
our parts we must be excused for saying that we have
good reason to believe, indeed we must believe our
own eyes, that in this interesting case, the business
adjourned to an alcove out of the moonlight, the
sound of fountains and the dancers faintly heard, and
our two young individuals sitting with excellent effect,
for a well-known scene in Retzsch's Song of the Bell,
to which we beg to refer our readers, old and young,
—it being observed that the 'parients' of both parties
are at a respectful distance, under an old *arbol
d'amore*, such as we have seen in the Royal Garden
at Aranjuez a-blessing of the young people. But
soberly, this was one of Mr. Halle's most perfect bits
of art, as it is one of the most perfect flowers of
the genius of that 'marvellous boy' who perished in
his bloom; it is full of the sweetness and the sadness,
the richness, the fresh blossoming of youth, like the
Eclogues of Collins, or the Endymion of Keats, the
'first crush of the grapes,' the 'odorous breath' and
the swift vanishing of the 'sweet hour of prime.'

Next came the *Allegro con molto expressione*, and

the *Allegretto ma non troppo e Cantabile,* from Beethoven's Sonata in E minor. This piece, especially the latter half, which was *cantabile* indeed, is the one which lingers most in our ear and mind; it took more possession of us—was to us 'more moving delicate, and full of life,'—was the one thing we would more have rather not lost than any of the others; its loveliness, its fulness, its happiness, its heavenliness can only be told by itself. It seemed as if it spoke out all its secret, told it to us and to itself for the first time, innocently as a child, or an angel, 'still quiring to the young-eyed cherubim;' or like an Æolian harp with a soul and a will and purpose of its own, and a tune which it made the vagrant winds play as it listed, not as they. It had the unexpectedness, the swells as of music from a far country, come and gone, of that witching but unsatisfying instrument. For, unlike it, this had a story to tell with all its caprice and swift changes, and was not a mere wandering voice, bent upon nothing. But we are too hard on the harps that we used long ago to get from Keswick, and which we pleased ourselves with thinking, sang to us the songs of 'Glaramara's inmost caves,' not to speak of a stave from Scafell and the Pikes, and a weird sough through 'the pining umbrage' of 'those fraternal Four of Borrowdale.' Do you remember Coleridge's lines, 'composed at Clevedon, Somersetshire?' when sitting with his 'pensive Sara'

they heard 'the stilly murmur of the distant sea telling
of silence ;' and then came the music of

> 'that simplest lute
> Placed length-ways in the clasping casement, hark !
> How by the desultory breeze caressed,
> Like some coy maid half yielding to her lover,
> It pours such sweet upbraiding as must needs
> Tempt to repeat the wrong !   And now, its strings
> Boldlier swept, the long sequacious notes
> Over delicious surges sink and rise—
> Such a soft floating witchery of sound
> As twilight elfins make when they at eve
> Voyage on gentle gales from Fairyland,
> Where melodies round honey-drooping flowers,
> Footless and wild, like birds of paradise,
> Nor pause, nor perch, hovering on untamed wing !
> O the one life within us and abroad,
> Which meets all motion and becomes its soul,
> A light in sound, a sound-like power in light,
> Rhythm in all thought and joyance everywhere,
> Methinks, it should have been impossible
> Not to love all things in a world so filled ;
> Where the breeze warbles, and the mute still air
> Is Music slumbering on her instrument.'

This is beautiful, is it not?   But we prefer
Beethoven's harping to that of Æolus ; there is
method in his madness ; there is a greatness in his
gentleness , it soothes our wild discontents and
regrets ; it sings them, like blind giants, to sleep,
like Ariel charming Caliban, the uncanny, clumsy
and glum.   Field's nocturne in E flat was pretty,
but we could see to the bottom, and we suspect the

21

kindly and modest reciter brought more out of it than Field ever put in. Heller's *Dans les Bois* was given *con amore*, as if Heller was Halle's brother; it is original without being odd, and we can wish the author few better pleasures than hearing it played by his friend. The pieces from Chopin were finely chosen, full of the subtlety, the quick life, the intense subjectivity of this supersubtle, supersensitive, great and odd genius, whom we would think as difficult and deserving of translation as the unique Jean Paul, who needs a language for himself.

This over, the delighted audience, like children only half full of pleasure, and asking for more, could not let their friend go without another last, and he gave the beautiful, lively, and most picturesque Spinning Wheel,' by Heller, the young maiden singing to herself and her wheel.

So ended this enjoyable concert, and so ends our rhapsody.

BIGGAR AND THE HOUSE OF FLEMING.[1]

March 12, 1863.

WE owe some amends to this excellent book—to its sensible and genial author—and to the shrewd

---

[1] Biggar and the House of Fleming; an account of the Biggar district, Archæological, Historical, and Biographical. By William Hunter. Biggar: David Lockhart.

and sturdy *auld-farrant* little capital of the Upper Ward, for having been so long in noticing 'Biggar and the House of Fleming.'

Biggar deserved a book to herself, and has now got it, and a good and a big one too, and a publisher of her own—a book written not like an article for a gazetteer, in the dull, plodding style, but as a work proper to itself, and having at the same time reference to the rest of Scotland and its history mainly as 'adjacent,' in the sense of the good old Greater and Lesser Cumbray story. To Biggar people, Biggar is the centre of the world; and this book is written by a Biggar man, and mainly for those who are or have been 'callants' there, and to whom the memories of the *Corse Knowe* and of *Daft Jenny*, *Johnny Minto*, *The West Raw*, *Bow's Well*, and the *Cadger's Brig* are sacred. But with all this —with the local colouring strong and keen—the book is good general reading, the work of a thinking, judging, well-knowledged, well-languaged man, who could write as well on many a wider subject. It is not a book to analyse; but we can assure our readers that, though they never saw Tinto, Coulter Fell, Cardon, or Bizzyberry, and never even heard the ancient joke, that 'London's big, but Biggar's bigger,' they will find much diversion, and not a little instruction, in this volume, especially under the chapters 'Prehistoric Remains,' 'Biggar a Burgh of

Barony,' 'The Romans in the Upper Ward ;' Its
Witches, Vagrants, and Crimes ; and, not the least
curious, 'The Battle of Biggar,' in which the question is ably and entertainingly handled—Was Blind
Harry right in asserting, in 'Ye Actis and Deidis of
ye illuster and vailyand Campioun, Shyr William
Wallace, knicht of Elrisle,' that Sir William and his
friend, Sir John Tinto, gave battle to and defeated
Edward I. and Sir Aylmer de Vallance, to east of
Biggar, on Guildie's Oxgait and the Stanehead, past
which runs the little burn, the Red Syke, which, of
course, all Biggar, past, present, and to come, held,
holds, and will for ever hold, to be proof positive of
the battle, as it ran of blood for days after? But,
seriously, this battle of Biggar is worthy of the
attention of these mighty expiscators and exploders
of myths, Sir George C. Lewis, and our own inevitable Burton. Let them clear up it and the Wigtown
martyrs. We shall now give 'a wheen swatches' of
this goodly volume :—

'GIEIN' HIMSEL' A FLEG.'

John Brown the fiddler, full of genius and music,
and also too frequently fou in the other sense, playing at the fairs, penny-weddings, and dancing-schools,
and leading a wild throughother life, had been up
all night fiddling and drinking at Broughton fair.

He had seen his 'neebors' all asleep, or prostrate, and betook himself in the cool, sober light of the morning, to the road. He was seized when near Heavyside with sudden qualms in the interior, and thought his end was come. Being a Calvinist as well as a fiddler and toper, he had sundry awful reflections on this subject; and to indulge them more fully, he sat down at the roadside, expecting every moment the final summons. After waiting and wondering, John got up with much alacrity, saying, 'If I maun dee, I may as well dee gaun as sittin',' and made victoriously for Biggar. Here is a good bit on the same drouthy genius:—'On another occasion, after indulging in a round of rather hard drinking, he fell into the horrors. He viewed his conduct with any-thing but complacency. He considered that a feeling of sorrow and regret was not a sufficient atonement for his delinquencies, but that he was fairly entitled to receive some personal chastisement. Labouring under this impression, he went forthwith to the late Mr. James Paterson, commonly called "Oggie," from having lived with his father on the farm of Oggscastle, near Carnwath. Having found him, he said, "Jeames, I maun hae the len o' a gun frae ye this mornin'; I'm gaun to tak' a bit daunder doon the length o' Bogha' castle." "The len o' a gun, John!" said James, "that's strynge. What on earth are ye gaun to dae wi' a gun? Ye dinna mean to shute yersel'?"

"No exactly that, Jeames," said John, "but of coorse I mean to gie mysel' a deevil o' a fleg."'

BIGGAR AS A MEDICAL SCHOOL.

'Biggar from a remote period has had a staff of medical men. So early as the fourteenth century, mention is made, in a charter, of Simon the physician of Biggar. We know very little regarding the Biggar doctors, however, prior to the beginning of last century. At that time Andrew Aikman flourished as a surgeon in Biggar. The earliest notice that we have of him is on the 28th June 1720, when he and James Thypland were brought before the Bailie's Court, and fined "in the soume of fyve punds Scots to the fiscall," for having, in the course of casting peats in Biggar Moss, encroached on their neighbour's room. In 1723, he and his family appear to have been greatly annoyed by William Liddell, a horse-couper, one of those restless and outrageous individuals who give their neighbours and the powers that be a great amount of trouble. He therefore arraigned him before the Bailie's Court, and Luke Vallange, the presiding magistrate, condemned him, under a penalty of "fyve hundred merks Scots," to keep the doctor, and his wife, bairns, family, and others, harmless and skeathless, in their bodyes, lives, goods, and geir, and not to molest him nor his in any sort, directly or indirectly, in tyme coming.

'Doctors William Baillie and William Boe were distinguished physicians at Biggar during a considerable part of last century. Biggar, during the time they flourished, acquired some celebrity as a medical school. It was a common practice at that time for young men who wished to acquire a knowledge of the medical art, to serve an apprenticeship to some eminent practitioner. The fame of these two Biggar worthies drew round them many young men, some of whom distinguished themselves in their profession in after years. We may specially refer to Dr. Robert Jackson, the well-known army medical reformer.'

ROBERT FORSYTH, ADVOCATE.

The following notice of this strong-brained man, whose huge frame and head were well known twenty years ago in the Parliament House, where he invariably appeared at 9 A.M., nobody ever being before him, is characteristic of the times and of the class out of which, by his own native force, he so nobly raised himself.

'His father was Robert Forsyth, bellman and gravedigger, to whom we have already referred; and his mother's name was Marion Pairman. This worthy couple were united in marriage in 1764, and their only child, Robert, was born on the 18th January 1766. Their condition in life was very humble, and they had to struggle with all the disadvantages and sorrows of extreme poverty; but they resolved to give their son, who early showed an aptitude for learning, a good education, in order to qualify him for the work of the ministry. He was sent early to the parish school, but being the son of a poor man, he was treated with marked neglect, and made small progress. He soon, however, became extremely fond of reading. He borrowed such books as his neighbours could supply, and read them in the winter nights to his parents, to Robert Rennie, shoemaker, and others, who commended him highly for his industry and ability, and thus encouraged him to renewed exertions. In this way he became acquainted with such works as *The History of the Devil, Satan's Invisible World Discovered*, the Histories of Knox, Crookshank, and Josephus, Ross's *View of all Religions*, the poems of Butler Young, Milton, Ramsay, Pennecuik, and Sir David Lindsay. It is remembered at Biggar, that one evening he was busily engaged in reading aloud the poems of Sir David Lindsay, by the blaze of a piece of Auchenheath coal, after his mother had gone to bed, when that worthy matron said, "O Robie man, steek the boords o' Davie Lindsay, and gie 's a blad o' the chapter buik (the Bible), or I 'll no fa' asleep the nicht."

'As he made slow progress in his classical studies at the parish school of Biggar, he was sent in his twelfth or thirteenth year to the burgh school of Lanark, then taught by Mr. Robert Thomson, a brother-in-law of the author of the *Seasons*. Here he made more advancement in a few months than he had done for years previously. When attending this seminary, he returned to Biggar every Saturday, and remained till Monday. His aged grandmother was wont to "hirple" out the Lindsaylands road to meet him on his way home; but young Forsyth sometimes spent a few hours in climbing trees at Carmichael, or looking for birds' nests at Thankerton, and this sorely tried the patience of the old dame as she sat by the wayside chafing at his delay, and longing for his return.

'Forsyth then studied four years at the University of Glasgow, and manfully struggled with all the obstructions arising from the *res angusta domi*. During one of these years, a severe and protracted storm of frost and snow occurred, and prevented all communication from place to place by means of carts. The Biggar carrier was consequently unable to pay his usual visits to Glasgow for several weeks. Old Forsyth was thrown into great distress regarding the state in which he knew his son would be placed from want of his ordinary supply of provisions. *He therefore procured a quantity of oatmeal, and carried it on his back along the rough tracks* on the top of the snow all the way to Glasgow, a distance of thirty-five miles, and just arrived when young Forsyth had been reduced to his last meal.'

He studied for the Church, but having no interest, though an eloquent preacher, and having then, perhaps, no great belief in what he preached, he gave up the ministry and took to the bar.

' At that time the men of the Parliament House were more exclusive than they are at present. They cared little for a new adherent to their ranks unless he came recommended by his connection with some aristocratic family. The idea of a *sticket* minister, and the son of a gravedigger, obtaining admission into their dignified order, was intolerable to the Dundases, the Forbeses, the Wedderburns, the Erskines, and others, who in those days ruled the roast in the Parliament House. One of their number connected with the Biggar district, but never distinguished for obtaining any great amount of practice, was specially opposed to Forsyth, and one day had the audacity to say, "Who are you, sir, that would thrust yourself into the Faculty? Are ye not the poor bellman's son of Biggar?" "I am so," said Forsyth coolly, but sarcastically, "and I have a strong suspicion that, had you been a bellman's son you would have been your father's successor."'

Mary Youston and Professional Ethics.

' William Baillie's (the tinker's) wife, Mary Youston, was also a remarkable character. In height she was nearly six feet, her eyes were dark and penetrating, her face was much marked with the smallpox, and her appearance was fierce and commanding. She was even more dreaded than her husband, as she was more audacious and unscrupulous. Few persons cared to give her offence, because, if they did, they were sure in the end to suffer some loss or injury. " It is like Mary Youston's awmous, gien mair for her ill than for her guid." She was, like her husband, a dexterous thief and pickpocket, so that it was a common observation regarding her, " Whip her up Biggar Street on a market day, wi' a man at ilka oxter, and she would steal a purse ere they got her to the head o't." Many stories of her sayings and exploits were at one time prevalent among the peasantry of the Biggar district. We give a specimen or two. One day Mary arrived at the village of Thankerton, with several juveniles, who were usually transported from place to place in the panniers of the cuddies. She commenced hawking her commodities amongst the inhabitants, when some of the children of the village came into the house where she was, and cried, " Mary, your weans are stealing the eggs out of the hen's nest." Mary quite exultingly exclaimed, " *The Lord be praised ! I am glad to hear that the bairns are beginning to show some signs o' thrift.* "

'LANGLEATHERS.

'John Thomson, commonly called "Langleathers," was a person of great strength, and carried a budget of old iron implements and other articles on his back that few persons could lift. He was decidedly fatuous; and the report was that he had received such a shock on witnessing the destruction of the city of Lisbon by an earthquake in 1755, that he never again entirely recovered his reason. He used, in his contemplative moods, often to mutter to himself, "I saw a city sunk." He was inoffensive, except when roused by the annoyances and tricks of mischievous boys. He then became exceedingly noisy and outrageous; and, being a dexterous "hencher" of stones, it required great nimbleness on the part of the youthful tormentors to avoid his aim. When he happened to be at Biggar on Sabbath, the boys and he were sure to come into collision, and then a great deal of noise and disturbance was the consequence. He had rather a fondness for these encounters, and was not easily prevailed on to give them up. When any person remonstrated with him, and said that he ought to pay more respect to the Sabbath, "Weel, weel, then," said Jock, "I'll aff to Crawfordjohn: there's nae Sabbath there."'

Jock Robertson, a clever ne'er-do-weel, who had been at Glasgow College with Campbell the poet, long haunted the Upper Ward, getting his bed, his supper, and his dram at the farm 'touns' for his tricks and his fortune-telling, of which he thus gives the *rationale:*—GOOD PHILOSOPHY.—'Such is the propensity of human nature to pry into futurity, that I am very successful as a spaeman; and as I take no money, I am less apt to be committed as a vagrant. I can hide my tongue in such a manner that it cannot be observed; and though I am dumb, I am not deaf; I hear in one house what is going on in another, and can easily make a tolerable history. I first kneel down on the floor, then draw a magic circle with my chalk; next I write the initials, J. S., which will serve for John Smith, James Sommerville, Joseph Sym, Jacob Simpson, and a thousand more. On seeing the initials, a girl perhaps whispers, "I'll wager that's our Johnnie that's at the sea." Having found a clew, I draw a ship, and write Mediterranean, or whatever can be elicited from the tattle of the maidens. If, on inspecting the initials, they look grave, or give a hint about death, I draw a coffin; but if the initials do not suit any absent friend of the parties, I make them a sentence, "I say," and follow it up with a new set of letters till I can fabricate a story.'

About a hundred years ago an old man, Adam Thomson, who made and sold heather besoms, and ' ranges,' and ' basses,'—mats of straw or rushes, ' threshes,' as they are called in that broad tongue which rejoices in Haup for Hope and Wull for Will —lived in a lonely cottage in the bleak muirland between Biggar and Carnwath. One night in mid-summer, when they were all in bed, Thomson, who had gone to the door to answer a loud knocking, was brutally murdered, his wife maltreated, and the house robbed :—

' Great efforts, by offering rewards, and otherwise, were made to discover the perpetrators of this foul outrage. Several persons were apprehended on sus-picion, and all manner of reports were put in circula-tion; but no satisfactory discovery was made, and most persons began to consider that further search was hopeless.

' Adam Thomson, a son of the deceased, a man of strange notions and eccentric habits, and then schoolmaster of the parish of Walston, after ponder-ing for a long time over the mysterious death of his father, resolved to make personal efforts to discover the murderers. From time to time, so often as his vocation would permit, he left his native locality, and travelled over the greater part of Scotland and England, making minute inquiries after suspicious characters, visiting jails, and mixing with thieves,

tinkers, and vagabonds of all sorts. Again and
again he returned home baffled and disappointed.
One evening as he lay in bed ruminating on the
painful subject which had taken so firm a hold of
his mind, he felt a strong and irresistible impulse
once more to renew his search. He rose early next
morning, and wended his way to Jedburgh, where,
as was his wont, he repaired to the Tolbooth. Here
he made the usual inquiries at the prisoners, if any
of them knew the perpetrators of his father's murder,
and it is understood that he obtained such information as enabled him to take effectual steps to appre-
hend them and bring them to justice. It was thus
ascertained that the murder was committed by two
men, John Brown and James Wilson, and two
women, Martha Wilson and Janet Greig. At what
place James Wilson was apprehended we have not
ascertained; but John Brown was captured in a
house near the Fort of Inversnaid, by a party of
soldiers from the garrison, on Sabbath, the 3d
January 1773, and conducted first to Stirling and
then to Edinburgh. As no person had seen them
commit the act, it would have been difficult to
obtain a conviction against them; but the two
women basely agreed to turn king's evidence. The
trial of the two men was fixed to take place on the
28th June; but it was postponed till the 12th
August, on the plea that at least one of the panels

could bring evidence to prove an *alibi.* The individual who at length came forward and made this
attempt was a person of their own kidney, called
William Robertson; but his statements were so
inconsistent and contradictory that the Court committed him to prison. The jury unanimously found
the prisoners guilty; and the sentence pronounced
upon them was, that they should be executed in the
Grassmarket, Edinburgh, on Wednesday, the 15th
September, and their bodies given to Dr. Monro for
dissection.

' The execution of Brown and Wilson took place
on the day appointed; and *Adam Thomson, it is said,
appeared with them on the scaffold and offered up a
solemn prayer, an exercise of which he was very fond,
and in which, it is allowed, he greatly excelled.* On
his return home, he erected a stone at the grave of
his father in Carnwath Churchyard, with an inscription in Latin. It was long an object of attraction,
and was visited by many persons at a distance who
had heard the story of the murder, the extraordinary
efforts made by young Thomson to discover the
perpetrators of it, and the singular epitaph which
he had composed. A relative of Thomson, some
years ago, removed the stone to the neighbouring
churchyard of Libberton, and there barbarously
caused the inscription to be defaced or erased, and
another one, regarding his own immediate relations,

to be put in its place. So far as can be remembered
the inscription ran as follows :—

'" Hic jacet Adamus Thomson, qui xv. ante Cal.
Julii 1771, cruentis manibus, Joannis Brown, Jacobi
Wilson, et duarum feminarum, apud Nigram Legem,
prope Novam Ædificationem, crudelissime trucidatus
erat. Illi, Adamo Thomson, defuncti filio et ludi-
magistro de Walston, detecti erant. Ob quod
crimen nefandum, Brown et Wilson, capitis damnati,
et xvii. Cal. Oct. 1773, suspensi erant.

'" Hoc monumentum extructum fuit Adamo
Thomson, rectore Academiæ de Walston."

'The late Rev. William Meek of Dunsyre was
wont to quote the above inscription as a curious
sample of the Latinity of the dominies of the Upper
Ward, putting special emphasis on the rendering of
Blacklaw, near Newbigging, by " Nigram Legem,
prope Novam Ædificationem," and the fine conceit
of Thomson in styling himself " ludimagister " and
" rector " of the Academy of Walston.'

Adam Thomson tracking his father's murderers
like a sleuth-hound, and then offering up a solemn
prayer—' an exercise of which he was very fond '—
at their gallows, is worthy of Matthew Wald and that
fell shoemaker M'Ewan, whose predestinarian meditations on the sands at Lamlash, none who have read
Lockhart's intense novel are likely to forget.

And now for a bit of the comic. Robert Forsyth,

22

the father of the advocate, and himself gravedigger, bellman, and minister's man, was asked by his master, who was knowing in pigs, to take one of a very fine litter to his friend, the then minister of Dolphinton. Rob was told to be sure to inform the receiver of everything about its 'blood and culture' —not only who its father and mother, but who its forebears generally were. 'And ye see, Rab, be shure ye tell this afore ye let it oot, for he'll never heed a word ye say after that for glowerin' at its perfections.' So off Rob trudged with his pock and its high-bred burden. When he came to Candy Burn, a little way out of Biggar, where a dram was then sold, he met Richie Robb, a humourist and wag, who, seeing the bedral, says, 'Whaur are ye gaun?' 'Oo, I'm gaun to Dowfintoun, wi' joost the wunnerfust pig ever was piggit; it's for the minister.' 'Ay, man! Come yer ways in and tak a dram, and let's see the pig.' The pig was seen and admired, and then the dram and a crack. Meantime, Richie takes out the pig and puts in a young puppy-dog about the same weight, and Robbie trudges off, arriving in the afternoon at the manse of Dolphinton. The minister was out looking about him, and knew Rob. 'What's this in the pock, Robbie, my man?' 'Ay, ye may well speir, Mr. Meek. It's joost the maist extraordnar pig ever was. My maister has sent it as a parteekler present to you, wi' his compliments.' 'Let us see 't, Robbie.' 'Na, na, sir, I maun first put ye up to its generation, sae to speak.' He then detailed its antecedents, and let it solemnly escape at the corner. Out came the puppy, *winking* and *lively*. 'That's a dowg, Robbie!' says the minister. 'A dowg! a dowg! as shure's daith it is a dowg; it was as shure, Mr. Meek—as fac's daith —it was a pig when it gaed in!' 'Weel, Robbie, it's a dowg noo, so you may tak' it back. But come in and hae yer four oors.' Robbie took a fearful look at the beast, returned it with much subdued blasphemy, astonishment, and cruelty to the pock, and, making a hearty meal, started again, giving a sceptical keek into the pock every now and then on his way when he thought nobody saw him, to see what further change was going on. He arrived once more, disgusted, bewildered, and weary, at Candy Burn, where, of course, Richie was waiting for him. 'Ye've been lang, Robbie, and what for are ye carryin' the pock ower yer shouther?' Robbie gave a grunt of disgust, and told his story. 'That's awfu', Robbie, perfectly fearsome; ye maun stap in and hae a dram. Oo maun tell Tibbie.' Rob flung down his pock with its portentous contents—which gave an unmistakeable *yowl*—and took his dram and told his woes. Of course Richie transposed the pig once more, and on went Rob, heartened by drink a little, but full of alarm as to his master, who met him at the door

eager to know what his friend thought of the pig.
Robbie flung down his pock with a desperate air, took
his stand, and, rubbing his forehead, poured out the
prodigious story—'A whaulp, an absolute whaulp, as
ye may see, sir, wi' yer ain een.' Opening the pock
and giving it a vindictive kick, out came the pig of
the morning! 'As fac's death, Mr. Watson, it was
a whaulp at Dowfinton, and I lookit in noos and
thans to see if it was turnin' into onything else; and
it was a whaulp at Candy Burn, and that Richie
Robb can aver and sweer.' 'Nae doot, Robbie,
Richie kens a' aboot it,' said the more knowing
minister. In its own small way, this is as good a
joke as any since Boccaccio. What a finished personation Matthews or Sir William Allan would have
made, and Macnee or Peter Fraser would make of it!
There was—'Ah for the change 'twixt now and then!'
—an institution in Biggar as peculiar to it as is the
Godiva procession to Coventry,—the '*Hurley-hacket!*'
It has ceased for ever, because its possibility is no
more. Forty years ago, the *Corse Knowe*, or Cross
Hill, was as essential a feature in Biggar as St. Paul's
in London, St. Regulus' Tower at St. Andrews,
the Campanile in Venice, or our own Castle here.
Biggar is no more Biggar as it was than the Apollo
would be himself without his nose. This *knowe*
was in the centre of the town, and middle of the
street, and the market cross was on its top; and

when there was a hard frost, it was the pleasure of the entire town, young and old, to go mad, and take to hurling themselves down the frozen slopes, 'keepin' the puddin' het' in an astonishing way. As were the saturnalia to old, and the Carnival to present Rome, so was this short insanity to the staid town— its consummation being the Hurley-hacket, a sort of express train, headed by one or two first-raters, 'perfect deevils,' who could descend the steep stand- ing, like Hamlet in 'To be or not to be,' calm, and with their arms crossed, and their feet close heel-and- toe, shod with iron ; one fellow—he was afterwards hanged—was generally the leader, straight as an arrow shooting the rapids, and yielding, like a con- summate rider, to the perilous ups and downs ; behind him came the lads and lasses, scudding on their hunkers ; then their elders on their creepies, turned upside down, and then the ruck. Away it swept, yelling and swaying to-and-fro, like a huge dragon, lithe and supple—'swingeing the horror' of its mul- titudinous tail—down across the street, heedless of everything, running, it may be, right into Mr. Pairman's shop, or down on the other side into William John- stone's byre, and past the tail of his utmost coo. Then the confusion and scrimmage, and doubling of everybody up at the ending ! that was the glory, like emptying an express train into a 'free toom.' All this is gone, the Cross Knowe is levelled, the Hurley-

hacket is unknown, no longer flames down the steep
with half the town, and it may be the minister and
the dominie secretly at its tail, with a fragment of a
tar barrel flourishing and blazing at its head. It was
worthy of the pen of him who sang of Anster Fair.
The old Biggar callants may say, with their native
poet Robert Rae—

> 'Syne fancy leads me back to some
>   Tremendous Hurley-hacket row,
> When "Roarin' Billie," langsyne dumb,
>   Gaed thunderin' doon the auld Corse Knowe.'

'London's big, but Biggar's Biggar.'—*Joke of the
District.*

THE ENTERKIN.

THE ENTERKIN.

IF you have a holiday, and can trust your *aneroid*
when it promises fair—if you can do twenty-one
miles in seven hours, and wish, moreover, to see
what you never saw before, and what you will never
forget—then take six brown biscuits in your pocket,
and a return ticket to *Abington*, on the Caledonian,
starting at 6.20 A.M.

There is not much from Edinburgh to Abington
that everybody does not know; but as you pass
Kirknewton you will not be the worse of remembering that the beautiful little wooded glen—'dingle or
bushy dell or bosky bourne'—on the left, into whose
recesses you get a brief, surreptitious glimpse, with
the young Gogar trotting cheerily through it, is the
once famous 'PROCUL NEGOTIIS' of the great philosophic physician Dr. Cullen, where it was his delight
to walk, and muse, and delve. You may see the
maze of his walks still. It was part of his little estate
of Ormiston Hill. Behind the present handsome
and sensible mansion the old house may still be seen,
with its magnificent outlook across the Vale of the

Almond to the Ochils, and the outlying Grampians
from Benlomond to Schiehallion, and across the Firth
to Benarty and the Lomonds; above its door are
the words 'EST ULUBRIS,' from the well-known
lines :—

> 'Cœlum, non animum, mutant qui trans mare currunt;
>   Strenua nos exercet inertia : navibus atque
>   Quadrigis petimus bene vivere.   Quod petis, hic est;
>   Est Ulubris, animus si te non deficit æquus.'

This is untranslateable, but we give its bones : 'It is
clime not character they change, who run across the
sea; a strenuous idleness keeps us at work; in our
yachts and "drags" we seek a happy life.   What
you seek is here.   Even in this our Ulubræ—our
own homely out-of-the-way Ormiston Hill, if we but
bring with us the even mind.'   It is pleasant to think
of this great old Doctor, leaving his town work and
books, and giving himself up to gardening—the
records of which, in outlandish plants and shrubs,
still remain—and to farming, testing those original
speculations as to soils and manures which he
expounded in his lectures on chemistry, and which
were in much anticipatory of the new doctrines and
practice.   You may—to while away the time past
Carnwath and its dreary *Lang Whang*—fancy the
old Doctor, as Dr. Benjamin Rush sketches him—
'tall and slender, and with a stoop in his shoulders,
his face long, his under lip protruded a little beyond

the upper, his nose large and inclined to a point downwards, his eye of a blue colour, penetrating but soft,
and on his whole face an air of mildness and thought'
—walking in his glen, and repeating to himself or to
a friend his favourite beatitude of the old usurer—
'*Beatus ille qui procul negotiis,*' etc., or that of Poli-
tian :—

> '   Felix ille animi, divisque simillimus ipsis,
>   Quem non mendaci resplendens gloria fuco
>   Solicitat, non fastosi mala gaudia luxus.
>   Sed tacitos sinit ire dies, et paupere cultu
>   Exigit innocuæ tranquilla silentia vitæ.'

We are glad, by the by, to learn that that our College
of Physicians is about to repair the tomb of this, one
of their greatest fellows ; it is in the old burying-
ground of Kirknewton, and had fallen sadly into ruin
and forgetfulness.

We are now past Carnwath, and got to that station
which a shivering Cockney, who was kept waiting
some hours on a windy winter night in the old shed,
said was well-named *Curst airs* (Carstairs), and past
Thankerton—Tancred's Town—and Symington—
Symon's—and are at Abington before nine. There
is Mrs. Hunter's comfortable little roadside inn,
where, in the Eglinton Tournament year, the present
Emperor of the French arrived one evening alone,
wet, hungry, and weary, having been grouse-shooting
all day on Crawford Muir. He asked for a room,

but was told the only one was occupied by some young men who were surveying the Caledonian line. He sent up his card asking to be allowed to join them, and was requested to go to the place whence Mr. Kinglake seems to think his Majesty has a return ticket. He sat down by the kitchen fire, got his supper, slipped away to bed, and was off early next morning on foot.

You now take the road to Leadhills by the Glengonar Burn, which, like the river Pison in the Eden of Genesis, 'compasses the land where there is gold.' Indeed this region was called in olden times 'God's treasure-house in Scotland,' and the four petty burns in which the precious yellow grains were found— Glengonar, Short Cleuch, Mennock, and Wanlock— were compared to the four rivers in the Garden of the Lord—Pison, Gihon, Hiddekel, and Euphrates! Here was got the gold of which King James's *bonnet-pieces* were made, hundreds of workmen being then employed in its search. The glittering sand is still occasionally to be found, and every now and then a miner, smit with the sacred hunger, takes to the deluding, feckless work, and seldom settles to anything again.

It is six miles of a pleasant glen road from Abington to Leadhills—a dreary, unexpected little town— which has lain great part in ruins for many years, owing to the suspension or spiritless working of the mines, during a long, baffling House of Lords lawsuit. Things are better now under the new Company, and we may soon see it as tidy and purpose-like as the Duke's neighbouring Wanlockhead. The people are thoughtful and solid, great readers and church-goers. They have a capital library. Like all natives of such forlorn, out-of-the-world places, they cannot understand how any one can be happy anywhere else; and when one of them leaves the wild, unlovely place, they accompany him with wondering pity to the outskirts of their paradise, and never cease to implore and expect his return for good.

If you have a keen eye, you will not fail to observe something you never before didn't see in a Scottish village. There are the usual dogs and children about the doors, but *there is not a hen to be seen !*— they would be all poisoned by the lead in the gravel they pick up.

You are now some twelve hundred feet above the sea, and as you pass the door of the good doctor— an old Peninsular surgeon, and a thoroughbred gentleman, who has returned to his birthplace, and is the honoured friend and healer of that solitary upland—you may see what is now a broken-down byre, in which the author of *The Gentle Shepherd* was born.

Take now the road to the left; the other goes to Wanlockhead and down Mennock to Sanquhar;

yours leads you by the shoulder of the huge Lowthers through the Enterkin Pass to Durrisdeer and Dalveen. The road is little more than a bridle one. You ascend steadily and gently, to a great height, the high hills lying all around—not sharp and ridgy like the Highland mountains, 'curling their monstrous heads, and hanging them,' like the fierce uplifted waves of a prodigious sea—they are more like round-backed, lazy billows in the after-swell of a storm, as if tumbling about in their sleep. They have all a *sonsy*, good-humoured, *buirdly* look. As compared with Ben Lomond, our young *Jacobus* pronounced them 'slow.' This must, however, be a perilous road in snow and drift; for we passed several *cairns*, marking where some shepherd or bewildered traveller had stumbled on, blinded and sleepy, and taken his final rest.

The east side of the Lowthers is an easy ascent, and the effect of this vast expanse, stretching miles in smoothest surface, when covered with new-fallen snow, is said to be wonderful; shapely and rounded like some great recumbent creature, 'white, radiant, spotless.' At this time of the year, as we saw it, covered with thick, short, tawny grass and moss, one unbroken surface to the summit of 2377 feet, it was like the short close-grained fur of a lioness—the hills lying like her cubs, huddling round their mighty mother. On its summit the counties of Lanark and

Dumfries meet, as also three lairds' lands, and here it was the custom, up to fifty years ago, to bury suicides. Any more solitary and out-of-the-world place could hardly be conceived. The bodies were brought from great distances all around, and, in accordance with the dark superstitions of the time, the unblest corpse was treated with curious indignity —no dressing with grave-clothes, no *strieking* of the pitiful limbs ; the body was thrust, with the clothes it was found in, into a rude box, not even shaped like a coffin, and hurried away on some old shattered cart or sledge, with ropes for harness.

One can imagine the miserable procession as it slunk, often during night, through the villages, and past the farmsteads, every one turning from it as abhorred. Then, arrived at this high and desolate region, the horse was taken out, and the weary burden dragged with pain up to its resting-place, and carried head foremost as in despite ; then a shallow hole dug, and the long, uncouth box pushed in—the cart and harness left to rot as accursed. The white human bones may sometimes be seen among the thick short grass ; and one who was there more than fifty years ago remembers with a shudder still, coming —when crossing that hill-top—upon a small outstretched hand, as of one crying from the ground ; this one little hand, with its thin fingers held up to heaven as if in an agony of supplication or despair.

What a sight, seen against the spotless sky, or cross-ing the disc of the waning moon !

We are now nearing the famous Enterkin Pass ; a few steps and you are on its edge, looking down giddy and amazed into its sudden and immense depths. We have seen many of our most remark-able glens and mountain gorges—Glencroe and Glencoe—Glen Nevis, the noblest of them all—the Sma' Glen, Wordsworth's Glen Almain (Glen-almond), where Ossian sleeps—the lower part of Glen Lyon, and many others of all kinds of sublimity and beauty ; but we know nothing more noticeable, more unlike any other place, more impressive, than this short, deep, narrow, and sudden glen. There is only room for its own stream at its bottom, and the sides rise in one smooth and all but perpendicular ascent to the height, on the left, of 1895 feet, *Thir-stane Hill*, and on the right, of 1875, the exquisitely moulded *Stey Gail*, or Steep Gable—so steep that it is no easy matter keeping your feet, and if you slip you might just as well go over a *bona fide* mural pre-cipice. 'Commodore Rogers' would feel quite at home here ; we all know his merits :—

'Commodore Rogers was a man—exceedingly brave—par-
  ticular ;
  He climbed up very high rocks—exceedingly high—per-
  pendicular ;
  And what made this the more inexpressible,
  These same rocks were quite inaccessible.'

This sense of personal fear has a finely idealistic effect upon the mind, makes it impressionable and soft, and greatly promotes the after-enjoyment of the visit. The aforesaid *Stey Gail* makes one dizzy to look at—such an expanse of sheer descent. If a sheep dies when on its sides it never lies still, but tumbles down into the burn ; and when we were told that Grierson of Lagg once rode at full gallop along its slope after a fox, one feels it necessary to believe that either he or his horse were of Satanic lineage. No *canny* man or horse could do this and live.

After our first surprise, we were greatly struck with the likeness of the place to a picture of it by Mr. Harvey, exhibited in our Academy in 1846, and now in Mr. Campbell of Blythswood's collection. This was one of the great painter's first landscapes, and gives the spirit, the idea of the place with wonderful truth and beauty—its solemnity and loneliness, its still power, its gentle gloom, its depth and height, its unity, its sacred peace—

> ' It is not quiet, is not ease,
>   But something deeper far than these,
>   The separation that is here
>   Is of the grave ; and of austere,
>   Yet happy feelings of the dead.'

We have heard that the artist, who sat alone for hours sketching, got so *eerie*, so overpowered with the loneliness and silence, that he relieved himself

23

from time to time by loud shouts, and was glad to hear his own voice or anything. It must be a wonderful place to be alone in on a midsummer's midnight, or at its not less witching noon—

> ' In such a glen as this, on such a day,
>   A poet might in solitude recline,
> And, while the hours unheeded stole away,
>   Gather rich fancies in the art divine,
> Great thoughts that float through Nature's silent air,
> And fill the soul with hope and love and prayer.'

The glen is peculiar in being closed in, to all appearance, as much at the lower as the upper end —you feel utterly shut in and shut out. Half-way down is a wild cascade called Kelte's Linn—from Captain Kelte, one of Claverhouse's dragoons, who was killed here.

Defoe's account of the affair and of its wild scene, in his *Memoirs of the Church of Scotland*, is so homely and to the quick, that we give it in full. It is not unworthy of Robinson Crusoe, and is unexaggerated in local description :—

' This *Entrekein* is a very steep, and dangerous Mountain ; nor could such another Place have been easily found in the whole Country for their Purpose; and, had not the Dragoons been infatuated from Heaven, they would never have entered such a Pass, without well discovering the Hill above them. The Road for above a Mile goes winding, with a moderate Ascent on the side of a very high, and very steep Hill, 'till on the latter part, still ascending and the Height on the left above them being still vastly great, the Depth on their right below them makes a prodigious Precipice, descending steep and ghastly into a narrow deep Bottom, only broad enough for the Current of Water to run that descends upon hasty Rain : From this Bottom the Mountain rises instantly again steep as a Precipice on the other side to a stupendous Height. The passage on the side of the first Hill, by which, as I said, the Way creeps gradually up, is narrow ; so that two Horsemen can but ill pass in Front : And, if any Disorder should happen to them, so as that they step but a little a-wry, they are in danger of falling down the said Precipice on their right, where there would be no stopping 'till they came to the Bottom. And the writer of this has seen, by the Accident only of a sudden Frost, which had made the way slippery, 3 or 4 Horses at a Time of Travellers or Carryers lying in that dismal Bottom, which slipping in their way, have not been able to recover themselves, but have fallen down the Precipice, and rolled to the Bottom, perhaps, tumbling 20 Times over, by which it is impossible but they must be broken to pieces, ere they come to stop.

' In this Way the Dragoons were blindly marching 2 and 2 with the Minister and 5 Countrymen, whom they had taken Prisoners, and were hauling them

along to *Edinburgh ;* the Front of them being near
the Top of the Hill, and the rest reaching all along
the steep part; when on a sudden they heard a
Man's Voice calling to them from the side of the
Hill on their left a great Height above them.

' It was misty, as indeed it is seldom otherwise on
the Height of that Mountain ; so that no Body was
seen at first : But the Commanding Officer hearing
some Body call, halted, and call'd aloud, *What d'ye
want, and who are ye?* He had no sooner spoke,
but 12 Men came in sight upon the side of the Hill
above them, and the Officer call'd again, *What are
ye ?* and bad *Stand :* One of the 12 answer'd by
giving the Word of Command to his Men, *Make
Ready ;* and then calling to the Officer, said,
Sir, Will ye deliver our Minister ? The Officer
answer'd with an Oath, *No, Sir, an ye were to
be damn'd.* At which the Leader of the Countrymen fir'd immediately, and aim'd so true at him,
tho' the Distance was pretty great, that he shot him
thro' the Head, and immediately he fell from his
Horse ; His Horse fluttering a little with the Fall of
his Rider, fell over the Precipice, rolling to the
Bottom, and was dash'd to pieces.

' The rest of the 12 Men were stooping to give
Fire upon the Body ; when the next Commanding
Officer call'd to them to *hold their Hands*, and
desir'd *a Truce.* It was apparent, that the whole

Body was in a dreadful Consternation ; not a Man of them durst stir a Foot, or offer to fire a Shot. And had the 12 Men given Fire upon them, the first Volley, in all Probability, would have driven 20 of them down the side of the Mountain into that dreadful Gulph at the Bottom.

'To add to their Consternation, their 2 Scouts who rode before, gave them Notice, *That there appear'd another Body of Arm'd Countrymen at the Top of the Hill in their front;* which however was nothing but some Travellers, who, seeing Troops of Horse coming up, stood there to let them pass, the Way being too narrow to go by them : It's true, there were about 25 more of the Countrymen in Arms, tho' they had not appear'd and they had been sufficient, if they had thought fit, to have cut this whole Body of Horse in pieces.

'But, the Officer having ask'd a *Parley,* and demanded, *What it was they would have?* they replied again, *Deliver our Minister. Well, Sir,* says the Officer, *Ye's get your Minister, an ye will promise to forbear firing : Indeed we'll forbear,* says the good man, *We desire to hurt none of ye : But, Sir,* says he, *Belike ye have more prisoners : Indeed have we,* says the Officer, *and ye mon deliver them all,* says the honest Man. *Well,* says the Officer, *Ye shall have them then.* Immediately the Officer calls to *Bring forward the Minister :* But the Way was so narrow and crooked he could not be brought up by a Horseman, without Danger of putting them into Disorder : So that the Officer bade them *Loose him, and let him go ;* which was done : So the Minister stept up the Hill a step or two, and stood still ; Then the Officer said to him, *Sir, and I let you go, I expect you promise to oblige your People to offer no Hindrance to our March.* The Minister promis'd them, *He would do so. Then go, Sir,* said he, *You owe your Life to this Damn'd Mountain. Rather, Sir,* said the Minister, *to that God that made this Mountain.* When their Minister was come to them, their Leader call'd again to the Officer, *Sir, We want yet the other Prisoners.* The Officer gave Orders to the rear, where they were, and they were also deliver'd. Upon which the Leader began to march away, when the Officer call'd again, *But hold, Sir,* says he, *Ye promised to be satisfied if ye had your Prisoners : I expect you'll be as good as your Word. Indeed shall I,* says the Leader, *I am just marching away ;* it seems he did not rightly understand the Officer. *Well, Sir, but,* says the Officer, *I expect you call off those Fellows you have posted at the Head of the Way. They belong not to us,* says the honest Man, *they are unarm'd People, waiting till you pass by. Say you so?* said the Officer ; *Had I known that, you had not gotten your Men so cheap, or have come off so free :* Says the Countryman, *An ye are for Battle,*

Sir, We are ready for you still, if you think you are
able for us, ye may trye your Hands; we'll quit the
Truce, if you like. NO, says the Officer, *I think ye*
be brave Fellows, e'en gang your Gate.'

In his curious account of his travels in Scotland,
Defoe gives a more detailed description of the glen
and of his own visit to it, saying with true London
naïveté, that the hills on each side 'are nearly as
high as the Monument !' [1]

[1] 'From *Drumlanrig* I took a Turn to see the famous Pass
of *Enterkin,* or *Introkin* Hill : It is indeed, not easy to describe ; but by telling you that it ascends through a winding
Bottom for near half a Mile, and a Stranger sees nothing
terrible, but vast high Mountains on either Hand, tho' all
green, and with Sheep feeding on them to the very Top ; when,
on a suddain, turning short to the left, and crossing a Rill of
Water in the Bottom, you mount the Side of one of those
Hills, while, as you go on, the Bottom in which that Water
runs down from between the Hills, keeping its Level on your
Right, begins to look very deep, till at Length it is a Precipice
horrible and terrifying ; on the left the Hill rises almost perpendicular, like a Wall ; till being come about half Way, you
have a steep, unpassable Height on the Left, and a monstrous
Casm or Ditch on your Right ; deep, almost, as the Monument is high, and the Path, or Way, just broad enough for you
to lead your Horse on it, and, if his Foot slips, you have
nothing to do but let go the Bridle, least he pulls you with him,
and then you will have the Satisfaction of seeing him dash'd to
Pieces, and lye at the Bottom with his four Shoes uppermost.
I pass'd twice this Hill after this, but the Weather was good,
and the Way dry, which made it safe ; but one of our Company was so frighted with it, that in a Kind of an Extasy,
when he got to the Bottom, he look'd back, and swore heartily
that he would never come that Way again.'

We now escaped by a secret path which we defy the uninitiated to discover—we had a mountain nymph to guide us—out of this strange, deep place, which, if it were any longer, would weigh the traveller down with its solemnity and seclusion— into Dalveen, down which flows the Carron, and the road from Edinburgh to Dumfries, by Biggar and Thornhill. It is an exquisite scene—great steep green hills opening and shutting the winding valley. It is well known as one of the finest and most romantic passes in the south of Scotland—it must have been something worth one's while to descend it on the box seat in the old four-horse-coach days. It is six miles from Leadhills to Lower Dalveen, and nine from that to Elvanfoot, where you must catch the train due at 4.20—most provokingly early. Any one fearing lest the twenty-one miles may be too much for his legs or his time, may shorten the walk two or more miles by going to Elvanfoot and walk- ing up the Elvan, instead of the Glengonar Burn. If he has our sky and our willingness to be happy, he will mark the Enterkin day with a white stone.

We have said that the miners at Leadhills are a reading, a hard-reading people ; and to any one looking into the catalogue of their ' Reading Society,' selected by the men themselves for their own uses and tastes, this will be manifest. We have no small gratification in holding their diploma of honorary membership—signed by the preses and clerk, and having the official seal, significant of the craft of the place—of this, we venture to say, one of the oldest and best village-libraries in the kingdom, having been founded in 1741, when the worthy miners of that day, headed by James Wells and clerked by William Wright, did, on the 23d November, 'condescend upon certain articles and laws'—as grave and thorough as if they were the constitution of a commonwealth, and as sturdily independent as if no Earl was their superior and master. 'It is hereby declared that no right is hereby given, nor shall at any time be given to the said Earl of Hopetoun, or his aforesaids, or to any person or persons whatever, of disposing of any books or other effects whatever belonging to the Society, nor of taking any concern with the Society's affairs,' etc. As an indication of the wild region and the distances travelled, one of the rules is, 'that every member not residing in Leadhills shall be provided with a bag sufficient to keep out the rain.' Here is the stiff, covenanting dignity cropping out—'Every member shall (at the annual meeting) deliver what he hath to say to the preses; and if two or more members attempt to speak at a time, the preses shall determine who shall speak first;' and 'members guilty of indecency, or unruly, obstinate behaviour,' are to be punished 'by fine.

suspension, or exclusion, according to the nature of the transgression.' The Westminster Divines could not have made a tighter job.

If Charles Lamb had, by any strange chance— such as dropping from a balloon, hailing from Hampstead—strayed into this reading and *howking* village, and put up at Mr. Noble's for a day or two, with his pipe (of peace and more, for he used to say with a sad smile between the earnest puffs, 'Other men smoke for pleasure; I (puff) smoke (puff) for my (puff) sal- (puff) va-va-vation,'[1]) well-provisioned, and a modicum of old Madeira and Hollands, and had he been driven into his inn by stress of weather and fear of the mountains (we all rememember how, when visiting Southey at Keswick, he ran away from Skiddaw and the rest of the big fellows, back to 'the sweet security of streets,')—how he would have enjoyed this homely working-man's library with its 2200 volumes! Fancy him and 'Papaverius' (De Quincey) and 'The Bookhunter' storm-stayed, all three here, and discussing over their toddy, and through their fragrant reek, its multifarious books,

[1] 'When Dr. Parr,—who took only the finest tobacco, used to half fill his pipe with salt, and smoked with a philosophic calmness,—saw Lamb smoking the strongest preparation of the weed, puffing out smoke like some furious enchanter, he gently laid down his pipe and asked how he had acquired his power of smoking at such a rate? Lamb replied, "*I toiled after it, Sir, as some men toil after virtue.*"'—Talfourd's *Life of Lamb.*

from Cudworth's 'Intellectual System' and Grotius
'on Christianity,' to Spurgeon's 'Gems' and Wylie's
'Seventh Vial.' Fancy *Carloagnulus* beseeching The
Bookhunter to enlighten him upon the Marrow
Controversy, and the Old and New Lights, and the
Burghers and Antiburghers, the Glassites, Sande-
manians, Cameronians, and U.P.'s; and 'Papaverius'
entering curiously and delectably upon King's 'Origin
of Evil,' Thomas à Kempis, or 'Aspasio Vindicated.'
To hear 'Elia'[1] inquiring mildly and stammeringly
at The Bookhunter, as he turned over Erskine's
'Principles of the Law of Scotland,' whether 'multiple-
poinding' was a phrase which his friend Pierce Egan
—historian of the prize-ring—might not advantage-
ously adopt; and during the mixing of another
tumbler, asking his opinion as to the two Histories
of the *Concilium Tridentinum*, in order to edge in
a small joke of Burton-upon-Trent. Then think
of the three discussing, with a single dip and a
blazing fire, 'Humphrey Clinker,' 'The Adventures of a Guinea,' and 'The Bravo of Bohemia.'
Fancy their awe when they found upwards of 140
volumes of sermons, graduating from Butler, Sterne,
Horsley, and Robert Hall, down to Drs. Dodd and
Cumming. How Charles would expatiate upon
'Queen Street, a poem'—what 'on earth' it might
mean and what it might not;—how curious he would

[1] See note, p. 360.

be upon Clark's 'Hundred Wonders' and 'Extracts of C. L., Esq.'—were these *his* Essays taken down in his sleep—all unbeknown to himself? Who wrote 'Juniper Jack?' and 'The Land of Sinim?' and who ever allowed 'Count Fathom' to slip into such decent company? But seriously, we have been greatly struck with the range of subjects and of authors in this homely catalogue; and it is impossible to think with anything but respect of the stout-hearted, strong-brained men who, after being in the bowels of the earth all day, sat down to wrestle with John Owen or Richard Baxter, or dream of heaven and holiness with Scougall and Leighton, or refresh themselves with Don Quixote, the Antiquary, the Fool of Quality, and Daubuisson on 'The Basalts of Saxony' —besides eviscerating, with the help of Jonathan Edwards and Andrew Fuller, their own gloomy and masculine theology as mercilessly as they did the stubborn galena and quartz.

Note by 'The Bookhunter' on Papaverius.

Papaverius would have scunnered at the decent 'good book' appearance of Fisher's 'Marrow,' or Gib's 'Display of the Secession Testimony.' To bring him round about to the manner by a learned-like congenial path, I would have put into his hands, to bring him up to the seventeenth century, the ' *Tremulantes sive Quakeri*,' and the *Independentes*, by means of ' *Speculum Abominationum*,' and then have shipped him in the ' Histoire des Sectes Religieuses ' of Bishop Grégoire, where he would have found ' Methodistes, Seceders, Burghers, Reliefs, Bereans, Glassites, Balchristes, Hutchensonians, Tunkers, Shakers, Skevikares, Buchanistes, Brugglerians, Mamillaires, Venchoristes,' with others equally familiar and unfamiliar, all discussed in fluent French.

SINCE our Leadhills ploy, four of us met one September morning at Abington to breakfast, and took our way up *Camps Water* and down *Glen Breck* into Tweed. It was a grey, demure day, gentle and serious,—' caught at the point where it stops short of sadness ;' the clouds well up and curdled— lying becalmed

' O'er the broad fields of heaven's bright wildernesse ;'

what of sunshine there was lay on the distant hills, moving slowly, and every now and then making darker the depths of some far-off *Hope*. There is something marvellous in the silence of these upland solitudes ; the burns slip away without noise ; there are no trees, few birds ; and it so happened that day

that the sheep were nibbling elsewhere, and the
shepherds all unseen. There was only 'the weird
sound of its own stillness,' as we walked up the glen.
It was refreshing and reassuring, after the din of the
town, this out-of-the-world, unchangeable place.

We got upon the Moffat road two or three miles
above Tweedsmuir Kirk; and one of us who had not
been there for three-and-thirty years—when,—taking
his time,—he walked from Edinburgh to Kendal and
back again,—could not but be moved at the deserted
look of that old mail road—hardly a trace of wheels,
like the bed of a stream that has ceased to flow,—
'the sound of a voice that is still.' Nature winning
it back to herself. Fancy the glory of coming there
upon the well-appointed Royal Mail with the music
of its team, the guard on his little seat, with its black
hairy skin, his horn and his tremendous blunderbuss.
What compactness! what a unity, power, and purpose
about the whole organism! what stories we used to
hear of what the driver could do, and what the
guard had done.[1] How Willie Lawson snuffed a
candle, and not out, with his whip at Penicuik Inn,
on a 'lown' night before starting. How the guard,
having in vain sounded his horn at Harestanes toll,

---

[1] 'An Edinburgh clergyman, of a rare and quaint genius,
was one day seen gazing at the Carlisle Mail as it came thundering down *The Bridges*. 'What are you thinking of?' said a
reverend brother. 'I'm thinkin' that, next to preachin' the
everlastin' gospel, I would like to drive the Mail.'

when some disorderly coal-carts were stopping the
royal way, their carters drinking heedless inside—
blew out the brains of the first horse, and got the
gate cleared forthwith. And what a peremptory,
'dread' horn it was, bringing somehow *Fontarabia*
into the schoolboy head.

One guard I remember well—M'George. He had
been in the army, and was a gentleman—stern and
not given to speak; even with his companion the
driver he would let a whole day pass in silence—a
handsome, firm, keen face. I remember well, too,
when I had gone day after day to meet the Mail, to
be taken into Edinburgh to school after my vacation
among the hills, and to my rapture the Mail was full,
and we came back rejoicing at the respite. 'Is she
full?' asked again my grave and dear old uncle, six
feet and more on his soles. 'Yes,' said M'George,
with a gentle grin, and looking me in the face; 'she's
full of emptiness!' whereupon the High School boy
was bundled inside, and left to his meditations. Our
guard, I must say, came and looked in upon me at
each stage, comforting me greatly with some jargonelle
pears, the smell and relish of which I can feel now.
I fell asleep, of course, and when we stopped at the
Black Bull, found myself snug in the potentate's
great-coat. All this impressed me the more, when I
heard of his death many years after. It was a snow-
storm—a night of wild drift—in midwinter : nothing

like it for years. The Mail from Dumfries was late, and the townspeople of Moffat had gathered at Mrs. Cranstoun's inn waiting for it. Up it came. They crowded round M'George, entreating 'him not to proceed—'At Tweedshaws it'll be awful.' But he put them aside. 'They' (meaning the Post-Office authorities) 'blamed me once; they'll never blame me again.' And saddling the two strongest horses, he and the driver mounted and took their way into the night, stumbling dumbly up the street. The driver returned, having at the *Beef-Tub,*—a wild hollow in the hills, five miles out of Moffat,—given it up in despair, and in time; M'George plunging on, and not to be spoken to. The riderless horse came back at midnight. Next morning at daybreak—the wind hushed, the whole country silent and white—a shepherd saw on the heights at Tweedshaws something bright like a flame. He made his way to it— it was the morning sun shining on the brass-plate of the post-bags, hung up on a bit of paling—we have seen the very stake—and out of the snow stretched a hand, as if pointing to the bags : M'George dead, and as the shepherd said, 'wi' a kind o' a pleesure on his face.'

> 'Stern daughter of the voice of God,
> We know not anything so fair
> As is the smile upon thy face.'[1]

---

[1] Wordsworth's *Ode to Duty.*

From Tweedsmuir we walked by the Bield, the old inn, where the Moffat carriers baited or slept; and could not help recalling a story worthy of *Humphrey Clinker.* Campbell the poet, in his young days, had walked out thus far, and had got snug into bed after his tumbler of toddy, when there was a knock at the door. 'Come in;' and behold, with a candle in her hand, stood the pretty maiden—who had given him his supper—in her short-gown and petticoat. 'Please, sir, could ye tak' a neebor into yer bed?' 'With all my heart,' said the imaginative, susceptible poet, starting gaily up. 'Thank ye, sir, for the Moffat carrier's just come in a' wat, and there's no a single ither place.' Up came the huge and reeking man; exit the dainty little woman.

There, on the river-side, is where once was *Linkumdoddie,* where *Willie Wastle* dwelt. There is the *Logan Water,* which, with superb exaggeration, the poet says, Willie's wife's face 'wad file.'

There is Mossfennan 'yett,' where 'lichtit doon' the lovers of the Lass of the Logan-lea. This ballad, which is still remembered as being sung entire, is gone, we fear irrecoverably, all but a few broken stanzas, for which we have to thank Miss Watson, who, in her *Bygone Days in our Village,* has so well described the old-world life of this pastoral region :—

'Some say that I lo'e young Polmood,
    An' some say he lo'es na me ;

24

But I think I 'm a match for the best o' his blude,
   Though I had never a ewe on the Logan-lea.

For wooers I 've had braw young men,
   Booted and spurr'd as ye may see,
A' lichtin at Mosfennan yett,
   Doon by the side o' the Logan-lea.

Three cam east, and three cam west,
   An' three cam out frae the north countrie,
The lave cam a' frae Moffat-side,
   An' lichtit doon at the Logan-lea.

John Paterson comes frae Holms-water head,
   An' he did come to visit me,
An' he cam in by the Mere-cleugh head,
   Wi' his spotted hounds and spaniels three.

Graham o' Slipperfield, on his grey mere,
   Charlie, an' his pistols clear,
Young Polmood, wi' his hounds three,
   Will ne'er heir a ewe on the Logan-lea.'

We closed our *Minchmoor* with *The Bush aboon Traquair*,—we close *The Enterkin* with the *Cry from Craigellachie*, which our companion the author recited with impassioned cadence, as we walked down Tweed to Broughton. After much urgency, we got him to put it in the *Scotsman*, from which we now take it.

May we not enjoy its fervour and beauty, and at the same time rejoice that the cottagers at Kingussie are getting their oatmeal and coals one-half cheaper, since the iron horse took his way down Badenoch?

A CRY FROM CRAIGELLACHIE.

(Written after travelling for the first time to Inverness by the Highland Railway last August.)

LAND of Bens, and Glens, and Corries,
   Headlong rivers, ocean-floods!
Have we lived to see this outrage
   On your haughty solitudes?

Yea! there burst invaders stronger,
   On the mountain-barrier'd land,
Than the Ironsides of Cromwell,
   Or the bloody Cumberland!

Spanning Tay and curbing Tummel,
   Hewing with rude mattocks down
Killiecrankie's birchen chasm,—
   What reck they of old renown

Cherish'd names! how disenchanted!
   Hark the railway porter roar,
Ho! Blair-Athole! Dalnaspidal!
   Ho! Dalwhinnie! Aviemore

Garry, cribb'd with mound and rampart,
   Up his chafing bed we sweep,
Scare from his lone lochan-cradle
   The charmed immemorial sleep.

Grisly, storm-resounding Badenoch,
   With grey boulders scatter'd o'er,
And cairns of forgotten battles,
   Is a wilderness no more.

Ha! we start the ancient silence,
   Thundering down the long incline
Over Spey and Rothiemurchus
   Forests of primæval pine.

Boar of Badenoch! Sow of Athole!
　Hill by hill behind us cast;
Rock, and craig, and moorland reeling—
　Scarce Craigellachie stands fast.[1]

Dark Glen More and clov'n Glen Feshie,
　Loud along these desolate tracts,
Hear the shriek of whistle louder
　Than their headlong cataracts.

Strange to them the train—but stranger
　The mixed throng it huddles forth—
Strand and Piccadilly emptied
　On the much-enduring North.

Cockneys, Frenchmen, swells, and tourists,
　Motley-garb'd and garish crew!
Belted pouches, knickerbockers,
　Silken hose and patent shoe.

While from carriage-window gazing,
　Eye-glass'd damsels, yawning, drawl,
'Strange these names of yours—Braeriach,
　Ben-Mac-Dhui, Cairntoul.'

What to them are birk-tree fragrance,
　Pine-wood scents, bog-myrtle balm!
What the burns down corries sounding,
　Or the solemn mountain calm!

Point not them to Loch-an-Eilan,
　Lochindorbh's grim island hold;
Tell them not wild tales of Comyn,
　Or the Badenoch Wolf of old.

---

[1] 'Stand fast Craigellachie,' is the war-cry of the Clan Grant.

O Cairngorum ! O Braeriach !
   Roll ye blinding swathes of cloud
Down your crags, that these insult not
   Your majestic foreheads proud.

On, still on—let drear Culloden
   For clan-slogans hear this scream,—
Shake the woods by Beauly river,
   Startle beauty-haunted Dhruim.

Northward still the iron horses,
   Naught may stay their destined path,
Till their snort, by Pentland surges,
   Stun the cliffs of far Cape Wrath.

———

Must then pass, quite disappearing
   From their glens, the ancient Gael ?
In and in must Saxon struggle ?
   Southron, Cockney more prevail ?

Clans long gone, and pibrochs going,
   Shall the patriarchal tongue
From these mountains fade for ever,
   With its names and memories hung ?

Oh ! you say, it little recketh,—
   Let the ancient manners go,
Heaven will work, through their destroying,
   Some end greater than you know !

Be it so ! but will Invention,
   With her smooth mechanic arts,
Raise, when gone, the old Highland warriors,
   Bring again warm Highland hearts ?

Nay ! whate'er of good they herald,
  Whereso comes that hideous roar,
The old charm is disenchanted,
  The old Highlands are no more !

———————

Yet, I know, there lie, all lonely,
  Still to feed thought's loftiest mood,
Countless glens undesecrated,
  Many an awful solitude !

Many a burn, in unknown corries,
  Down dark linns the white foam flings
Fringed with ruddy-berried rowans,
  Fed from everlasting springs.

Still there sleep unnumber'd lochans,
  Craig-begirt 'mid deserts dumb,
Where no human road yet travels,
  Never tourist's foot hath come !

Many a Scuir, like bald sea-eagle,
  Hoary-scalp'd with boulder piles,
Stands against the sunset, eyeing
  Ocean and the outmost Isles.

If e'en these should fail, I 'll get me
  To some rock roar'd round by seas,
There to drink calm nature's freedom,
  Till they bridge the Hebrides !

                         SHLIABHAIR.
                    (*Anglicè* Mountaineer.)

THE DUKE OF ATHOLE.

THE DUKE OF ATHOLE.

SOME men have character,—more or less,—others have none,—and some few *are* characters; it is of their essence and what they are made of. Such was the late Duke of Athole; he was a character, inscribed and graven by the cunning, inimitable, and unrepeating hand of Nature,—as original and as unmistakeable as his own Ben-y-Gloe.

He was a living, a strenuous protest, in perpetual kilt, against the civilisation, the taming, the softening of mankind. He was essentially wild. His virtues were those of human nature in the rough and unreclaimed, open and unsubdued as the Moor of Rannoch. He was a true autochthon, *terrigena*,—a son of the soil,—as rich in local colour, as rough in the legs, and as hot at the heart, as prompt and hardy, as heathery as a gorcock.[1] Courage, endurance, staunchness, fidelity and warmth of heart, simplicity, and downrightness were his staples; and with them he attained to a power in his own region and among his own people quite singular. The

[1] The cock grouse.

secret of this was his truth and his pluck, his kindliness and his constancy. Other noblemen put on the
kilt at the season, and do their best to embrown
their smooth knees for six weeks, returning them to
trousers and to town; he lived in his kilt all the year
long, and often slept soundly in it and his plaid
among the brackens; and not sparing himself, he
spared none of his men or friends,—it was the rigour
of the game,—it was Devil take the hindmost. Up
at all hours, out all day and all night, often without
food,—with nothing but the unfailing pipe,—there
he was, stalking the deer in Glen Tilt or across the
Gaick moors, or rousing before daybreak the un-
daunted otter among the alders of the Earn, the Isla,
or the Almond; and if in his pursuit, which was fell
as any hound's, he got his hand into the otter's grip,
and had its keen teeth meeting in his palm, he let it
have its will till the pack came up,—no flinching,
almost as if without the sense of pain. It was this
gameness and thoroughness in whatever he was
about that charmed his people,—charmed his very
dogs; and so it should.[1]

[1] Many years ago, when Lord Glenlyon, he was riding in a
hurdle race on the North Inch, when somehow his spectacles
(he was very shortsighted) fell off, and in taking the first leap
he and his horse fell heavily. Up he was and on again and
away, winning in spite of his lost time, and taking his hurdles
'like a lord.' His right arm was observed to hang useless,
and so it might, for he had broken his collar-bone.

There may be better pursuits for a man and a duke than otter-hunting, and crawling like a huge caterpillar for hours across bogs and rocks after a royal stag; but there may be worse; and it is no small public good to keep up the relish for and the exercise of courage, perseverance, readiness of mind and resource, hardihood,—it is an antidote against the softness and the luxury of a dainty world.

But he was not only a great hunter, and an organiser and vitaliser of hunting, he was a great breeder. He lived at home, was himself a farmer, and knew all his farmers and all their men; had lain out at night on the Badenoch heights with them, and sat in their bothies and smoked with them the familiar pipe. But he also was, as we have said, a thorough breeder, especially of Ayrshire cattle. It was quite touching to see this fierce, restless, intense man—*impiger, acer, iracundus*—at the great Battersea show doating upon and doing everything for his meek-eyed, fine-limbed, sweet-breathed kine. It was the same with other stock, though the Ayrshires were his pets to the end.

Then he revived and kept up the games of the country,—the throwing the hammer, and casting the mighty *caber*;[1] the wild, almost naked, hillrace; the Ghillie-Callum (sword dance) and the study of the eldritch, melancholy pipes, to which, we think, distance

---

[1] A huge tree, requiring great strength and knack to pitch it.

adds not a little enchantment; all the natural fruits of human industry—the dyes, the webs, the hose— of the district. There might be much for Adam Smith and the *Times* to laugh at in all this, but it had and did its own good; and it made him a living centre,—a king. And who that ever was there does not remember the wonderful ball that closed the Athole Gathering, when delicate London girls were endued with miraculous spunk, when reel succeeded reel like the waves of the sea,—all innocent, and all happy, and all light of heel,—and when the jocund morn, far up in heaven, saw them 'doun by the Tummel and banks o' the Garry,' or across into Lochaber by the grim Ben Aulder and utmost Dalnaspidal.

Let no man speak evil of those cordial and once-a-year jovialities. They did no harm to those who brought no harm with them, and they left the memory of honest mirth—of health and youth—rejoicing after its last Reel of Tulloch or Houlachan, to immerse itself in the loveliness of that nature which is the art of God, and go home to its bath, its breakfast, and its bed.

Then the Duke was a great organiser of men,—he was martial to the core; and had his body-guard dressed and drilled to perfection,—all mighty men of valour,—after whom at the Princess's marriage the lively and minute Cockneys gazed in an awful wonder.

Of all the men about him he was as much the friend as the master ; and this is saying much, as those who knew his peremptory nature can well confirm. This power over men, not from mere birth,—though he knew he was ' to the manner born,'—not by high intellect or what is called knowledge,—for, though he had a stout and keen understanding, it was not high or cultured,—not because he was rich, which he never was, but simply because he was immediate, honest, and alive,—up to anything, and always with them. This power gave him a hold over all about him, which, had it not been something deeper and better, would have been almost ludicrous. His Athole guard (many of whom, with Struan at their head, were his peers in birth) would have died for him, not in word, but in deed ; and a young, capable shepherd, who might have pushed his fortune anywhere and to any length, was more than rewarded for living a solitary deer-keeper at the far-end of Glen Tilt, or up some to us nameless wild, where for months he saw no living thing but his dog and the deer, the eagles and the hill fox, the raven and the curlew,—by his £18 a year, his £3 for milk, his six bolls and a half of oatmeal, with his annual coat of grey tweed, his kilt and his hose,—so that he had the chance of a kind word or nod from the Duke, or, more blessed still, a friendly pipe with him in his hut, with a confidential chat on the interests of the ' Forest.

He was habitually and curiously good to all below him, unrelenting in his requisition of service, but far more generous than just. He knew them every one, and all their interests and wants, and took his own odd but genuine ways of reaching their hearts and doing them good.

Every one knows the interest our Queen had in him, in his Duchess and in Blair,—where she first saw and loved the Highlands, when she and her husband were in their first young joys, and where she went when her friend and her friend's husband, and her husband's friend, lay dying by inches of that terrible malady against which he bore himself so patiently, we may now say so sweetly,—submitting that fierce restless spirit to the Awful Will, setting his house in order, seeing and comforting his friends, remembering his people, not even forgetting his Ayrshires,—why should he?—waiting steadfastly and like a man for the end. We all know—it is our possession—that meeting of the quick, honest, chivalrous, devoted chieftain with his sorrow-laden but sympathising Queen,—their mutual regards, their brief, measured words from the heart. The dying man rising from his final room and accompanying his Royal Mistress to the train,—kissing her hand, and bidding her, not without dignity, farewell; and when his amazed and loving people stood, silent and awed, almost scared, by something greater than

Majesty,—the presence of that Shade who is waiting for us all, and who 'the likeness of a kingly crown has on,'—as the Duke with his dying lips raised the parting cheer. Such a thing does a nation—does every one of us—good; it is that touch of nature which makes us we all know what, and which we are in this fast world of ours all too little and too seldom.

There must have been no ordinary worth in the man whom the Queen so regarded and honoured. Much of this honour he, in his simple-heartedness and his frank speech, would have returned to her, the admirable wife who now mourns him,—who had nursed him day and night for months as few women could even if they would,—to whom he was glad at all times to say he owed everything; and his marriage to whom he, in his blunt and strong way, said, at a dinner to him at Dunkeld some years ago, when the Duchess's health was drunk, was the wisest thing he ever did.

The Duke was by blood, inheritance, and education as pure a Tory as he allowed himself to be educated; but he had none of the meannesses, the tortuosities, of your partisan Tory. He was a cordial Palmerstonian, as his presence and his speech at his Lordship's dinner testified. He knew who could drive the coach, and he booked himself accordingly. Next to his deer, his Freemasonry and his belief in the Ayrshire breed, was his love for what he called

Toryism; but he was his own master in this as in everything, and his vote was at no man's bidding. Long will his well-known figure and gait, his hearty, ringing, shrill voice, his reckless daring, his unsparing energy, his hidden kindness, his genuine love of his hills and wilds and men, survive in his own noble region, where he lived and died as unsubdued by the hand of progress and city life,—as unhurt by luxury as Schiehallion or Ben Doran; for he was, as we at first said, a genuine character, with a look and a step, a set of his glengarry, an everything all his own, and a thoroughness, cordiality, and kindliness of nature all the more delightful and unforgetable that, like the honey in Samson's lion, it took us by surprise.

STRUAN.

STRUAN.[1]

ANOTHER Highland chief of the old breed has
been gathered to his fathers in the midst of
his years.   Struan Robertson—or, as he was best
known, *Struan*, not *the* Struan, the head of the clan
Donachie, and representative of one of the oldest
families in the North, who were Counts of Athole
before the Murrays, and once owned land from
the watershed of the Moor of Rannoch to within
a mile of Perth, and were always 'out' when
anybody was,—was laid in his grave on Monday
last, carried shoulder-high by his men and the
stout shepherds of Rannoch, and lowered into
his rest bv his brother-officers of the Athole
Guard.

A more exquisite place is not in all the Perthshire
Highlands,—of which it is the very heart,—a little
wooded knoll near Dunalister, within whose lofty
pines the shadow of death gently and for ever broods,
even at noon, over the few graves of the lords of the

[1] From the *Scotsman* of April 18, 1864.

clan and their kin ; at its foot the wild Rannoch,
now asleep, now chafing with the rocks ; and beyond,
the noble Schiehallion, crowned, as it was on that
day, with snow, and raked with its own pathetic
shroud-like mists.

Though he was but occasionally in Edinburgh,
Struan was better known than many men who never
leave it ; and all felt proud of watching the manly,
athletic, and agile chief, with his stern and powerful
look as of an eagle,—

> 'The terror of his beak, the lightning of his eye,'—

and his beard black as an Arab sheik's, as he strode
along Princes Street in his decorous kilt of hodden
grey,—for he detested the Cockney fopperies and
curt garments of what he called 'Sabbath-day
Hielandmen,'—as if he were on the heather in his
own 'Black Wood.' His last act before leaving this
country for the South, to die, was to give his thin,
trembling hand to lower his Duke and friend into
the grave at Blair ; and as he came home he said,
'I'll be the next;' and so he was. We may wait
long before we see such a pair.

Struan was in the Forty-Second when young.
Had he remained in the army he would have made
himself famous. He had a true military instinct,
and was pre-eminently cool and inventive in emer-
gencies. We remember well his sudden appearance

at the great fire in Leith Street some six-and-twenty
years ago,—as a stripling in Highland ball-dress,—
with a company of his men whom he had led from
the Castle; how he took, as if by right, the command of every one, and worked like Telamonian
Ajax (who we are sure was like him) at the engines;
how the boys gloried in him, saying, 'There's young
Struan; he works like six!' and so he did. He
and his men got the thanks of the Town-Council
next day. But his life was spent in his own Rannoch
and among his own people, taking part not only in
all their sports and games and strenuous festivities,
the life and soul of them all, but leading them also
in better ways,—making roads and building for
them schools and bridges.

Like all true sportsmen, he was a naturalist,—
studied Nature's ongoings and all her children with
a keen, unerring, and loving eye, from her lichens
and moths (for which Rannoch is famous) to her
eagles, red deer, and *Salmo ferox;* and his stories,
if recorded, would stand well side by side with Mr.
St. John's. One we remember. He and his keeper
were on a cloudless day in midwinter walking across
the head of Loch Rannoch, which, being shallow,
was frozen over. The keeper stopped, and, looking
straight up into the clear sky, said to his master,
'Do you see that?' Keen as he was, Struan said,
'What?' 'An eagle;' and there, sure enough, was

a mere speck in the far-off 'azure depths of air.' Duncan Roy flung a white hare he had shot along the ice, and instantly the speck darkened, and down came the mighty creature with a swoop, and not knowing of the ice, was 'made a round flat dish of, with the head in the centre.'

For one thing Struan was remarkable, even among good shots; he was the most humane sportsman we ever saw; he never shot but he hit, and he never hit but he killed. No temptation made him wound and lose a bird or deer as so many do,—he was literally a dead shot. He used to say that once when a boy he found a poor bird lying in the heather; he took it up, and it died in his hand,—he knew he had shot and lost it some days before. He said that bird's dying eye haunted him for months; and he made a covenant with himself that never again would his hand cause such long misery.

We have said he was in the Forty-Second; and his house, 'Ranach Barracks,' was the first rendezvous of that renowned corps, then known as the Black Watch.

He was as courtly and mannerly, as gentle and full of chivalrous service, as he was strong, peremptory, and hardy; and any one seeing him with ladies or children or old people would agree with one-half of King Jamie's saying, 'A' the 'sons' (men with names ending in *son* like Wilson, Nicholson, etc.)

'are carles' sons, but Struan Robertson's a gentleman's.' Those who knew and mourn him can never
hope to see any one like him again, with his abounding jokes and mirth, and his still more abounding
hospitality and heart.

THE TUMMEL

AT MOULINEARN.

. . . *Numerisque*
Lege solutis . . .

Past runs the sunlit Tummel,
  Strong from his wilds above,
Blue as 'the body of heaven,'
  Shot like the neck of a dove ;
He is fresh from the moor of Rannoch,
  He has drained Loch Ericht *dread,*
And mirror'd on Carie's *waters*
  Ben-y-Houlach's *stately head ;*
He has mourned round the graves of the Struans,
  Hid in the night of the wood,
He glides by the pleasant slope
  Where our old Dunalister stood.
Schiehallion has heard him chafing
  Down by his sunless steep,
And has watched the child of the mountains,
  Deep in his Loch *asleep.*
He's awake! and off by Bonskeid,
  He has leapt his Falls *with glee,*
He has married the swirling Garry,
  And they linger in Faskally.

DICK *MIHI*, OR *CUR*, WHY?

BEING VESTIGES OF THE NATURAL HISTORY OF THE
CREATION OF A HIGHLAND TERRIER; WITH A NEW
RENDERING OF '*de cespite vivo*,' AND A THEORY OF
BLACK AND TAN.

'*The reader must remember that my work is concerning the
aspects of things only.*'—RUSKIN.

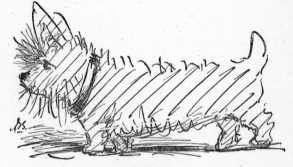

The Duchess.

THE MYSTERY OF BLACK
AND TAN.

W E,—the *Sine Quâ Non*, the Duchess, the
Sputchard, the Dutchard, the Ricapicticapic,
Oz and Oz, the Maid of Lorn, and myself,—left Crieff
some fifteen years ago, on a bright September morning, soon after daybreak, in a gig. It was a morning
still and keen : the sun sending his level shafts across
Strathearn, and through the thin mist over its river
hollows, to the fierce Aberuchil Hills, and searching
out the dark blue shadows in the corries of Benvorlich. But who and how many are 'we'? To
make you as easy as we all were, let me tell you we
were four ; and are not these dumb friends of ours
persons rather than things ? is not their soul ampler,
as Plato would say, than their body, and contains
rather than is contained?   Is not what lives and wills
in them, and is affectionate, as spiritual, as immaterial,
as truly removed from mere flesh, blood, and bones,
as that soul which is the proper self of their master?
And when we look each other in the face, as I now
look in Dick's, who is lying in his 'corny' by the

fireside, and he in mine, is it not as much the dog within looking from out his eyes—the windows of his soul—as it is the man from his?

The *Sine Quâ Non*, who will not be pleased at being spoken of, is such an one as that vainglorious and chivalrous Ulric von Hütten—the Reformation's man of wit, and of the world, and of the sword, who slew Monkery with the wild laughter of his *Epistolæ Obscurorum Virorum*—had in his mind when he wrote thus to his friend Fredericus Piscator (Mr. Fred Fisher), on the 19th May 1519, '*Da mihi uxorem, Friderice, et ut scias qualem, venustam, adolescentulam, probe educatam, hilarem, verecundam, patientem.*' '*Qualem,*' he lets Frederic understand in the sentence preceding, is one '*quâ cum ludam, quâ jocos conferam, amœniores et leviusculas fabulas misceam, ubi sollicitudinis aciem obtundam, curarum æstus mitigem.*' And if you would know more of the *Sine Quâ Non*, and in English, for the world is dead to Latin now, you will find her name and nature in Shakespeare's words, when King Henry the Eighth says, 'go thy ways.'

The Duchess, alias all the other names till you come to the *Maid of Lorn*, is a rough, gnarled, incomparable little bit of a terrier, three parts Dandie-Dinmont, and one part—chiefly in tail and hair—Cocker : her father being Lord Rutherfurd's famous 'Dandie,' and her mother the daughter of a Skye, and a light-hearted Cocker.   The Duchess is about the size and weight of a rabbit; but has a soul as big, as fierce, and as faithful as had Meg Merrilies, with a nose as black as Topsy's; and is herself every bit as game and queer as that delicious imp of darkness and of Mrs. Stowe. Her legs set her long slim body about two inches and a half from the ground, making her very like a huge caterpillar or hairy *oobit*—her two eyes, dark and full, and her shining nose, being all of her that seems anything but hair. Her tail was a sort of stump, in size and in look very much like a spare fore-leg, stuck in anywhere to be near. Her colour was black above and a rich brown below, with two dots of tan above the eyes, which dots are among the deepest of the mysteries of Black and Tan.

This strange little being I had known for some years, but had only possessed about a month. She and her pup (a young lady called *Smoot*, which means smolt, a young salmon), were given me by the widow of an honest and drunken—as much of the one as of the other—Edinburgh street-porter, a native of Badenoch, as a legacy from him and a fee from her for my attendance on the poor man's deathbed. But my first sight of the Duchess was years before in Broughton Street, when I saw her sitting bolt upright, begging, imploring, with those little rough fore leggies, and those yearning, beautiful eyes, all the world, or any one, to help her master, who was lying 'mortal' in the kennel. I raised him, and with the help of a ragged Samaritan, who was only less drunk than he, I got Macpherson—he held from Glen Truim—home ; the excited doggie trotting off, and looking back eagerly to show us the way. I never again passed the porters' stand without speaking to her. After Malcolm's burial I took possession of her ; she escaped to the wretched house, but as her mistress was off to Kingussie, and the door shut, she gave a pitiful howl or two, and was forthwith back at my door, with an impatient querulous bark. And so this is our second of the four ; and is she not deserving of as many names as any other Duchess, from her of Medina Sidonia downwards?

A fierier little soul never dwelt in a queerer or stauncher body : see her huddled up, and you would think her a bundle of hair, or a bit of old mossy wood, or a slice of heathery turf, with some red soil underneath ; but speak to her, or give her a cat to deal with, be it bigger than herself, and what an incarnation of affection, energy, and fury—what a fell unquenchable little ruffian !

The Maid of Lorn was a chestnut mare, a broken-down racer, thoroughbred as Beeswing, but less fortunate in her life, and I fear not so happy *occasione mortis :* unlike the Duchess, her body was greater and finer than her soul ; still she was a ladylike creature, sleek, slim, nervous, meek, willing, and fleet. She had been thrown down by some brutal half-drunk Forfarshire laird, when he put her wildly and with her wind gone, at the last hurdle on the North Inch at the Perth races. She was done for, and bought for ten pounds by the landlord of the Drummond Arms, Crieff, who had been taking as much money out of her, and putting as little corn into her as was compatible with life, purposing to run her for the Consolation Stakes at Stirling. Poor young lady, she was a sad sight—broken in back, in knees, in character, and wind—in everything but temper, which was as sweet and all-enduring as Penelope's or our own Enid's.

Of myself, the fourth, I decline making any account. Be it sufficient that I am the Dutchard's master, and drove the gig.

It was, as I said, a keen and bright morning, and the S. Q. N. feeling chilly, and the Duchess being away after a cat up a back entry, doing a chance stroke of business, and the mare looking only half breakfasted, I made them give her a full feed of meal and water, and stood by and enjoyed her enjoyment. It seemed too good to be true, and she looked up every now and then in the midst of her feast, with a mild wonder. Away she and I bowled down the sleeping village, all overrun with sunshine, the dumb idiot man and the birds alone up, for the ostler was off to his straw. There was the S. Q. N. and her small panting friend, who had lost the cat, but had got what philosophers say is better—the chase. '*Nous ne cherchons jamais les choses, mais la recherche des choses,*' says Pascal. The Duchess would substitute for *les choses—les chats.* Pursuit, not possession, was her passion. We all got in, and off set the Maid, who was in excellent heart, quite gay, pricking her ears and casting up her head, and rattling away at a great pace.

We baited at St. Fillans, and again cheered the heart of the Maid with unaccustomed corn—the S. Q. N., Duchie, and myself, going up to the beautiful rising ground at the back of the inn, and lying on the fragrant heather, looking at the Loch, with its mild gleams and shadows, and its second heaven looking out from its depths, the wild, rough mountains of Glenartney towering opposite. Duchie, I believe, was engaged in minor business close at hand, and caught and ate several large flies and a humble-bee ; she was very fond of this small game.

There is not in all Scotland, or as far as I have seen in all else, a more exquisite twenty miles of scenery than that between Crieff and the head of Lochearn. Ochtertyre, and its woods ; Benchonzie, the headquarters of the earthquakes, only lower than Benvorlich ; Strowan ; Lawers, with its grand old Scottish pines ; Comrie, with the wild Lednoch ; Dunira ; and St. Fillans, where we are now lying, and where the poor thoroughbred is tucking in her corn. We start after two hours of dreaming in the half sunlight, and ramble ever and anon over an earthquake, as the common folk call these same hollow, resounding rifts in the rock beneath, and arriving at the old inn at Lochearnhead, have a *tousie* tea. In the evening, when the day was darkening into night, Duchie and I,—the S. Q. N. remaining to read and rest,—walked up Glen Ogle. It was then in its primeval state, the new road non-existent, and the old one staggering up and down and across that most original and Cyclopean valley, deep, threatening, savage, and yet beautiful—

> ' Where rocks were rudely heaped, and rent
>   As by a spirit turbulent ;
>   Where sights were rough, and sounds were wild,
>   And everything unreconciled ; '

with flocks of mighty boulders, straying all over it. Some far up, and frightful to look at, others huddled down in the river, *immane pecus*, and one huge unloosened fellow, as big as a manse, up aloft watching them, like old Proteus with his calves, as if they had fled from the sea by stress of weather, and had been led by their ancient herd *altos visere montes*—a wilder, more ' unreconciled ' place I know not ; and now that the darkness was being poured into it, those big fellows looked bigger, and hardly 'canny.'

Just as we were turning to come home—Duchie

26

unwillingly, as she had much multifarious, and as usual fruitless hunting to do—she and I were startled by seeing a dog *in* the side of the hill, where the soil had been broken. She barked and I stared; she trotted consequentially up and snuffed *more canino,* and I went nearer : it never moved, and on coming quite close I saw as it were the *image* of a terrier, a something that made me think of an idea *un*realised ; the rough, short, scrubby heather and dead grass, made a colour and a coat just like those of a good Highland terrier—a sort of pepper and salt this one was—and below, the broken soil, in which there was some iron and clay, with old gnarled roots, for all the world like its odd, bandy, and sturdy legs. Duchie seemed not so easily unbeguiled as I was, and kept staring, and snuffing, and growling, but did not touch it,—seemed afraid. I left and looked again, and certainly it was very odd the *growing* resemblance to one of the indigenous, hairy, low-legged dogs, one sees all about the Highlands, terriers, or earthy ones.

We came home, and I told the S. Q. N. our joke. I dreamt of that visionary terrier, that son of the soil, all night ; and in the very early morning, leaving the S. Q. N. asleep, I walked up with the Duchess to the same spot. What a morning ! it was before sun-rise, at least before he had got above Benvorlich. The loch was lying in a faint mist, beautiful exceedingly, as if half veiled and asleep, the cataract of Edinample roaring less loudly than in the night, and the old castle of the Lords of Lochow, in the shadow of the hills, among its trees, might be seen

'Sole sitting by the shore of old romance.'

There was still gloom in Glen Ogle, though the beams of the morning were shooting up into the broad fields of the sky. I was looking back and down, when I heard the Duchess bark sharply, and then give a cry of fear, and on turning round, there was she with as much as she had of tail between her legs, where I never saw it before, and her small Grace, without noticing me or my cries, making down to the inn and her mistress, a hairy hurricane. I walked on to see what it was, and there in the same spot as last night, in the bank, was a real dog —no mistake; it was not, as the day before, a mere surface or *spectrum*, or ghost of a dog; it was plainly round and substantial; it was much developed since 8 P.M. As I looked, it moved slightly, and as it were by a sort of shiver, as if an electric shock (and why not?) was being administered by a law of nature; it had then no tail, or rather had an odd amorphous look in that region; its eye, for it had one—it was seen in profile—looked to my profane vision like (why not actually?) a huge blackberry (*vaccinium Myrtillus*, it is well to be scientific) black and full;

and I thought,—but dare not be sure, and had no time or courage to be minute,—that where the nose should be, there was a small shining black snail, probably the *Limax niger* of M. de Férussac, curled up, and if you look at any dog's nose you will be struck with the typical resemblance, in the corrugations and moistness and jetty blackness of the one to the other, and of the other to the one. He was a strongly-built, wiry, bandy, and short-legged dog. As I was staring upon him, a beam—Oh, first creative beam !—sent from the sun—

> ' Like as an arrow from a bow,
> Shot by an archer strong '—

as he looked over Benvorlich's shoulder, and piercing a cloudlet of mist which clung close to him, and filling it with whitest radiance, struck upon that eye or berry, and lit up that nose or snail : in an instant he sneezed (the *nisus* (*sneezus ?*) *formativus* of the ancients) ; that eye quivered and was quickened, and with a shudder—such as a horse executes with that curious muscle of the skin, of which we have a mere fragment in our neck, the *Platysma Myoides*, and which doubtless has been lessened as we lost our distance from the horse-type—which dislodged some dirt and stones and dead heather, and doubtless endless beetles, and, it may be, made some near weasel open his other eye, up went his tail, and out he came, lively, entire, consummate, *warm*, wagging his tail, I was going to say like a Christian, I mean like an ordinary dog. Then flashed upon me the solution of the *Mystery of Black and Tan* in all its varieties : the body, its upper part grey or black or yellow, according to the upper soil and herbs, heather, bent, moss, etc. ; the belly and feet, red or tan or light fawn, according to the nature of the deep soil, be it ochrey, ferruginous, light clay, or comminuted mica slate. And wonderfullest of all, the Dots of Tan above the eyes—and who has not noticed and wondered as to the philosophy of them ?—*I saw made* by the two fore feet, wet and clayey, being put briskly up to his eyes as he sneezed that genetic, vivifying sneeze, and leaving their mark for ever.

He took to me quite pleasantly, by virtue of 'natural selection,' and has accompanied me thus far in our 'struggle for life,' and he, and the S. Q. N., and the Duchess, and the Maid, returned that day to Crieff, and were friends all our days. I was a little timid when he was crossing a burn lest he should wash away his feet, but he merely coloured the water, and every day less and less, till in a fortnight I could wash him without fear of his becoming a *solution*, or fluid extract of dog, and thus resolving the mystery back into itself.

The mare's days were short. She won the Consolation Stakes at Stirling, and was found dead next morning in Gibb's stables. The Duchess died in a good old age, as may be seen in the history of 'Our Dogs.' The S. Q. N., and the parthenogenesic earth-born, the *Cespes Vivus*—whom we sometimes called Joshua, because he was the Son of None (Nun), and even Melchisedec has been whispered, but only that, and Fitz-Memnon, as being as it were a son of the Sun, sometimes the Autochthon αὐτό-χθονος (indeed, if the relation of the *coup de soleil* and the blaeberry had not been plainly causal and effectual, I might have called him *Filius Gunni*, for at the very moment of that shudder, by which he leapt out of non-life into life, the Marquis's gamekeeper fired his rifle up the hill, and brought down a stray young stag) ; these two are happily with me still, and at this moment she is out on the grass in a low easy chair, reading Emilie Carlen's *Brilliant Marriage*, and Dick is lying at her feet, watching, with cocked ears, some noise in the ripe wheat possibly a chicken, for, poor fellow, he has a weakness for worrying hens, and such small deer, when there is a dearth of greater. If any, as is not unreasonable, doubt me and my story, they may come and see Dick. I assure them he is well worth seeing.

E. V. K.

TO HIS FRIEND IN TOWN.

E. V. K.

TO HIS FRIEND IN TOWN.

THE following verses were written by my dear friend Andrew Coventry Dick—a member of the Scottish Bar, and for many years resident Sheriff of Bute—a man of the finest gifts and culture and affections, who, had his life not been maimed by long years of shattered health—bringing languor and suffering not to be recalled even now, without pain and wonder—he died in 1870—would have risen to the highest honours in his profession, and enriched literature with his wise and lively thought.

He was the author of two small Treatises, which, in the opinion of good judges, contain the essence of the questions they take up : one 'A Dissertation on Church Polity,' the calmest and most thorough vindication of what is called Voluntaryism I ever read ; the other, 'On the Nature and Office of the State,' in which 'the things that are Cæsar's' are clearly indicated. The verses are dated from Rothesay, and the letters E. V. K. stand for Edward Vincorcy Kent, which, Southey-like, he made out of his own name. Mightn't any man wish he had written that line, 'Dear prisoned spirits of the impassioned grape'? Some extracts from them have appeared in a paper on Vaughan's Poems, &c.

I SENT you late an urgent note, to pray
Your gladd'ning presence here some early day :—
You answered, yes ! But weeks have come and gone,
And still sad Rothesay waits th' unfaithful John.
You plead that business hinders : but the Muse,
Like knowing banker, won't discount th' excuse.
'Business !' she cries, 'if doctors plead their trade,
They may break every promise they have made;
There's always some one sickening : like a river
Disease flows down for ever and for ever ;
And is your friend a simple swain who stands
Till the lapsed stream shall leave him dryshod sands?
Nay, rather know him like those ancient Jews
Who neither wished to go nor to refuse,
And therefore conjured up a grave excuse :—
Now 'tis his wife—she can't be left alone ;
Now 'tis the *weans;* now business to be done.
The words are good ; but lifting up this blind
Of fair pretences, what's the truth behind ?
That nought detains the urger of these pleas,
But dinners, suppers, plays, and dancing teas.'

Thus speaks the Muse ;—but Muses *Pagan* be,
And *Christian* men should list to Charity.
That will I do : of you, I 'll *think no ill*,
Believe you could not come, and that you will come
     still.

O speed your coming !—Though its charms be few,
The place will please you, and may profit too ;
My house, upon the hillside built, looks down
On a neat harbour and a lively town.
Apart, 'mid screen of trees, it stands, just where
We see the popular bustle, but not share.
Full in our front is spread a varied scene—
A royal ruin, grey or clothed with green,
Church spires, tower, docks, streets, terraces, and
     trees,
Backed by green fields, which mount by due
     degrees
Into brown uplands, stretching high away
To where, by silent tarns, the wild deer stray.
Below, with gentle tide, the Atlantic Sea
Laves the curved beach, and fills the cheerful quay,
Where frequent glides the sail, and dips the oar,
And smoking steamer halts with hissing roar.
Thence lift your gaze, and to the right away,
The long recess of Striven Loch survey,
Whose girdling mountains, and whose tranquil seas,
Oft change their hues and shade, but ever please ;

Or, turning to the left, with straining eye
Through trees now bare, and o'er Loch Fad descry
Arran's peaked grandeur in the distant sky.

'Tis well, you say, but this is Winter time,
And folks look *hearthward* then in Scottish clime;
Fair shows without have wondrous little charm,
Unless the man within's well fed and warm.
True, I reply, and though I may not vaunt,
I think you'll suffer here nor cold nor want.
Not unattempted, sure, has been the expelling
Of the chill fiend, Discomfort, from our dwelling.
He's driven forth.   With all may keep him out
We've largely ammunitioned the redoubt;
And on the *qui vive*'s all the garrison
To hold for you the conquest we have won.

Lo! that high officer, big Kate the cook,
With brow all puckered, and most studious look;
She strictly meditates your table fare—
Hence her staid gait, and hence her anxious air.
Provident soul! already she has bound
In solemn treaty, half the country round,
The best of barns, byres, shops, and stands, and stalls,
To answer prompt her culinary calls:
New milk, fresh butter, tender fowls, fresh eggs—
Beef, mutton, veal, in chops, steaks, loins and legs,
Saddles and breasts—with fish of fin and shell,
Hams, tongues, game, venison, more than I can tell;

Besides, whate'er the grocery or the field,
Of spice, preserves, sauce, roots, fruits, stocks may
     yield—
All are bespoke.—With these, and with her skill,
Native, or learned from Soyer's Oracle,
She waits the day—all hopeful she may share
A festal triumph,—lolling on your chair,
(While from the table, Mary bears away
The ruined feast)—may hear you loudly say,
With smacks emphatic—' I have dined to-day!'

Lo! too, my Sister! conscious of the event,
Through her press-stores a searching glance has sent,
Unfolds and tests the packets which contain
What China's shrub yields, and the Indian cane;
And breaking up the soldierly array
Of jams and jellies, bears the best away,
Doomed—with a fragrant honeycomb—to be
Reft of sweet life at breakfast and at tea.
Then to the bedroom region, slow ascending,
(Obedient Mary at her heels attending,)
Settles by trial and reflection deep,
The nice arrangements of the hall of sleep;
And still to Mary anxious charge repeats,
Duly to dust its carpets, air the sheets,
Rightly to slope the mattress, trim the fire,
Blazing or glimmering just as you desire.

And I myself have looked into a bin
Of glass-bound brandy, whiskey, rum, and gin:

Of these, and those, different, though like in shape,
Dear prisoned spirits of th' impassioned grape,
Have noted which for you to disenthral,
And some fresh claret bought to crown the festival.

And here, methinks, that having lost all fear
Of lacking *creature*-comforts while you 're here,
You reassume the philosophic air,
And say, 'The body's *not* my chiefest care,'
Polite negation ! which affirms you think—
'My *soul* is not so sure of meat and drink—
Does not this Bute in Intellect's Arctic lie,
A rock of tempest, ice, and poverty,
"A dreary void at once of books and men,"
(To use a scrap (I think) of Churchill's pen,)
Thither from hence ? as kindly bid me go,
From genial Kashmeer's warmth to Boothia's snow.'

The tender townsman, used to breathe hot air,
To feed on spice, and gaze through gassy glare,—
At first, when from such pamperdom exiled,
Shrinks from a homelier life, as bleak and wild.
But tried awhile, he finds, with glad surprise,
It is not purgat'ry, but paradise,
All rife with joys ; and joys, which while they bless,
Strengthen his frame, not weaken by excess.
Your present home, our famed metropolis,
A very hotbed of the Intellect is ;

And you, its inmates, forced and fevered, shoot
Ten thousand overgrowths of flower and fruit ;
A brilliant show, but rotten at the core—
A blazing fire, mere ashes when 'tis o'er.
Say, can the mind be hale, be clear, be strong,
Which ferments in that stimulating throng?
Which compassed with blue women and pale men,
Each armed with tongue, brush, chisel, style, or pen,
Producers each of little wondrous things,
And cackling each, as forth his egg he brings—
Is forced to flutter to each offered flower,
And drink a drug of nostrums every hour?
No, 'hang it,' no ! Blank solitude is bad ;
But these pestiferous crowds, they turn men mad.
Insaned by them, the souls whom nature taught,
To keep, discreet, the pace of sober thought,
Must do some feat to startle and astound :
So, dervish-like, one whirligigs around,
One somersets, one stands upon his head—
The applauded antics through the circle spread,
Till none but shows some posture or grimace,
Twisting his limbs, or grinning on his face.
Even he, my friend, the man whom once I knew,
Loving with single mind the fair and true,
Even he perchance, by that contagion smit,
A peering critic prowls, or struts a wit,
Or as a frantic poet prances round,
Or stalks a sage in reverie profound—

Playing a part, and so he draw the gaze
Of fools, contented with the part he plays.
Ah! how unlike (if thus) his earnest youth!
Its artless joy in beauty, thirst for truth,
Its scorn of false praise; its resolvèd aim
On deathless works to build a lofty name,
And take an equal throne among the gods of fame.

Yet, if unchanged (and as I write, I hear
Indignant friendship chide the unduteous fear,)
Since still the same.——
——But, hark that sound! the mavis! can it be?
Once more! It is. High perched on yon bare tree,
He starts the wondering winter with his trill;
Or by that sweet sun westering o'er the hill
Allured, or for he thinks melodious mirth
Due to the holy season of Christ's birth.——
And hark! as his clear fluting fills the air,
Low broken notes and twitterings you may hear
From other emulous birds, the brakes among:
Fain would they also burst into a song;
But winter warns, and muffling up their throats,
They liquid—for the spring—preserve their notes.
O sweet preluding! having heard that strain,
How dare I lift my dissonant voice again?
Let me be still, let me enjoy the time,
Bothering myself or John no more with rugged rhyme.

E. V. K.

December 28th, 1847.

SIR HENRY RAEBURN.

SIR HENRY RAEBURN.[1]

SIR HENRY RAEBURN is the greatest of Scottish portrait-painters. Others may have painted one or more as excellent portraits: we have Sir George Harvey's Mrs. Horn—a veritable *Mater Scotorum*—and his Professor Wilson, and my father, the property of Mrs. Jas. Crum; Duncan's Dr. Chalmers and his magical likeness of himself; Geddes's Wilkie, so finely engraved in brown by Ward, also his old 'Sicily' Brydone reclining on his sofa—an exquisite piece—and his own 'couthy' old mother; the Provost of Peterhead by Sir John Watson Gordon; 'The Man of Feeling' by Colvin Smith; and Dr. Wardlaw by Macnee;[2] but none of

[1] Prefixed to a volume of ' Portraits of Sir Henry Raeburn.' Folio. Edin. 1874.

[2] I had just come from this excellent man's burial when the proof of this came in. He was a good painter, a great humourist, an incomparable *raconteur*, and a most loveable man—as unaffected as when I saw him fifty and more years ago, or as his own Touch Hills; and who ever saw and heard ' The hat,' or 'The gamekeeper's ghost story,' or his tremendous 'Sam Bough's railway journey to Port-Glasgow,' and indeed any of his perfect stories, can ever forget or tell them?—it is a lost delight and wonder.—[Jan. 21, 1882.]

these have given to the world such a profusion of masterpieces. Indeed, Sir Henry's name may stand with those of the world's greatest men in this department of Art—Titian and Tintoretto, Vandyck and Rubens, Velasquez and Rembrandt, Sir Joshua, Gainsborough, and Hogarth (witness his Captain Coram). There is a breadth and manliness, a strength and felicity of likeness and of character, and a simplicity and honesty of treatment, which are found only in men of primary genius.

Of the great masters of portraiture, Velasquez is the one whom Raeburn most resembles. Wilkie,— a first-rate Art critic,—writing from Madrid, where one must go to feel the full power of the great Spaniard, says, ' There is much resemblance between him and the works of some of the chiefs of the English school ; but of all, Raeburn resembles him most, in whose square touch in heads, hands, and accessories I see the very counterpart in Velasquez.' Nothing can be happier than the expression ' square touch' as characteristic of the handling of both, and with Raeburn it must have been like-mindedness, not imitation, as there is no reason to think he saw almost any of the works of this great master.

Raeburn stands nearly alone among the great portrait-painters, in having never painted anything else. This does not prove that he was without the ideal faculty. No man can excel as a portrait-painter—no man can make the soul look out from a face, who wants it. Richmond pleasantly put it, and truly, to Professor Syme, when he first showed him the drawing of himself, well known by Holl's engraving; the great surgeon, after scrutinising it with his keen and honest eyes, exclaimed, laughing, 'Yes, it is like; but then—it is good-looking!' 'Ah! you see,' said the artist, 'we do it *lovingly*.' The best likeness of a man should be the ideal of him realised. As Coleridge used to say, 'A great portrait should be liker than its original;' it should contain more of the best, more of the essence of the man than ever was in any one living look. In these two qualities Raeburn always is strong; he never fails in giving a likeness at once vivid, unmistakeable, and pleasing. He paints the truth, and he paints it in love.

This eminent Scotsman was born in Stockbridge, on the Water of Leith—now a part of Edinburgh—on the 4th of March 1756. His ancestors were of the sturdy Border stock—reiving, pastoral lairds—and probably took their name from Raeburn, a hill-farm in Annandale still held by Sir Walter Scott's kinsfolk.[1] Raeburn was left an orphan at six, and was educated in Heriot's Hospital or 'Wark,' as it

[1] His grandson tells me that Sir Henry used to say he was a Raeburn of that Ilk—his forebears having had it before the Scotts, whose it is now. His crest is a Rae or Roe deer.

was called. He is one of the curiously few of those brought up in this Scottish Christ's Hospital who became distinguished in after life—a contrast to the scholars of the great London School. At fifteen he was apprenticed to a goldsmith. He early showed his turn for Art. He caricatured his comrades, and by and bye, without any teaching, made beautiful miniatures of his friends. After his time was out, he set himself entirely to portrait-painting, giving up miniature, and passing from its delicacies and minuteness at once to his bold 'square touch' in oil. He had to teach himself everything,—drawing, the composition of colours, in which doubtless he employed largely Opie's well-known mixture, 'With Brains, Sir.' About this time the young Herioter became acquainted with the famous cynic, lawyer, and wit, John Clerk, afterwards Lord Eldin, then a young advocate, fond of pictures and of painting, in which he had some of that family gift which in the case of Mrs. Blackburn has blossomed out into such rare and exquisite work. Allan Cunningham tells a good story of this time. Both were then poor. Young Clerk asked Raeburn to dine at his lodgings. Coming in, he found the landlady laying the cloth and setting down two dishes, one containing three herrings, and the other three potatoes. 'Is this a'?' said John. 'Ay, it's a'!' 'A'! didn't I tell ye, wumman, that a gentleman is to dine wi' me, and that ye were to get six herrin' and six potatoes ?'

When twenty-two, the following romantic incident, as told by Allan Cunningham, occurred :—' One day a young lady presented herself at his studio, and desired to sit for her portrait ; he instantly remembered having seen her in some of his excursions, when, with his sketch-book in his hand, he was noting down fine snatches of scenery ; and as the appearance of anything living and lovely gives an additional charm to a landscape, the painter, like Gainsborough in similar circumstances, had admitted her readily into his drawing.' He found that she had, besides beauty, sensibility and wit—he fell in love with his sitter, and made a very fine portrait, now at Charlesfield. The lady, Ann Edgar, daughter of the Laird of Bridgelands, became in a month after this his wife, bringing him a good fortune, good sense, and an affectionate heart. He now resolved to visit London and improve himself in his art. He was introduced to Sir Joshua, and often told how the great painter counselled him to go to Rome and worship Michael Angelo in the Sistine Chapel, and study his ' *terribile via*,' and how in parting he said, ' Young man, I know nothing of your circumstances—young painters are seldom rich— but if money be necessary for your studies abroad, say so, and you shall not want it.' There is little

record of his life at Rome. Byres, Barry's antago-
nist, gave him an advice he ever after followed, and
often spoke of : ' Never paint any object from
memory, if you can get it before your eyes.'

From his return to Edinburgh until his death, his
life was busy, happy, and victorious. Full of work,
eager, hospitable, faithful in his friendships, homely
in his habits, he was one of the best-liked men of
his time. The following is Cunningham's account
of him :—' Though his painting-rooms were in York
Place, his dwelling-house was at St. Bernard's, near
Stockbridge, overlooking the Water of Leith—a
romantic place. The steep banks were then finely
wooded ; the garden grounds varied and beautiful ;
and all the seclusion of the country could be enjoyed,
without the remoteness. The motions of the artist
were as regular as those of a clock. He rose at
seven during summer, took breakfast about eight
with his wife and children, walked up to his great
room in 32 York Place, now occupied by Colvin
Smith, R.S.A., and was ready for a sitter by nine ;
and of sitters he generally had, for many years, not
fewer than three or four a day. To these he gave
an hour and a half each. He seldom kept a sitter
more than two hours ; unless the person happened—
and that was often the case—to be gifted with more
than common talents. He then felt himself happy,
and never failed to detain the party till the arrival of

a new sitter intimated that he must be gone. For a head size he generally required four or five sittings : and he preferred painting the head and hands to any other part of the body : assigning as a reason that they required least consideration. A fold of drapery, or the natural ease which the casting of a mantle over the shoulder demanded, occasioned him more perplexing study than a head full of thought and imagination. Such was the intuition with which he penetrated at once to the mind, that the first sitting rarely came to a close without his having seized strongly on the character and disposition of the individual. He never drew in his heads, or indeed any part of the body, with chalk—a system pursued successfully by Lawrence ; but began with the brush at once. The forehead, chin, nose, and mouth were his first touches. He always painted standing, and never used a stick for resting his hand on ; for such was his accuracy of eye, and steadiness of nerve, that he could introduce the most delicate touches, or the utmost mechanical regularity of line, without aid, or other contrivance than fair off-hand dexterity. He remained in his painting-room till a little after five o'clock, when he walked home, and dined at six.'

One of his sitters thus describes him :—' He spoke a few words to me in his usual brief and kindly way —evidently to put me into an agreeable mood ; and then, having placed me in a chair on a platform at the end of his painting-room, in the posture required, set up his easel beside me with the canvas ready to receive the colour. When he saw all was right, he took his palette and his brush, retreated back step by step, with his face towards me, till he was nigh the other end of his room; he stood and studied for a minute more, then came up to the canvas, and, without looking at me, wrought upon it with colour for some time. Having done this, he retreated in the same manner, studied my looks at that distance for about another minute, then came hastily up to the canvas and painted a few minutes more. I had sat to other artists; their way was quite different— they made an outline carefully in chalk, measured it with compasses, placed the canvas close to me, and looking me almost without ceasing in the face, proceeded to fill up the outline with colour. They succeeded best in the minute detail—Raeburn best in the general result of the expression; they obtained by means of a multitude of little touches what he found by broader masses; they gave more of the man—he gave most of the mind.'

'Like Sir Joshua, he placed his sitters on a high platform, shortening the features, and giving a pigeon-hole view of the nostrils. The notion is that people should be painted as if they were hanging like pictures on the wall, a Newgate notion, but it was Sir Joshua's. Raeburn and I have had good-humoured disputes about this : I appealed to Titian, Vandyck, etc., for my authorities ; they always painted people as if they were sitting opposite to them, not on a mountebank stage, or dangling on the wall.'

This great question we leave to be decided by those who know best. His manner of taking his likenesses explains the simplicity and power of his heads. Placing his sitter on the pedestal, he looked at him from the other end of a long room, gazing at him intently with his great dark eyes. Having got the idea of the man, what of him carried furthest and 'told,' he walked hastily up to the canvas, never looking at his sitter, and put down what he had fixed in his inner eye ; he then withdrew again, took another gaze, and recorded its results, and so on, making no measurements. His hands are admirably drawn, full of expression, and evidently portraits. He was knighted by George the Fourth at Hopetoun House, and made His Majesty's Limner for Scotland soon after. He was a Royal Academician for some years before his death, and Member of the Academies of New York and South Carolina, as well as of Florence and Athens.

Sir Henry died, after a short illness, on the 8th of July 1823, beloved and honoured by all.[1] 'Honest

---

[1] He is buried in the mortuary of St. John's, Edinburgh, but to our shame there is not a word to say where he lies.

Allan' sums up his personal character thus :—' The character of Raeburn appears to have been every way unblemished ; he was a candid modest man, ever ready to aid merit, and give a helping hand to genius in art. His varied knowledge, his agreeable manners, his numerous anecdotes, and his general conversation, at once easy and unaffected, with now and then a touch of humorous gaiety, made him a delightful companion ; he told a Scotch story with almost unrivalled *naïveté* of effect, and did the honours of a handsome house and elegant table with all the grace of a high-bred gentleman. Through life he discharged, with blameless attention, all the duties of a good citizen. His pencil never kept him from his place in church on Sunday, and in the days of trouble he was a zealous volunteer. First and last, among all the children of art no one was ever more widely respected than Sir Henry Raeburn ; and his tall, handsome figure, and fine open manly countenance, will not be forgotten for many a day in "the place which knew him." '

The remarkable collection of Photographs from Raeburn's Portraits now given in this volume, though wanting the charm of colour, and most of them from engravings—-masterly indeed, but still inexpressive in some degree of the full power and sweetness of the original—gives us a good sample of this great master's faculty of rendering the human countenance. Judging from those we know, we may say that the cardinal virtue of making a strong, true likeness is pre-eminent in Raeburn's work; he seizes the essential features and expression, which make the man to differ from all other men; and he gives the best of him. Take that of Dr. Nathaniel Spens as a Royal Archer; we do not know a nobler portrait; look at his eye, at his firm legs, at his gloved hands, at the cock of his bonnet. At his feet is a sturdy Scotch thistle, bristling all over with *Nemo me.* This great picture is done to the quick, tense with concentrated action, and that arrow, 'shot by an archer strong,' you know the next instant will be off and home. There is true genius here. This picture is now in Archers' Hall; we grudge them it—it should be seen of all men.

There is Dr. Adam of the High School—the perfection of a Rector—firm, reasonable, loving. The holding out the hand to still the unseen boys brings to mind that fine story of him when dying: lifting up his thin hand he said—'But it grows dark, boys; you may go.' Then there is Scott, sitting on ruins, his dog Camp—the English bull-terrier on whose death-day he wrote saying he could not dine out, because 'a very dear friend' had died—at his feet; the stern old keep of Hermitage in the distance—was there ever a more poetic picture of a poet? Look at his child-mouth—his rapt, brooding eyes, seeing things invisible, peopling the past. Camp with his unreflex, animal eyes is looking, as only dogs look, into the visible and the near. What cares he for knights of old and minstrelsy and glamourye? he is snuffing up some possible *foumart*, or watching the twinkling *fud* of a vanishing rabbit. The *replica* of this portrait has in it two favourite greyhounds of Sir Walter, 'Douglas' and 'Percy,' and the Braes of Yarrow for the background.

Then look at Sir Harry Moncreiff. What a thorough gentleman—what a broad, sunny-hearted Churchman! Look at the hands, how expressive! Again, there's Professor Robison. Did you ever see a dressing-gown so glorified? and the nightcap, and the look of steady speculation in the eyes—a philosopher all over.

John Tait and Grandson. Mr. Tait was grandfather to the present Archbishop of Canterbury, and the little *mannie* gazing at the watch is the present Sheriff of Perthshire.

There is another of Scott—quite different but very fine—the bluff, cordial man of the world—with his pleasant mouth that has a *burr* in it. This must have been done in his prime.

Francis Horner—gentle and immovable—the Ten Commandments written all over his face, as Sydney Smith said.

John Clerk, his 'herrin'' friend, ugly and snuffy, shrewd and subtle; the crouching Venus among the law-papers—beautifully drawn—indicating John's love of Art.

Archibald Constable, the handsome, buirdly bookseller of genius, to whom the world owes more of its enjoyment from Scott than it is aware of, and to whose powers and worth and true place in the literature of this century, his son, I rejoice to see, has done a long-delayed act of justice and of filial affection, and done it well.

Lord Newton, full-blooded, full-brained, taurine with potential vigour. His head is painted with a Rabelaisian richness; you cannot but believe, when you look at the vast countenance, the tales of his feats in thinking and in drinking, and in general capacity of body and of mind.

Jamie Balfour, in the act of singing 'When I hae a saxpence under my thoom.' You hear the refrain —'Toddlin' hame, toddlin' hame, round as a neep she cam' toddlin' hame.' Mr. Melville of Hanley, with whom have perished so many of the best Edinburgh stories, used to tell how he got this picture, which for many years hung and sang in his hospitable dining-room. It was bought, at the selling off of the effects of the old Leith Golf-House, by a drunken old *caddy*, for 30s. Mr. Melville heard of this, went to the ancient creature, and got it for 40s. and two bottles of whisky. James Stuart of Dunearn offered him (Mr. Melville) £80 and two pipes of wine for it, but in vain. Sir David Wilkie coveted it also, and promised to pay for it by a picture of his own, but died before this was fulfilled.

Raeburn's own portrait—handsome, kindly, full of genius. How is it that all painters glorify themselves so delightfully? Look at Vandyck, Nicolas Poussin, Hogarth, Rubens, Sir Joshua, and our own Duncan.

Like Sir Joshua, Raeburn has been well engraved on the whole. The number of his engraved portraits is remarkable, greater than any British painter except Reynolds. Mr. Drummond had 125, and there may be ten or fifteen more. Beugo's vigorous and crisp graver has rendered worthily Dr. Spens, 'lord of the unerring bow;' and Charles Turner's brown mezzotint of Sir Walter, and those of Sir Harry Moncreiff and Professor Jardine and Robison, and many others, and Walker's stippling of Lord Hopetoun and Scott, are masterpieces of their art. There is also one head in line by the famous Sharpe, besides Ward (painter of the famous Bull) in mezzotint.

Raeburn is generally said to have failed in painting ladies. I think this a mistake. He certainly is mainly a painter of men; but this arose very much from his having more men than women as sitters.

Can anything be more homely—more like a Scottish *gudewife*, more *auld-farrant*—than Mrs. Hamilton, the author of *The Cottagers of Glenburnie* and 'Mrs. M'Clarty' and 'I canna be fash'd,'—what sweeter, more 'full of all blessed conditions,' than Mrs. Scott Moncrieff, now in our National Gallery, and one of the loveliest female portraits we know? as also is Mrs. Gregory, now in Canaan Lodge, a beautiful woman and picture, and Mrs. Kennedy, mother of the staunch intrepid old Whig of Dunure.

I shall mention only one other portrait, it is of the true heroic type—the full-length of Lord Duncan, in the Trinity House of Leith, which might without misgiving hang alongside of Sir Joshua's Lord Heathfield, holding the key of Gibraltar in his hand. It is, as we have said, a heroic picture. The hero of Camperdown and captor of De Winter is standing at a table with his left hand resting on the finger-tips— a favourite posture with Raeburn; the right hanging quietly at his side and its distended veins painted to the life. It is the incarnation of quiet, cheerful, condensed power and command. The eyes, bright, almost laughing and at their ease—the mouth, fixed beyond change, almost grim,—the whole man instinct with will and reserved force. The colouring is exquisite, and the picture in perfect condition.

I end with the following excellent estimate of

28

Raeburn's merits as an artist :—' His style was free
and bold, his colouring rich, deep, and harmonious.
He had a peculiar power of rendering the head of
his figure bold, prominent, and imposing. The
strict fidelity of his representations may in a great
degree be attributed to his invariable custom of
painting, whether the principal figure or the minutest
accessory, from the person or the thing itself—never
giving a single touch from memory or conjecture.
It has been judiciously said that all who are con-
versant with the practice of the Art must have observed how often the spirit which gave life and vigour
to a first sketch has gradually evaporated as the
picture advanced to its more finished state. To
preserve the spirit, combined with the evanescent
delicacies and blendings which nature on minute
inspection exhibits, constitutes a perfection of art to
which few have attained. If the works of Sir Henry
Raeburn fail to exhibit this rare combination in that
degree, to this distinction they will always have a
just claim, that they possess a freedom, a vigour, and
a spirit of effect, and carry an impression of grace,
life, and reality, which may be looked for in vain
amidst thousands of pictures, both ancient and
modern, of more elaborate execution and minute
finish.' He recorded men rather as Fielding than
as Richardson,—had they handled the brush instead
of the pen,—would have done ; still the perfection

is when both qualities are at their best in one man, as in Da Vinci and Titian and Holbein.

Since writing the above I have been to Charles-field, the residence of Sir Henry's grandson, L. W. Raeburn. I wish I had been there before. It is a snug, old Scotch house near Mid-Calder, on a burn of its own, which paraffin has defiled with its stench and prismatic films. I shall never forget it, nor the kindness of the three friends—who showed me their cherished treasures, and who inherit the simplicity, heartiness, and glowing, rich eyes of their grand-father. The house is overrun with the choicest Raeburns.

In the lobby there is a big man, as many stones weight as the Claimant, who is handed down as an Irish Duke. Then there is Francis Jeffrey when in his prime—very fine—keen and kindly, the beautiful, sweet, mobile mouth, the rich, brown eyes. A head of the Duke of Gordon—finished and noble. There was a comico-tragic story attached to this. The head was once on a full-length body in the Highland dress; there being so little room in the house, or rather so many pictures in it, this, the last Duke of Gordon, the 'Cock of the North,' was put in the nursery, and my friend the master of the house said, ashamedly, that he and his brother used to send sundry pennies through the person of his Grace, and shot arrows plentifully into his sporran, and all over him, so much so that the body had to be destroyed. Our friend is penitent to this day. In the lobby are several of the animal-painter Howe's spirited oil sketches of cart-horses and ploughmen, full of rough genius and 'go.' In the dining-room are the heads of his familiars—whose full portraits he had done—painted from love and for himself. I question if any such record of pictorial genius and friendship exists. The walls are literally covered. There is Cockburn with his melancholy, wonderful eye, with a joke far in; Skirving, the crayon portrait-painter, full of fire and temper, fit son of the man who wrote 'Hey, Johnnie Cope' and challenged one of his affronted troopers to combat.

Rennie, the great engineer—the large, powerful, constructive *beaver*-like face of the inspired millwright of East Linton.

Professor Dalzel—exquisite for delicate, refined expression and sweetness—the *lactea ubertas* of the dear old man,—his *Analecta Majora* and *Minora* lying on the table.

Besides many others, over the fireplace is a life-size portrait of Mr. Byres of Tonley,[1] whom we have mentioned as at Rome with Raeburn; this was painted long after, and is of the first quality, done with the utmost breadth of felicity. The ruffles of his shirt are still of dazzling whiteness, as if bleached

[1] He was the cicerone of Gibbon in Rome.

by the burn-side. At the fireside is a small head of
Ferguson the poet, by Runciman—intense and painful, the eyes full of perilous light and coming frenzy,
—in colour dingy beside the glow of Raeburn. It is
not the same portrait as the one engraved in his
works, also by Runciman. In a bedroom is Professor
Playfair—very fine ; Mr. Edgar ; and a most curious
.portrait of Raeburn's son and his horse : the horse
is by Sir Henry — strong, real, perfectly drawn
the son, painted after his father's death, s by John
Syme, remembered by some of us for his wooden
pictures. Anything more ludicrous than the strength
of the horse's portrait and the weakness of the man's
I never saw ; it is like meeting with a paragraph by
the worthy Tupper, or some other folk we know, in
a page of Thackeray or Swift. A comical incongruity of the same kind was shown to me by Mr.
James Drummond, R.S.A., who knew and had so
many things that nobody else had or knew. It is
the record of a clever dodge. Mr. Hatton, the
printseller, had a fine print of Dr. Thomas Hope,
Professor of Chemistry in the University,—whose
only joke, by the bye, I well remember, and apply
it, sometimes to other than gaseous bodies,—when
lecturing upon hydrogen, he used to end with ' In
fact, gentlemen, in regard to this remarkable body,
we may almost say that it is possessed of absolute
levity.' Well, Hatton, when George the Fourth

came to Scotland, and we were all mad about him, from Sir Walter downwards, having made his utmost out of the plate as Dr. Hope, scraped his head out and put in that of the bewigged and becurled 'First Gentleman in Europe.' The rest of the plate remains unchanged, except the royal arms on the book, and the Star of the Garter on the Doctor's breast! Dr. Hope had not much of the heroic in his face or nature, but his head by Raeburn keeps its own and more against that of His Most Gracious Majesty—by Mr. Hatton; it is altogether one of the best of jokes. Maxwell of Pollok—the head finished on the naked canvas—amazing freshness and vigour, as if done at a heat. Henry Mackenzie, 'The Man of Feeling'——very fine.

Up-stairs on the landing, Lady in green silk pelisse, through whose body had gone another nursery penny, now neatly healed.

Mrs. Vere of Stonebyres, Sir Henry's stepdaughter, lying asleep, her head on a pillow—a very fine study.

My eye was arrested by a portrait above a door; it was the head and neck, life-size, of a young man of great beauty. This, my friends told me, was the portrait of Peter Raeburn, Sir Henry's eldest son, painted by himself, when he knew he was dying of consumption, and given by him to his mother! His father used to say that if he had lived he would have far surpassed him.

The drawing-room is crowded with perfections. When you enter, above the fireplace is his own incomparable portrait, than which—as our President of the Royal Academy says—no better portrait exists : it glorifies the little room, and is in perfect condition ; the engraving gives no full idea of the glow of the great dark eyes, the mastery of touch, the ardour and power of the whole expression. Opposite him is his dear little wife, comely and sweet and wise, sitting in the open air with a white head-dress, her face away to one side of the picture, her shapely, bare, unjewelled arms and hands lying crossed on her lap.

Boy with cherry—very like Reynolds. Then there is another funny incongruity : Mrs. Raeburn, his son's wife, a woman of great beauty, a sister of that true humourist to whom we owe 'Sir Frizzle Pumpkin,' and much else—the Rev. James White—is sitting with two young Edgars at her knees. Her head and bust are by Sir J. Watson Gordon, the youngsters by Raeburn, and oh ! the difference !

Dr. Andrew Thomson, the great preacher and ecclesiastical pugilist—very powerful.

Next him, in the corner, is the gem of all, a little oval picture of Eliza Raeburn, his eldest granddaughter, who died at six ; there she is—lovely, her lucid blue eyes, her snowy bosom, her little mouth, just open enough to indicate the milk-white teeth, the sunny hair, the straightforward gaze, the sweetness! It is not possible to give in words the beauty of this; Correggio or Giorgione need not have been ashamed of it, and there is a depth of human expression I have never seen in them; she was her grandfather's darling, and she must be of every one who looks at her, though she has been fifty years in her grave.

Thomson of Duddingston—heavy and strong.

I was confirmed by the grandchildren as to the simple, frank, hearty nature of the man, his friendliness and cheery spirit, his noble presence—six feet two—and his simple, honest pleasures and happy life.

I am indebted to Mrs. Ferrier, widow of Professor Ferrier of St. Andrews, and eldest daughter of Professor Wilson, the renowned 'Christopher North,' for the following recollections of St. Bernard's House and the Raeburn family. She was then about six years of age. Our first parents 'skelpin' aboot' before the Fall, and before 'Shelly' in his old white hat, is a great idea.

'More than half a century ago I was frequently in my childhood at St. Bernard's House, on the banks of the Water of Leith, which were in those days green and smooth to the river's edge. This old house was reached by a broad avenue of trees and shrubbery from Ann Street, where we lived for some years; this would be about 1820. This interesting old house was surrounded by large green fields, a fine orchard of apple and pear trees, and leading from this was another avenue of old stately elms, part of which still remain with the rookery in St. Bernard's Crescent. On the right hand of this avenue was a nice old garden, well stocked, and with hot-houses.

' In this ancient mansion lived the Raeburn family, with whom we were very intimate as children and likewise school companions, though there were some years between our ages. Sir Henry and Lady Raeburn, and their son and his wife, with three children, comprised the family party at this time. The great portrait-painter, as far as I can recollect him, had a very impressive appearance, his full, dark, lustrous eyes, with ample brow and dark hair, at this time somewhat scant. His tall, large frame had a dignified aspect. I can well remember him, seated in an arm-chair in the evening, at the fireside of the small drawing-room, newspaper in his hand, with his family around him. His usual mode of address to us when spending the evenings, while he held out his hand with a kind smile, was "Well, my dears, what is your opinion of things in general to-day?" These words always filled us with consternation, and we all huddled together like a flock of scared sheep, vainly attempting some answer by gazing from one to the other; and with what delight and sense of freedom we were led away to be seated at the tea-table, covered with cookies, bread and butter and jelly! From this place of security we stole now and then a fearful glance at the arm-chair in which Sir Henry reclined. After tea we were permitted to go away for play to another room, where we made as much noise as we liked, and generally managed to disturb old Lady Raeburn, not far from the drawing-room, where we had all been at tea on our best behaviour, in the presence of her great husband. This old lady was quite a character, and always spoke in broad Scotch, then common among the old families, now extinct. I can never forget the manner in which we uproarious creatures tormented her, flinging open the door of her snug little room, whither she had fled for a little quiet from our incessant provocations and unwearied inventions at amusement, which usually reached the climax by throwing bed-pillows at her and nearly smothering her small figure. At this juncture she would rise up, and, opening the door of a cupboard, would bring out of it a magnificent bunch of grapes, which she endeavoured to divide among us with these words of entreaty, 'Hoot, hoot, bairns, here's some grapes for ye; noo gang awa' an' behave yersels like gude bairns, an' dinna deave me ony mair.' For a short time the remedy effected a lull in the storm, which,

at the least hint, was ready to set in with renewed
vigour. She would then throw out of a wardrobe
shawls, turbans, bonnets, and gear of all sorts and
colours, in which we arrayed ourselves to hold our
court, Anne Raeburn being very often our Queen.
Beyond the walls of the house we used to pass hours
of a sunny forenoon in drawing a yellow child's
coach, which held two of us, who were as usual
enveloped in shawls and decorated with feathers and
flowers for our masquerading. There was a black
pony; I remember well its being led up and down
the long avenue by an old nurse with some one of
the Raeburn children on it. When we were in
quieter moods at play we used to go up four or five
steps at the end of the passage leading to the great
drawing-room, which was seldom entered except on
company days. We children never quite felt at our
ease when we stealthily opened the door of this
large apartment; we imagined there might be a
ghost somewhere. There was a curious old beggar-
man, I must not forget to mention, who was fed and
supported by the family, by name Barclay, *alias*
SHELLY, so called not from the poet, but from his
shelling the peas, and who lived in some outhouse.
This old creature was half-witted, and used to sweep
the withered leaves from the lawn, manage the pigs,
etc. ; short of stature, of a most miserable aspect, on
his head an old grey hat crushed over his face, which

was grizzly with unshaven beard. He wore a long-tailed coat, probably one of Sir Henry's, and always had a long stick in his hand. We wished to be very familiar with him, but were never at our ease, owing to his strange appearance and his shuffling gait. He exercised a great fascination over us, and we used to ask him to tell us stories, although he was nearly idiotic—"silly," to use a common Scotch phrase. He often said, as he turned round and pointed to the banks of the river, "Ou aye, bairns, I can weel remember Adam and Eve skelpin' aboot naket amang the gowans on the braes there." At times this dirty, uncanny old man got hold of a fiddle, on which he scraped with more energy than success.

'After Sir Henry's death and our removal from Ann Street, the old house of St. Bernard's passed into the silence of memory, but I have all my life been intimate with the family.'

We now part with regret from this fine old friend. We have been nobly entertained; it has been a quite rare pleasure to rest our mind and eyes on his character and works—to feel the power of his presence—his great gifts—his frank, broad, manly nature. We have come to know him and his ways and be grateful to him. We see him in his spacious room in York Place, hearty and keen, doing his best to make his sitters look themselves and their best, instead of looking ' as if they couldn't help it.' He had a knack of drawing them out on what their mind was brightest, and making them forget and be themselves. For is it not this self-consciousness— this reflex action, this tiresome *ego* of ours which makes us human, and plays the mischief with so much of us, to which man owes so much of his misery and greatness? What havoc it makes of photographs, unless they be of dogs or children, or very old people, whose faces like other old houses are necessarily picturesque. Sir Joshua used to suffer, as all portrait-painters must who wish to get at the essence of their man, from this self-conscious-ness in his sitters. He used to tell that the happiest picture he ever painted was done in this wise : some Sir John had been importuned by his family year after year to sit to him. He never would. One day a friend came and said *he* was going to sit to Reynolds, and wished Sir John to come and keep him company. He was delighted, went day after day with his friend, and was most agreeable. He was not allowed to see the picture till it was finished, and then he beheld—himself! a perfect likeness. If we could get the sun to take us in this unbeknown sort of way, he would make a better thing of us than he generally does.

In looking over Raeburn's portraits, one feels what would we not give to have such likenesses of

Julius Cæsar and Hannibal, Plato, and Alcibiades, of Lucian and Æsop, Moses and St. Paul, as we have here of Dugald Stewart and Dr. Adam, Horner and Scott? What we want is the eyes, the soul looking out. There are genuine busts of the great ancients, men and women ; we know the snub nose of Socrates, the compact skull of Hannibal, and we have a whole row of these tremendous fellows the Roman Emperors, but we want to see the *eyes* of Cæsar and the keen, rich twinkle of Aristophanes. What would a Burns be without the eyes?

SOMETHING ABOUT A WELL.

SOMETHING ABOUT A WELL.

WHEN a boy I knew, and often still think, of a
well far up among the wild hills—alone,
without shelter of wall or tree, open to the sun and
all the winds. There it lies, ever the same, self-
contained, all-sufficient; needing no outward help
from stream or shower, but fed from its own unseen
unfailing spring.

In summer, when all things are faint with the
fierce heat, you may see it, lying in the dim waste, a
daylight star, in the blaze of the sun, keeping fresh
its circle of young grass and flowers.

The small birds know it well, and journey from far
and near to dip in it their slender bills and pipe
each his glad song.

The sheep-dog may be seen halting, in his haste
to the uplands, to cool there his curling tongue.

In winter, of all waters it alone lives ; the keen ice
that seals up and silences the brooks and shallows
has no power here. Still it cherishes the same grass

and flowers with its secret heat, keeping them in perpetual beauty by its soft warm breath.

Nothing can be imagined more sweetly sudden and beautiful than our well seen from a distance, set with its crown of green, in the bosom of the universal snow. One might fancy that the Infant Spring lay nestled there out of grim Winter's way, waiting till he would be passed and gone.

Many a time, as a boy, have I stood by the side of this lonely well, 'held by its glittering eye,' and gazing into its black crystal depths, until I felt something like solemn fear, and thought it might be *as deep as the sea!* It was said nobody knew how deep it was, and that you might put your fishing-rod over head and not find the bottom.

But I found out the mystery. One supremely scorching summer day, when the sun was at his highest noon, I lay poring over this wonder, when behold, by the clear strong light, I saw far down, on a gentle swelling like a hill of pure white sand (it was sand), a delicate column, rising and falling and shifting in graceful measures, as if governed by a music of its own. With what awful glee did I find myself the sole witness of this spectacle! If I had caught a *Soul*, or seen *it* winking at me out of its window, I could have scarcely been more amazed and delighted.

What was it? May be *the Soul of the Well?* May

be *Truth?* found at last where we have been so often told to seek for it. How busy, how nimble, how *funny!* Now twisting, now un-twisting, now sinking on its bed as if fainting with ecstasy, then starting bolt upright and spinning round like a top; again it would curl up like a smooth pillow, and anon pause for a moment as if hovering with out-stretched wings, and then fold itself once more on its bed.

I have often seen it since, and it was always at its work, and is so doubtless still, morn, noon, and night incessantly, and its out-flow all the year round was the same.

Such is our well, at all times the same, full, clear, deep, composed; its only motion a gentle equable heaving, its only sound the liquid gurgle of its over-flowings among the roots of the flowers, its open face reflecting the heavens, calm or in storm, and though disquieted by every wandering wind, or dipping fly, or scampering 'well-washer,' soon recovering its placid face, while its depths rest for ever untroubled.

Pray you have a heart like this well, full, deep, clear, unchangeable, with Truth at the bottom; and a merry dancing elf there too, dancing to himself, 'ever wealthy with the treasure of his own exceeding pleasure.'

In the time of hot raging passion, a fountain of coolness. In shivering grief and bleak misery, a refuge from the storm, a covert from the tempest, and at all times a 'balm that tames all anguish, that steeps in rich reward all suffering, a saint that evil thoughts and aims taketh away.' Fearless alike of fire and frost, cool, not cold, warm, not hot. How many such hearts are at this moment beating in the bosoms of our mothers, wives, sisters, daughters, as little known, it may be, as this wilderness well, as full of goodness and love that never fails, passing away in silence, and telling no tale of all the good they do, and known only by the verdure that conceals their course.

> Long may thy springs,
> Quietly as a sleeping infant's breath,
> Send up cool waters to the Traveller
> With soft and easy pulse ; nor ever cease
> Yon tiny cone of sand its soundless dance
> Which at the bottom, like a fairy's page,
> As merry and no taller, dances still.

And long may our wells of living water find duty and affection, and making the wilderness and the solitary place to rejoice, their exceeding great reward, and elsewhere spring up into everlasting life.

12th April 1836.
1874.   J. B.

ANTESCRIPT

To the Sixtieth Thousand of ' Rab and his Friends.'

My dear Publisher—and Friend, for I don't agree with Tom Campbell's grim joke about Napoleon and the bookseller,[1]—what business has this inquisitive simpleton with his tongue out, this cordial little ruffian,—what has he to do on the cover of ' Rab and his Friends' ?   Rightly he is one of ' Our Dogs,' and wasn't born for many a year after Rab was dead(ed).   Nevertheless I like to see him looking out of the carriage-window at the general world of dogs and men.   He was a queer fellow, a thoroughbred ' mustard' Dandie Dinmont of the old breed, big enough to tackle with an otter.   His great-grandsire was the famous ' Crib,' whom Sir Walter got from Davidson of Hyndlee (the original Dandie Dinmont), and gave to his Constable, as his son, my Constable (tam carum caput !) told me.   ' Bob' was like King James I[st] and VIth, and Oliver Goldsmith—' an inspired idiot' —he could do little that other dogs did, and much that no other dog ever did,—a sort of bornnatural.   If Bob had known Rab, he would have respected him, but, being irritable and plucky, he might have run the risk of being throttled by that unceremonious old warrior—whose temper, like his tail, was of the shortest ; and so I allow you your frontispiece under protest—denying the railevancy, as Dr. Chalmers would say.*

[1] *At a booksellers' dinner Campbell proposed Napoleon's health, 'for he hanged a bookseller.'*

23 RUTLAND STREET,
    August 8, 1881.

MORE OF 'OUR DOGS.'

THE printer's devil—a very small and black and gentle one, whose name is Snowdon, whom I like to tease before he is off by giving him a small coin and then taking it and seeing how he looks, ending with making him haul it out of my fingers with his teeth, a great joke to us two—was asleep in the lobby, and I was trying to be pleased with the last sheet of *Our Dogs*, when the door opens and in trots a hairy little fellow, with all the gaiety and assurance proper to puppies, responsible and not. He, at one bound, for he is as springy as *Jock*, was on the table, and staring at me and then at the proof, with his head on one side, as much as to say, 'Oh! do put *me* in,—*Cur non?*' whisking off my spectacles with an ingenious jerk of his tail, wh'ch same tail I have no doubt he will soon be able to crack like a whip, so long, so plentiful, so handy it is already. Who could resist him? Recovering my spectacles and my understanding, for if not identical they are with me co-existent, I sketch him as he is now asleep at the fireside.

Knowing the pangs of bereavement and under the dread of that *ineluctabile fatum* which compels dogs and men, we have often spoken of appointing an assistant and successor to *Dick;* but we were ill to please, and we felt a delicacy as to him, for he is as compact of love and jealousy as was the Moor, or the elder *Peter* or *Fussy* or *Wasp*—to whose memory and to whose Mistresses and Master I dedicate *Our Dogs.* One day lately, however, a friend sent in a young Skye puppy for our judgment. We kept him for a day to study him, and the upshot is that we keep him still. He was so funny, so confidential, so plucky, his nose and the roof of his mouth were so black and comely, his genius for oddity, for unexpectedness so decided, his tail so glorious, that we could not let him go; and then, best of all, Dick tolerated him, adopted him, allowed him to take liberties with *his* tail that no mortal dog had ever before dared to do unbitten. Not that Dick played with him, or showed any approach to hilarity or acute interest, but he permitted himself and his dignity and his tail to be interfered with by this inveterate imp in a way that made the question of succession clear. You'll observe that I give him no name; this was our distress—no name would fit him. You know doubtless what one comes through in selecting a

name for a dog; it is infinitely worse than doing the
same by a child; if it is your seventeenth, you can
fall back upon Scripture, or the Anglo-Saxons, or the
cardinal virtues; but with a dog there must be what
Goethe calls an elective affinity between the dog and
the name. Well, we tried him for a week in vain
with all sorts of compact and cordial words, till one
evening after dinner, when we were sleepy and the
room darkening, this young and genial ruffian was
seen perched in the arm-chair. 'Peter!' we all
exclaimed, and *Peter* he is—not any particular Peter,
but Peter absolute. I don't know him well enough
yet to speak definitely, but I incline to think well of
him, he is an original, and stands on his own bottom.
Dogs, like men, have generally some dominant
quality; thus Toby was eminently wide-awake, though
he was much else; Wylie, in the same way, was more
eident than any one other thing; Wasp more impassioned; Jock more *daft;* Crab more deep—a very
deep dog was Crab; John Pym more full o' fechtin;
Puck more of a simpleton; Rab more huge (in head,
in heart, and in affliction); and Dick, like another
Richard, more judicious; but Peter is, in his essence
and in every action—especially of his tail—which he
waves aloft like a feather or banner—*ludicrous*, he
can't help it, he does not mean it, he is it; he is like
the great actor Liston, his mere look makes you
laugh; not that you laugh at him, or in any way

think lightly of his understanding; he is the cause, not the object of laughter, as many a good man and great has been before him; he is not the least of a foolish or hare-brained dog,—he is a dog of affection and *nous*. He is a dark brindle, and as plucky and procacious as Mr. Roebuck, whom I am told he resembles, but then he is young. If I survive him, which I almost hope may not be, I shall perhaps write his life, which I promise will not be so long as his tail and shorter than his temper, which, with all his boyish wilfulness, I can see is as sweet and faithful as was Jonathan's (the grandson of Kish) or Colonel Newcome's. If he survive me, I am sure of one true mourner. *Macte esto puer!*

'Man is the god of the dog,' says Burns after Lord Bacon; it were well for us if we served our Master as our dog serves his.

PETER.

Peter died young; very quick and soon that bright thing came to confusion. He died of excess of life; his vivacity slew him. Plucky and silent under punishment, or any pain from without, pain from within, in his own precious, brisk, enjoying body, was an insufferable offence, affront, and mystery—an astonishment not to be borne; he disdained to live under such conditions.

One day he came in howling with pain. There

was no injury, no visible cause, but he was wildly ill, and in his eyes the end of all things had come. He put so many questions to us at each pang—what is this?—what the —— can it be?—did you ever? As each paroxysm doubled him up, he gave a sharp cry, more of rage and utter exasperation than of suffering; he got up to run away from it—why should he die? Why should he be shut up in darkness and obstruction at that hour of his opening morn—his sweet hour of prime? And so raging, and utterly put out, the honest, dear little fellow went off in an ecstasy of fury at death, at its absurdity in his case.

We never could explain his death; it was not poison or injury; he actually expired when careering round the green at full speed, as if to outrun his enemy, or shake him off. We have not yet got over his loss, and all the possibilities that lie buried in his grave, in the Park, beneath a young chestnut-tree where the ruddy-cheeked, fat, and cordial coachman, —who of old, in the grand old Reform days, used to drive his master, Mr. Speaker Abercromby, down to 'the House' with much stateliness and bouquet —and I dug it for him; that park in which Peter had often disported himself, fluttering the cocks and hens, and putting to flight the squadron of Gleneagle's wedders.

Dick.

He too is dead; he who, never having been born,

we had hoped never would die; not that he did—like Rab—'exactly' die; he was slain. He was fourteen, and getting deaf and blind, and a big bully of a retriever fell on him one Sunday morning when the bells were ringing. Dick, who always fought at any odds, gave battle; a Sabbatarian cab turned the corner, the big dog fled, and Dick was run over—there in his own street, as all his many friends were going to church. His back was broken, and he died on Monday night with us all about him; dear for his own sake, dearer for another's, whose name—Sine Quâ Non—is now more than ever true, now that she is gone.

I was greatly pleased when Dr. Cotting of Roxbury came in yesterday and introduced himself to me by asking, 'Where is Dick?' To think of our Dick being known in Massachusetts!

BOB.

If Peter was the incarnation of vivacity, Bob was that of energy. He should have been called Thalaba the Destroyer. He rejoiced in demolition —not from ill temper, but from the sheer delight of energizing.

When I first knew him he was at Blinkbonny toll. The tollman and his wife were old and the house lonely, and Bob was too terrific for any burglar. He was as tall and heavy as a foxhound, but in every other respect a pure old-fashioned, wiry, short-haired Scotch terrier,—red as Rob Roy's beard,—having indeed other qualities of Rob's than his hair—choleric, unscrupulous, affectionate, stanch,—not in the least magnanimous, as ready to worry a little dog as a big one. Fighting was his 'chief end,' and he omitted no opportunity of accomplishing his end. Rab liked fighting for its own sake too, but scorned to fight anything under his own weight; indeed, was long-suffering to public meanness with quarrelsome lesser dogs. Bob had no such weakness.

After much difficulty and change of masters, I bought him, I am ashamed to say, for five pounds, and brought him home. He had been chained for months, was in high health and spirits, and the surplus power and activity of this great creature, as he dragged me and my son along the road, giving battle to every dog he met, was something appalling.

I very soon found I could not keep him. He worried the pet dogs all around, and got me into much trouble. So I gave him as night-watchman to a goldsmith in Princes Street. This work he did famously. I once, in passing at midnight, stopped at the shop and peered in at the little slip of glass, and by the gas-light I saw where he lay. I made a noise, and out came he with a roar and a bang as of a sledge-hammer. I then called his name, and in an instant all was still except a quick tapping within that intimated the wagging of the tail. He is still there,—has settled down into a reputable, pacific citizen—a good deal owing, perhaps, to the disappearance in battle of sundry of his best teeth. As he lies in the sun before the shop door he looks somehow like the old Fighting Téméraire.

I never saw a dog of the same breed ; he is a sort of rough *cob* of a dog—a huge quantity of terrier in one skin ; for he has all the fun and briskness and failings and ways of a small dog, begging and hopping as only it does. Once his master took him to North Berwick. His first day he spent in careering about the sands and rocks and in the sea, for he is a noble swimmer. His next he devoted to worrying all the dogs of the town, beginning, for convenience, with the biggest.

This aroused the citizens, and their fury was brought to a focus on the third day by its being reported alternatively that he had torn a child's ear off, or torn and actually eaten it. Up rose the town as one man, and the women each as two, and, headed by Matthew Cathie, the one-eyed and excellent shoemaker, with a tall, raw divinity student, knock-kneed and six feet two, who was his lodger, and was of course called young Dominie Sampson ; they bore down upon Bob and his master, who were walking calmly on the shore.

Bob was for making a stand, after the manner of

Coriolanus, and banishing by instant assault the 'common cry of curs;' but his master saw sundry guns and pistols, not to speak of an old harpoon, and took to his heels, as the only way of getting Bob to take to his. *Aurifex*, with much *nous*, made for the police station, and, with the assistance of the constables and half a crown, got Thalaba locked up for the night, safe and sulky.

Next morning, Sunday, when Cathie and his huge student lay uneasily asleep, dreaming of vengeance, and the early dawn was beautiful upon the Bass, with its snowy cloud of sea-birds 'brooding on the charmed wave,' Bob was hurried up to the station, locked into a horse-box—him never shall that ancient Burgh forget or see.

I have a notion that dogs have humour, and are perceptive of a joke. In the North, a shepherd, having sold his sheep at a market, was asked by the buyer to lend him his dog to take them home. 'By a' manner o' means tak' Birkie, and when ye're dune wi' him just play so' (making a movement with his arm), 'and he'll be hame in a jiffy.' Birkie was so clever and useful and gay that the borrower coveted him ; and on getting to his farm shut him up, intending to keep him. Birkie escaped during the night, and took the entire hirsel (flock) back to his own master ! Fancy him trotting across the moor with them, they as willing as he.

PITY THE SOR-
ROWS OF US
HOMELESS DOGS

PLEA FOR A DOG HOME.

EDINBURGH, *December* 8, 1862.

SIR,[1]—I am rejoiced to find Mr. William Chambers has taken up this matter. There is no fear of failure of Glenormiston sets himself to organise a home for our destitute four-footed fellow-creatures, from whom we get so much of the best enjoyment, affection, and help. It need not be an expensive institution—if the value of the overplus of good eating that, from our silly over-indulgence, makes our town dogs short-lived, lazy, mangy, and on a rare and enlivening occasion *mad*, were represented by money, all the homeless, starving dogs of the city would be warmed and fed, and their dumb miseries turned into food and gladness. When we see our Peppers, and Dicks, and Muffs, and Nellys, and Dandies, and who knows how many other cordial little ruffians with the shortest and spiciest of names, on the rug, warm and cosey—pursuing in their dreams that imaginary cat—let us think of their wretched brethren or sisters without food, without shelter, without a master or a bone. It only needs a beginning, this new ragged school and home, where the religious element happily is absent, and Dr. Guthrie may go halves with me in paying for the keep of a rescued cur. There is no town where there are so many thorough-bred house-dogs. I could

30   [1] Addressed to the Editor of the *Scotsman*.

produce from my own dog acquaintance no end of
first-class Dandy Dinmonts and Skyes; and there is
no town where there is more family enjoyment from
dogs—from Paterfamilias down to the baby whose
fingers are poked with impunity into eyes as fierce
and fell as Dirk Hatteraick's or Meg Merrilies's.

Many years ago, I got a proof of the unseen and
therefore unhelped miseries of the homeless dog. I
was walking down Duke Street, when I felt myself
gently nipped in the leg—I turned, and there was a
ragged little terrier crouching and abasing himself
utterly, as if asking pardon for what he had done.
He then stood up on end and begged as only these
coaxing little ruffians can. Being in a hurry, I curtly
praised his performance with 'Good dog!' clapped
his dirty sides, and, turning round, made down the
hill; when presently the same nip, perhaps a little
nippier—the same scene, only more intense—the
same begging and urgent motioning of his short,
shaggy paws. 'There's meaning in this,' said I to
myself, and looked at him keenly and differently.
He seemed to twig at once, and, with a shrill cry, was
off much faster than I could. He stopped every now
and then to see that I followed, and by way of putting
off the time and urging me, got up on the aforesaid
portion of his body, and, when I came up, was off
again. This continued till, after going through
sundry streets and by-lanes, we came to a gate, under

which my short-legged friend disappeared. Of course
I couldn't follow him. This astonished him greatly.
He came out to me, and as much as said, 'Why the
—— don't you come in?' I tried to open it, but in
vain. My friend vanished and was silent. I was
leaving in despair and disgust, when I heard his
muffled, ecstatic yelp far off round the end of the wall,
and there he was, wild with excitement. I followed
and came to a place where, with a somewhat burglari-
ous ingenuity, I got myself squeezed into a deserted
coachyard, lying all rude and waste. My peremptory
small friend went under a shed, and disappeared in a
twinkling through the window of an old coach body,
which had long ago parted from its wheels and become
sedentary. I remember the arms of the Fife family
were on its panel; and, I daresay, this chariot, with
its C springs, had figured in 1822 at the King's visit,
when all Scotland was somewhat Fifeish. I looked
in, and there was a pointer bitch with a litter of five
pups; the mother like a ghost, and wild with maternity
and hunger; her raging, yelling brood tearing away
at her dry dugs. I never saw a more affecting or
more miserable scene than that family inside the
coach. The poor bewildered mother, I found, had
been lost by some sportsman returning south, and
must have slunk away there into that deserted place,
when her pangs (for she has her pangs as well as a
duchess) came, and there, in that forlorn retreat, had

she been with them, rushing out to grab any chance garbage, running back fiercely to them—this going on day after day, night after night. What the relief was when we got her well fed and cared for—and her children filled and silent, all cuddling about her asleep, and she asleep too—awaking up to assure herself that this was all true, and that there they were, all the five, each as plump as a plum,—

> 'All too happy in the treasure,
> Of her own exceeding pleasure,'—

what this is in kind, and all the greater in amount as many outnumber one, may be the relief, the happiness, the charity experienced and exercised in a homely, well-regulated *Dog Home*. *Nipper*—for he was a waif—I took home that night, and gave him his name. He lived a merry life with me—showed much pluck and zeal in the killing of rats, and incontinently slew a cat which had—unnatural brute, unlike his friend— deserted her kittens, and was howling offensively inside his kennel. He died, aged sixteen, healthy, lean, and happy to the last. As for *Perdita* and her pups, they brought large prices, the late Andrew Buchanan, of Coltbridge, an excellent authority and man—the honestest 'dogman' I ever knew—having discovered that their blood and her culture were of the best.

I have subscribed to the London 'Home' ever since I knew of it, and will be glad to do as much more for one of our own, as Edinburgh is nearer and dearer than the city of millions of dogs and men. And let us remember that our own dogs are in danger of being infected by all the dog-diseases, from the tragic *rabies* down to the mange and bad manners, by these pariah dogs; for you know among dogs there is in practical operation that absolute equality and fraternity which has only been as yet talked of and shot at by and for us.—I am, &c.

RANDOLPH.

Orat, plorat et adorat.

Edinburgh University Press:
THOMAS AND ARCHIBALD CONSTABLE, PRINTERS TO HER MAJESTY.

BY THE SAME AUTHOR.

Now ready, uniform with John Leech, etc.

HORÆ SUBSECIVÆ,

FIRST SERIES.

LOCKE AND SYDENHAM, Etc.

CONTENTS.

Fourth Edition, in one Vol., with a portrait, 7s. 6d.

EDINBURGH : DAVID DOUGLAS.

Now ready, uniform with John Leech, etc.

HORÆ SUBSECIVÆ,

SECOND SERIES.

RAB AND HIS FRIENDS, Etc.

CONTENTS.

Twelfth Edition, in one Vol. Crown 8vo, 7s. 6d.

EDINBURGH : DAVID DOUGLAS.